JE01 '93

COLORADO MOUNTAIN COLLE
D763.I82C264
Mo

D1473165

D
763
I82
C264

HAPGOOD, D.
Monte Cassino

ofile

Keep - 2013

Mte. Cairo

Colle Majola

COLORADO MOUNTAIN COLLEGE
LEARNING CENTER--WEST CAMPUS
Glenwood Springs, CO 81601

Drawing adapted from a sketch drawn by a Polish artilleryman.
(Looking northwest toward Rome)

COLORADO MOUNTAIN COLLEGE
LRC--WEST CAMPUS
Glenwood Springs, Colo 81601

MONTE CASSINO

COLORADO MOUNTAIN COLLEGE
LRC--WEST CAMPUS
Glenwood Springs, Colo. 81601

MONTE CASSINO

BY
DAVID HAPGOOD
AND
DAVID RICHARDSON

CONGDON & WEED, INC.

NEW YORK

COLORADO MOUNTAIN COLLEGE
LRC--WEST CAMPUS
Glenwood Springs, Colo. 81601

Copyright © 1984 by David Hapgood and David Richardson

Library of Congress Cataloging in Publication Data

Hapgood, David.
Monte Cassino.

Bibliography: p.
Includes index.
1. Cassino (Italy), Battle of, 1944. I. Richardson,
David, 1935–   II. Title.
D763.I82C264   1984   940.54'21   83–24074
ISBN 0-86553-105-6
ISBN 0-312-92537-9 (St. Martin's Press)

PHOTO CREDITS
Following page 8: courtesy of Henry M. Willard; Cassino Tourist Agency;
Alinari; Cassino Tourist Agency; Abbey of Monte Cassino; courtesy of
Maximilian J. Becker; U.S. Signal Corps. *Following page 29:* Signal Corps;
Imperial War Museum (IWM); Bundesarchiv (BA); BA. *Following pages 36, 51,
and 70:* BA. *Following page 85:* IWM; Signal Corps; IWM; Signal Corps.
Following page 123: IWM; IWM; Signal Corps. *Following page 144:* Signal
Corps; U.S. Army Pictorial Service; New Zealand Consulate General; IWM;
IWM. *Following page 187:* Signal Corps; IWM; BA; Signal Corps. *Following
page 203:* U.S. Air Force; Air Force; BA; Air Force. *Following page 218:* Air
Force; BA; BA; BA; BA; IWM; BA. *Following page 224:* BA; BA; Pvt. George
Aarons for *Yank.*

Published by Congdon & Weed, Inc.
298 Fifth Avenue, New York, N.Y. 10001
Distributed by St. Martin's Press
175 Fifth Avenue, New York, N.Y. 10010
Published simultaneously in Canada by Methuen Publications
2330 Midland Avenue, Agincourt, Ontario M1S 1P7

All Rights Reserved
Printed in the United States of America
Designed by Irving Perkins
Maps by David Lindroth
First Edition

One day the whole world will learn the truth about what happened at Monte Cassino.

—*Abbot Gregorio Diamare,*
January 6, 1944

CONTENTS

MONTE CASSINO

PART ONE
PORTENT

1

October 14, 1943: It was midmorning when Dr. Becker first saw his objective. Becker—Maximilian J. Becker, 33, a handsome, dark-haired captain in the elite Hermann Goering Division—and his two companions were driving north on the road from Naples to Rome in his little Fiat convertible. As Becker years later remembered that October day, the sun was shining and it was warm enough to put down the top of the convertible.

When the car rounded the eastern side of a small, steep hill, a spectacular mountain landscape unfolded before the three travelers. Directly ahead of them two valleys joined in a V to form a single plain. One valley, the Rapido, rose to their right and disappeared into the snow-capped peaks of the Abruzzi, the rugged, inhospitable mountains of central Italy. Along the valley to their left, beside the Liri River, ran the road that led to Rome, 80 miles to the north. This was Route 6, the ancient Via Casilina. The plain before them was farmland and pasture dotted with farmhouses and clumps of trees beginning to turn gold and brown. In the center of the V formed by the two valleys a massive mountain ridge rose abruptly 1,500 feet from the plain below. It jutted out into the plain like the prow of a ship. That ridge was the keystone of the entire landscape. It dominated the valley plain and the road to Rome. From the top of that ridge a man could look down—and *shoot* down, Becker thought— at anything or anyone on the plain below him.

On the ridge, facing out over the two valleys, stood a gigantic stone building. Its rows upon rows of windows sparkled like so many eyes in the morning sun. The size of the stone building—four stories covering the area of a city block—was underscored by its total isolation. From the hillside where Becker was now looking, 5 miles away across the plain, no human structure of remotely comparable size was visible on that mountain or any of the other mountains within his sight. People in this region clustered in the fertile plains. Few lived on the mountains, and fewer still built buildings of any size there, with that one gigantic exception. The building was the Abbey of Monte Cassino, and it was Dr. Becker's destination.

The Abbey of Monte Cassino was one of the most sacred of Christian sites. In the year 529, it is said, the wandering Saint Benedict chose that mountain to found the monastery that became the model for monasteries in the Western European world. The site he chose was already sacred and strategic, as well as spectacular. The Roman road passing below was then ten centuries old; the Romans had built a citadel upon the crest, which in Benedict's time had become a temple to Apollo. "Round about it likewise on all sides" —in the words of the third-hand account that is history's only record of Benedict's life—"there were woods for the service of devils, in which even till that very time, the mad multitude of infidels did offer most wicked sacrifice." Benedict converted the infidels, the chronicler tells us, settled with his followers on that mountain "that seems to touch the very heavens," and wrote the Rule of Benedict, the extraordinary constitution that ever since has governed most of Western monastic life.

Over the centuries the Abbey of Monte Cassino grew to be the largest and most important of Western monasteries. From this cradle of the Benedictine order, missionary monks fanned out and founded monasteries throughout the Christian world. During the Dark Ages its scholar monks preserved and copied the writings of their own and previous times; many ancient authors were known only through documents saved at Monte Cassino. In the early Middle Ages Monte Cassino was one of the most important seats of learning and art in the West; the miniatures and frescoes produced elsewhere, notably at Cluny in France, were based on styles created by the monks of Monte Cassino. The abbey was richly adorned and its abbot was a powerful voice in the affairs of the Church. By the twentieth century the archive of Monte Cassino was known to be a treasure literally without price.

That treasure was what brought Becker to the abbey that day. The young German doctor wanted to save the archive of Monte Cassino. Medicine was Becker's profession and war was now his occupation, but his passion was art and archeology. In the last years of peace he had gone to the Middle East on an archeological dig, and even during the war—a war which for his Hermann Goering Division nowadays consisted of defeat and retreat, followed by another defeat and another retreat—the young doctor had managed to keep his sketchbook handy; only a few weeks earlier he had taken advantage of a military traffic jam south of Naples to get in some sketching in the ruins of Pompeii.

Becker was no military strategist, but a single glance around the Liri Valley ahead of him was enough to tell him why the abbey and its treasures were now in danger. The Allies, after their successful landing at Salerno, had captured Naples and were pushing north toward their inevitable objective: Rome. Already they had reached the Volturno River, only 40 miles south of Monte Cassino. There was only one practical way from Naples to Rome through the mountains of central Italy, and that was along the road Becker was now traveling. The key to the road to Rome was the great mountain ridge on which the abbey stood. The Germans would have to defend that keystone; the Allies would have to attack it; the abbey would be engulfed in the battle. Becker's self-appointed mission that day was to convince the Benedictine monks of their danger and then to arrange to move their treasures to some place safe from the advancing war.

Becker's traveling companions in the little Fiat were two Franciscan monks from a small monastery to the south where Becker had his quarters and where he ran a first-aid station for his unit of the Hermann Goering Division. Becker, whose Italian was far from fluent, had asked the monks along to help him make his case to the abbot of Monte Cassino. He expected them to give him, a German officer, some credibility with the monks by testifying to his earlier effort to save another Italian treasure. When he was setting up his quarters in the monastery of San Antonio in Teano, Becker had run across several hundred boxes which, it turned out, contained the archives of the national library of Naples. Becker had arranged to move these archives to a location outside the probable line of combat. It was one of the very few truly worthwhile, satisfying things Becker had accomplished in three grim years of war. Now he wanted to do the same for the Abbey of Monte Cassino.

As they drove through Cassino, the town of 25,000 nestled at the foot of Monte Cassino, Becker saw in the destruction left by a recent Allied bombing added evidence of the urgency of his mission: the war was coming close indeed. The road then wound in a series of hairpin turns up the steep, rocky slope of the mountain. Above them, the abbey appeared, vanished, and reappeared, looming with each turn larger in Becker's field of vision. Around them scrubby trees clung

5

to what soil they could find in the rocky ravines. As he drove up the winding road, he reviewed in his mind the moves he had made in preparation for the sensitive negotiation that lay ahead. Rescuing the treasure of Monte Cassino had been his own idea. His unit was not in combat at the moment, thank God, so the doctor had some time on his hands; and members of the Hermann Goering Division, whose patron was, of course, the number two man in the Nazi hierarchy, had a freedom of action denied to officers in the regular Wehrmacht.

Becker, a mere captain, had no power to order the resources he needed, but, after three years, he knew how things got done in his division. The commander of his unit, Major Hans Sandrock, readily gave the young doctor the time off he requested: there was little for Becker to do when the unit was not in action. Next, Becker went to the quartermaster of the division, Lieutenant-Colonel Ulrich Bobrowski. Bobrowski had arranged for Becker to use the trucks that moved the books from the monastery at Teano. Now the quartermaster told Becker he would approve this second project of his but that he would have to work out the details with the division's supply officer. So the day before he drove to Monte Cassino Becker went to see the supply officer, one Lieutenant-Colonel Jacobi, in the house trailer Jacobi had fixed up as his quarters.

They chatted; Jacobi had offered the doctor a drink. Becker had led the conversation around to the treasure of the Abbey of Monte Cassino, mentioning the credit that rescuing the treasure would bring to the Hermann Goering Division. The thought that hung unspoken between them was that they would need that credit if the war ended, as seemed ever more likely, in a German defeat. Becker also mentioned that he had heard of some Italian trucks that might be available for the mission he had in mind. He said he thought he would need only a few of them, and Jacobi agreed to let him use the trucks. Becker then said the abbot might ask him to save other valuable possessions—the abbey also had a number of important works of art—and perhaps even to move the monks themselves. Could Becker promise that to the abbot? As the doctor later recalled it, Jacobi then answered: "Yes, of course, as far as I'm concerned. But if we're supposed to do all that, there'll have to be something in it for us, too. Just a couple of paintings. Such an old monastery is sure to have enough. Just cut them out of the frames and roll them up." Becker, dismayed at that suggestion and yet not wanting to

6

jeopardize the rescue, had murmured something about hinting to the abbot that a gift would be in order. Jacobi then laughed, made a gesture of dismissal, and said, "Nonsense, forget about my suggestion. I just thought you'd understand a joke." Nothing more was said, but the exchange had left a bad taste in Becker's mouth, a suggestion of trouble to come.

Soon the three men—Becker and the two Franciscans—were driving up the oak-lined approach to the great gate of the abbey. Seen close up, the abbey, with its massive stone walls and rows and rows of windows gazing down, was even more impressive than it had been when they saw it from across the valley. Over the gate, the single word PAX was carved in stone. A monk in the black cowl of the Benedictines opened the gate, and the young German military doctor entered a world far removed from his own.

The monks of the Abbey of Monte Cassino were men who had withdrawn from the world into which they were born. That withdrawal was the essential commitment of Benedictine life. The monks —some fifty-five at the time of Becker's visit—lived a life defined for them in great detail in the Rule of Benedict, which prescribed a daily cycle of very early rising and a waking day divided equally between prayer and work. Each day of the year the monks gathered eight times in the carved walnut choir stalls of the basilica to chant and recite the "hours," the daily rituals that began before dawn with matins and ended at bedtime with compline.

The first requirement of the monks' work was that they feed and clothe themselves. Living in a time when organized society was falling apart, Benedict insisted that each monastery be self-sufficient. From the earliest times, however, the temporal powers endowed Monte Cassino and other monasteries with extensive lands, so the monastic community lived largely off the work of its tenant farmers. This freed the priest-monks, who were mostly of upperclass origin, from the need for manual labor. In modern times, the monks who worked in the fields and olive groves and vineyards that belonged to the abbey, and cared for its animals, were lay brothers: monks who were not trained as priests and who usually came from lower levels of society than the priest-monks. Some of the priest-monks were scholars working in the great archive; others specialized in the Gregorian chant that was the musical glory of Monte Cassino; still others taught in the boys' boarding school and the seminary that were housed within the walls of the abbey.

The monks' life was plain and hard, but it was not the hair-shirt asceticism of such stricter orders as the Trappists, or those solitary monks who lived like the early hermits of the Egyptian desert. Each monk had his own comfortable room, the food in normal times was good and plentiful, and the wine of Monte Cassino—a Frascati—was of excellent quality. (Benedict, a realist, allowed wine, because "though we read that wine is not at all suitable for monks, in our day it is not possible to persuade the monks of this truth.") Nor was the monastery's isolation as complete as Benedict had intended. Over the centuries, as the outside world evolved from the simple economy of the sixth century, Benedict's rule that each monastery must be self-sufficient came to be interpreted as self-supporting. By the mid-twentieth century Monte Cassino was dependent on the outside world for manufactured goods and heating fuel, electricity, and gasoline for its vehicles and was linked to it by telephone and mail. Many people passed through the abbey's gates daily. Students came and went. Local people worked for the abbey in return for food. In normal times the abbey received a constant stream of visitors—tourists and monks visiting from other monasteries. Yet in its essence, Monte Cassino was a world apart, and all that the monks really asked of that other, outside world was that it leave them alone. Now Dr. Becker had come to tell them it could no longer be.

A monk summoned the doctor, but told him he would have to see the abbot alone. Disappointed—the absence of the two Franciscans would only make his task harder—Becker followed the monk down a long corridor to the abbot's workroom. The door opened and, to Becker's surprise, a German officer emerged; he was a lieutenant-colonel and Becker saw by the distinctive stripes on his right cuff-band that he was from his own Hermann Goering Division. The officer introduced himself as Julius Schlegel and said Jacobi—the supply officer Becker had seen the day before—had told him to go see the abbot. Schlegel told the doctor he had informed the abbot that the monastery was to be "cleared out," whether the abbot agreed or not, and so there was no purpose to Becker's own visit. Becker was both puzzled and disturbed by this news: why had Jacobi sent this other officer on his mission? Becker said he would see the abbot anyway, and as he strode into the workroom a monk said to him in fluent German, "Come, come! The abbot is waiting for you."

ABOVE: The Abbey of Monte Cassino, in a seventeenth-century engraving. BELOW: The abbey seen from the northwest, along the ridge, in a prewar photo.

Montecassino - Lato esterno nord-ovest del Collegio di S. Benedetto

LEFT: A prewar photograph of the main cloister of the abbey and the monumental stairs—flanked by statues of Saint Benedict and Saint Scholastica—that lead to the basilica. OPPOSITE, BOTTOM: Another prewar view of the interior of the abbey. BELOW: The interior of the basilica, looking toward the altar.

RIGHT: Dr. Maximilian J. Becker of the Hermann Goering Division. BELOW: The Monte Cassino ridge and the abbey, from across the Liri valley, in a photograph taken February 6, 1944. The town of Cassino is at the foot of the ridge, and the castle on Rocca Janula is above it at far right.

The abbot held out his hand in greeting. Gregorio Diamare was 79 years old, a short, stooped man with sagging jowls and a pendulous lower lip. He carried his paunchy frame with the assurance of a man who for 34 years had been the ruler of the community of Monte Cassino. At his invitation, Becker took a seat at a large round table. Also seated at the table were three other monks, one of whom, to Becker's relief, was the German-speaking monk, who would act as interpreter. The monks were all considerably older than Becker; their rough homespun black robes and ascetic features were in sharp contrast to the worldly air of the handsome young German in his dashing uniform. Abbot Diamare looked sharply at the doctor through his horn-rimmed glasses and opened the conversation: "Now what news are you bringing us? Do you too come from General Conrath [commander of the division] to convey the order that the monastery will be cleared out?"

"Not an order," said Becker, and he then outlined his plan for removing the archive to safety. As he was speaking, one of the monks, a bald man with a jutting chin who had been eyeing the German with obvious hostility, burst in excitedly, but Becker could not understand what he was saying. The abbot heard Becker out with apparent interest, but then dismissed his plan as both impossible and unnecessary. The archive could not be moved; the monastery lacked even crates in which to pack it. Anyhow, it was safe at Monte Cassino. The Germans would not use the abbey for military purposes; Field Marshal Albert Kesselring himself, commander of all German forces in the south of Italy, had personally assured the abbot of that. The Allies would not bomb the abbey. Among the many thousands of American and English visitors before the war had been prominent people who would use their influence to prevent such a crime against civilization. Besides, much of the archive belonged to the Italian state,* so its fate was not up to the abbot to decide.

Becker vigorously put forward the arguments he had prepared on the road to the monastery. No doubt the Germans would not use the abbey itself, but the ridge on which it stood was the best defensive position south of Rome; in fact, the Germans were already digging in at the foot of the mountain. The Allies might not deliberately

---

*The property of Monte Cassino and other monasteries was nationalized in 1866. Monte Cassino was made a "national monument" with the monks as its custodians.

bomb the abbey, but they would bomb and shell the German positions all around it, and bombs often did not land where they were supposed to. Becker told the abbot about the accidental destruction of religious places he had seen in Sicily during the recent fighting there. In this total war, he concluded, there were no islands of safety.

The monks did not need to be told that the war was drawing nearer to their isolated home. In the early years of the conflict, when the Axis powers were winning, life at Monte Cassino had gone on much as usual, except that most of the visitors wore German uniforms. But now the monks were feeling the foreshocks of approaching battle. For about four months now, and ever more intensively, the Allies had been bombing targets in the valleys below. They had bombed the town of Cassino twice, most recently four days before Becker's visit, and an occasional stray bomb had fallen on the mountain itself. More than once the monks had been forced by an alarm to leave their tables in the refectory during a meal and flee to the vaults and chapels that lay deep beneath the ground. The funicular that connected the monastery with the town had been destroyed just a few days earlier (though in fact this was the work of a stunting German pilot, not an Allied bomb). The bombing of Cassino had disrupted Monte Cassino's electricity and telephone service. The monks had moved their evening service up to 6:30 so they would not have to use candles in the basilica. The lives of their students had been disrupted too, and so the seminary and the *collegio,* the monastery's boys' boarding school, had not reopened after the summer.

The worst problem was the refugees. Bombed out of their homes, terrified, the local people had been streaming to the abbey in the hope of finding safety there. The monks could not deny them hospitality, and now families were living in shelters improvised in the arched passageways of its three great cloisters. Among the refugees were nuns and orphans from the three Benedictine convents in Cassino, who were now living in the dormitory of the *collegio.* There were about a thousand refugees already. This added population was far beyond the capacity of the abbey's food supply, and the monks thought some of the refugees were troublemakers. The water level in the abbey's great cistern was dangerously low. Winter was coming. The situation that faced Abbot Diamare was increasingly difficult.

The old abbot now got to his feet and went to the window from which one could look out over the valleys and plains below. He stood, his head bowed, seeming to gaze down at the bomb-damaged town of Cassino; Diamare was bishop of Cassino as well as abbot of the monastery. There was a long silence in the room; any decision was the abbot's alone to make. At last the abbot turned to Becker and asked: "What is to happen to my monks? What will be the fate of all these refugees in the abbey?" The German doctor said he might be able to arrange transportation for the monks, including, if he so desired, Abbot Diamare himself.

At that the old monk drew his stooped figure erect, and, in a suddenly confident voice, said: "Tell me, doctor, would your general leave his soldiers in the lurch in battle?"

"No," said Becker.

"I am the general, the bishop here, the shepherd of my people. I dare not leave them in the lurch in their time of need, even if battle breaks out. I will stay here with my refugees and a few of my younger monks, and we will wait it out, come what may."

2

That evening Becker was drinking with his fellow officers at a big house outside Teano, the town halfway between Naples and Cassino where the Hermann Goering Division had its headquarters. The house was now occupied by Julius Schlegel, the lieutenant-colonel Becker had met that morning at the Abbey of Monte Cassino. Half a dozen officers were sitting around a table in what had been the living room. Across the room another officer was playing a piano. The men around the table were talking animatedly about how to move the treasures of Monte Cassino.

Becker had arrived late, indeed had almost not come at all. That afternoon he had almost given up his self-appointed mission. When he had returned to his room at the monastery he had found a letter from his wife in Berlin on the pillow of his cot. Becker had written her to say he would not be coming home on leave, as they had planned, because of his involvement in moving the Naples library. He had expected his wife to be angry, and when he opened her letter he found out that she was very angry indeed. On his leave Becker was supposed to move her and their little daughter from Berlin to the comparative safety of her parents' home in Tecklenburg, near the Rhine. The bombing of Berlin, she wrote, was getting worse every day. Two streets nearby had just been hit; their street was sure to get it soon. If Becker wasn't worried about his wife and child, how about all his valuable things in Berlin? Aunt Christine and Uncle Heinrich and all their friends just couldn't understand his failure to come home when he had the chance.

Becker had sat on his cot, brooding, his wife's letter still in his hand. Should he drop this Monte Cassino project and take his leave while he still could? If he waited, it might be too late for either his family or himself. As he brooded, the young doctor's thoughts turned to his earliest connection with the Abbey of Monte Cassino. It was through, of all people, the American poet Henry Wadsworth Longfellow. Becker's father had lived for some years in St. Louis, and he had brought home with him a taste for Longfellow's romantic poetry. Becker's mother was English and the boy grew up bilingual. When Becker was about ten his father had promised him a toy train if he would memorize Longfellow's "Psalm of Life." The boy duly committed Longfellow's lush verses to memory, picked out the most expensive train in the catalogue, and found it under the tree at Christmas. As an adult Becker always carried a volume of Longfellow with him; it was here in his room at the monastery in Teano. In it was the poem Longfellow wrote after his visit to Monte Cassino in 1869. Titled "Monte Cassino," the poem included a verse that Becker suddenly found prophetic:

> *The conflict of the Present and the Past,*
> *The ideal and the actual in our life,*
> *As on a field of battle held me fast,*
> *Where this world and the next world were at strife.*

Becker's thoughts had returned to the present. There was something peculiar about his fellow officers' behavior in this Monte Cassino business. Why had Jacobi agreed to let Becker handle it, and then sent this other man, this Schlegel? What was their game? Whatever it was, Becker didn't like it. That was a good reason, despite his guilty conscience about his wife and child, to stay and see it through. There was more. Becker's work for three years of war had consisted of patching up men smashed in senseless combat. It was disheartening and futile work, done in a cause in which Becker did not believe, a cause, moreover, that was doomed—he was by now convinced—to inevitable defeat. Now he had the opportunity to give meaning to his life, to show that a German officer could do something worthwhile: to save a priceless piece of Europe's civilization. He might never have another such opportunity. He might be killed tomorrow.

His mind made up, Becker had again sought out Jacobi in his trailer. He had found the supply officer, a former Berlin policeman, in a surly mood. Jacobi evaded the doctor's question whether their commander, Major-General Paul Conrath, had in fact ordered the monastery "cleared out," as Becker had been informed that morning by Schlegel. Becker concluded there was no such order. Why had Jacobi sent this Schlegel on a mission that, after all, had been Becker's own inspiration? (Schlegel, in his postwar account, claimed that the rescue was his idea.) Jacobi pointed out that Schlegel was a transport man, in charge of maintaining the division's vehicles, and so could resolve problems that were beyond the resources of a medical officer. "Don't you want to work together with Schlegel?" he asked. Becker agreed that this made sense, and Jacobi said they would talk it over that evening at Schlegel's quarters.

Schlegel was the life of the party. As they sat around the table drinking, he regaled his fellow officers with stories of his earlier days. He was an Austrian from Vienna, now in his late forties, whose broad face was usually wreathed in an engaging grin. Schlegel was also a committed Nazi. Becker recalled that Schlegel boasted he was one of the founding members of Hitler's party in Austria; his party card bore the number seven, and he held two Nazi decorations, the Order of Blood and the Golden Party Badge. He boasted of his exploits in the Austrian horse artillery during the First World War, and said he had also been a flier. He dropped famous names in his stories, and he talked about his visits to the Uffizi and Pitti galleries of Florence.

13

Schlegel said he had owned a transport business in Vienna before the war, and that experience, plus his present job as a transport officer, made him the right man to supervise the removal of the Monte Cassino archives. They talked about the need for crates, and one officer said there was a soft-drink plant nearby with some already-cut boards. Someone else said they could get skilled workers from a German detachment that was now in reserve.

Schlegel, in high spirits, waved off all the problems. He would handle them. He was already in charge.

3

The day after their first visit the two officers were waiting to see Abbot Diamare. Dr. Becker was sitting, absorbed in his thoughts. Schlegel was pacing around looking at the paintings on the walls of the anteroom. His restlessness was getting on the doctor's nerves.

Schlegel stopped to examine a wooden sculpture. It was an unpainted figure, in the Romanesque style, of a seated Madonna with the infant Jesus on her lap. It stood about three feet tall. Both officers admired the sculpture, and Schlegel asked, "How old could it be?"

"Early Middle Ages," Becker guessed.

"That would be something for the Iron Man," Schlegel said.

Although Hermann Goering was more blubber than metal, the doctor knew that was who Schlegel meant. He also knew that Goering, the patron of their division, was the prime looter of art in Nazi-occupied Europe. Did Becker's fellow officers want to loot the Abbey of Monte Cassino on behalf of their patron? And was that why they seemed to be trying to ease Becker out of the affair?

"How do you mean that?" Becker asked.

"Don't you know that the Reichsmarshal collects such Madonnas?" Schlegel replied.

"Probably he has enough of them already," Becker said.

Becker's fear that loot, not rescue, was Schlegel's main motive was all the greater because of something the two had learned when they entered the monastery for their second interview with the abbot. At the entrance they had met two big Italians dressed in the uniform of museum guards. One of the guards came forward, exclaimed "Dottore, dottore!" and embraced Becker. The man looked vaguely familiar, but the doctor could not place him till the guard said simply, "Pompeii." Becker remembered. It was only a couple of weeks ago.

Becker had been driving in his little Fiat from Naples to the Salerno front, where his unit was in action. He was in a long line of military vehicles that had been immobilized by an Allied air attack. The drivers and passengers in the vehicles had taken refuge off the road. Becker had then driven his maneuverable little car off the road and had found himself at the ruins of Pompeii. He took out his sketchbook and pencil with the idea of passing the air raid sketching some ruins. In the ruins, Becker had encountered the big Italian guard. Soon a bomb fell near them, and the guard suffered a slight wound on his upper arm. Becker patched him up with the supplies in his car, gave him some cigarettes, and went on his way back to the front. Now, at the entrance to the abbey, Becker asked the guard what he was doing at Monte Cassino.

The big Italian took Becker aside and explained in a semi-whisper. He and his fellow guard were there to look after some valuables from Naples. After the first Allied bombing of Naples, the works of art from its national gallery and its archeological museum had been sent to Monte Cassino for safekeeping. There were, the guard said, more than 200 crates, including 30 crates of archeological finds from Pompeii and Herculaneum. No one knew exactly what was in the sealed crates, because in addition to art from Naples they held paintings loaned for the Naples Triennial Exposition, but it was said they contained eleven Titians (including his nude *Danae*), an El Greco, and the only two Goyas in Italy.

In the abbot's waiting room, the two Germans had spoken about the art from Naples only long enough to decide to ask the abbot if

15

they could take it to safety along with the other treasures. (Schlegel's account of this episode, which omits Becker entirely, says that it was he, Schlegel, who first learned of the Naples treasure, from a guard he had met at Pompeii the previous May.*) Now, after Becker's suspicions had been fanned by his Austrian colleague's remark about the wooden Madonna, it occurred to the doctor that looters would find the art of Naples a far more inviting target than the old documents of Monte Cassino.

The art of Naples, and what he had seen of Monte Cassino itself, made Becker realize that what he had undertaken was far bigger and more important than he had imagined when he first decided to drive up and talk to the abbot. Like any educated European, Becker had heard of the artistic wealth of Monte Cassino. But nothing he had heard quite prepared him for what he saw when a monk took him around the buildings after his first visit. The monastery was a great museum, a memorial to the medieval splendor of the mother house of the Benedictines. Everywhere the young doctor went he saw objects of inestimable value: the ancient illuminated scrolls and the intricately carved cases that held them; the mosaics and frescoes of the multitude of crypts and chapels, many of them executed by Germans from the monastery at Bueron in a severely formal style that was intended to produce a visual counterpart to the Gregorian chant. Hanging on the walls of rooms and corridors he saw paintings by Italian masters of the late Renaissance. The basilica, with its robin's-egg-blue cupola, stood alone on its mountaintop. Its bronze doors bore reliefs depicting the three destructions of Monte Cassino, and inside, over the entrance, hung a great painting by Luca Giordano showing the crowds gathered for *The Dedication of the Basilica* in the eleventh century. All this was wealth untold that must somehow be saved from war or looting.

Becker's thoughts were interrupted when the German monk sum-

*After the war Becker and Schlegel both wrote accounts of the rescue of the treasures. Each man claimed the idea of the rescue was his alone, and they disagree in several other respects. Becker's account is far more factual and more internally convincing. On several key points of disagreement Becker is corroborated by the accounts of the monks at Monte Cassino and Teano and other members of the Hermann Goering Division. The monk Tommaso Leccisotti wrote: "Becker's account seems more believable, because Schlegel's contains several inaccuracies." Becker, who is still alive, has supplied more details in correspondence with the authors.

moned them into Abbot Diamare's workroom. The German officers told the elderly abbot they would take the Naples treasure to the Vatican for safekeeping. No, said Diamare, the art of Naples belonged to the Italian state, and the Vatican was not Italian soil. He intended to hand the art over to Marshal Badoglio, who would soon be arriving at Monte Cassino with his army. Pietro Badoglio was head of the ephemeral Italian government that had succeeded Mussolini and, six weeks earlier, had signed an armistice with the Allies. In fact, as Becker and Schlegel knew, Badoglio had no army and his government existed only on paper; the only power that mattered in Italy was the Germans—and the Allies.

They now offered to take the art somewhere to the north of Rome, perhaps to Assisi. But suppose the war reached Assisi, the abbot asked. Becker's private opinion was that the war would end when the Allies captured Rome, but it could have cost him his life to say so in front of a fellow officer—a Nazi at that—so he simply said the art could be moved further north.

The old abbot then peered at Becker suspiciously through his horn-rimmed glasses. "Do you mean to Germany?" he asked.

Of course, Becker thought unhappily, the abbot thinks we Germans want to loot the treasure, and, considering Schlegel's remark about the wooden Madonna, Becker could not be certain the abbot was wrong. Still, it was increasingly urgent to move the treasure. Time was running out. In the last 48 hours the Allies had broken the barrier of the Volturno River, 40 miles to the south, and the Germans expected an enemy landing on the nearby coast any day. Soon the abbot would be able to look out his window and see the Allied soldiers rounding the hillside, across the valley, from which Becker had first seen Monte Cassino. And then it would be too late: the abbey would be surrounded in the battle, and there would be no treasure to save or loot.

As Becker recalled it, he and Schlegel finally won the abbot's consent to their plans by standing before him to deliver their solemn personal pledges to protect the treasures. (The account by Emmanuel Munding, the German monk who served as interpreter, implied that the abbot merely conceded the Germans' superior power to impose their will). The abbey's own possessions, and the monks themselves, would be taken to the Benedictine monasteries at St.

Paul's Outside the Walls and San Anselmo in Rome. The much larger amount that belonged to the state of Italy—most of the archive and all the art from Naples—would be taken to the supply depot of the Hermann Goering Division at Spoleto, 70 miles north of Rome, and would be turned over to the Italian authorities as soon as arrangements could be made. They would begin work the next day, with Schlegel in charge.

Schlegel renewed the offer to evacuate the abbot himself. The old man again refused, and Schlegel said, "Then you must be prepared to die here with your monks."

"I will remain here," the abbot repeated.

Abbot Diamare then asked the two Germans where those who stayed—he and a few of his monks—would be best protected in the event of bombing. Schlegel offered to look over the monastery from that point of view. Becker left, and the German monk, Munding— a short, bald man of about sixty—took Schlegel on a tour of the abbey grounds.

The abbey consisted of a complex of four-story buildings around three large cloisters. From the gallery of the first of these, the Loggia del Paradiso, a visitor could look out over the panorama of the Liri Valley and the road to Rome. A staircase at the end of the central cloister, flanked by statues of Saint Benedict and his sister, Saint Scholastica, led to the basilica, located at the opposite end of the complex from the entrance. Beneath the basilica and its neighboring buildings was a subterranean maze of chapels, crypts, and storerooms: the abbey had almost as much space below the ground as above it. When Schlegel and his escort came to a room with a heavily arched ceiling that lay 30 feet below ground level and under a 60-foot stone tower, the Austrian officer turned to the monk and said: "Here you will be safe from bombs."

4

The great palace at Caserta always had about it an air of the faintly ridiculous. When Charles IV, the Bourbon king of the Two Sicilies, set out in the mid-eighteenth century to build a palace in this town 30 miles north of Naples, he wanted to outdo the Versailles of his French cousins. The effort was enormous. But, impressive as the result was—the building with its 34 monumental stairs; the park, gardens, waterfalls, and artificial lakes—critics from Baedeker ("pompous") on sniffed at Charles's work as just an imitation, not the real thing. All the critics conceded, though, that the palace was big—so big, indeed, that, as was said in the fall of 1943, its 1,200 rooms could have housed the entire wartime population of Caserta. What the palace housed, that fall, was not the people of Caserta but the headquarters of the invading Allied armies: the Fifth Army, commanded by an American, Lieutenant-General Mark W. Clark, and the commander of all the Allied forces, the British general Sir Harold Alexander.

It was entirely typical of Mark Clark—typical both of his natural instincts and of his careful cultivation of his public image—that he refused to stay in the royal palace itself. A European palace was no home for an American cowboy, and this tall, raw-boned man with the open shirt resembled nothing so much as a European's conception of the hero of a Western movie. Clark set himself up in a trailer out in the formal gardens behind the palace. It was a converted truck, and, as Clark let the world know, it had room only for a bunk, a small desk, and a bucket of water. This shunning of luxury got him a lot of press attention, though it was in fact a repeat performance. Earlier that month Clark had refused to stay in the royal palace in Naples, because, as he wrote his wife, Maurine—who promptly and to no one's surprise read the letter at a war-bond rally—"I just felt lost in a big city so went back to where I belonged and could be with my men." Clark was raised in Chicago: no matter, it was a good story and the crowds cheered.

Now 47, Mark Wayne Clark—"Wayne" to his friends—had been at 46 the youngest lieutenant-general the U.S. Army had ever known.

His rise had been sudden and rapid; among his fellow officers only his friend Dwight D. Eisenhower had risen faster than he. Son of a career man, Clark was graduated from West Point in 1917, just in time to see combat for a few days in the First World War. Between the wars his career was in the doldrums; Clark was a captain for sixteen years. As the second war cast its shadow on America, Clark, by now a lieutenant-colonel, was assigned to plan training for the expanding U.S. Army. His diligence and competence in that assignment so impressed his superiors, including General George C. Marshall, the army chief of staff, that Clark was promoted directly to brigadier-general. When Eisenhower was sent to England to plan for the North African landing of November 1942, he asked for Clark, and the two men shared an apartment in London. Before the landing Clark made a dramatic, secret trip by submarine—later much publicized—to Vichy-ruled Algiers. Little more than two years earlier he had been an unknown lieutenant-colonel. Now he held the army's second highest rank and, after North Africa, his long, thin face, with its noteworthy nose and high cheekbones, was a familiar portrait in the gallery of wartime military leaders.

In Italy in October of 1943, Mark Clark had reached the supreme moment of his career. After the slow obscure decades of peacetime, the meaning of that career would be determined by a handful of decisions fused in the heat of combat over the next few months. Through a series of political and military negotiations among the Allied leaders, each pursuing different if not contradictory goals, Clark had been assigned a compromise mission that satisfied no one. He had, moreover, been given command of a polyglot army, with far fewer resources than logic would dictate, and told to carry out his mission at the wrong time of the year.

Clark's mission was to conquer Rome, from the south. It was the wrong way to go about it. That much had been plain more than two thousand years earlier when Hannibal, based like the Allies in North Africa, had circled all around through Spain and the Alps to avoid approaching Rome through the mountains of southern Italy. Many months and many lives later a Roman princess would tell Clark that he was "only the second barbarian to conquer Rome from the south." No doubt the princess had in mind not Garibaldi, who accomplished the feat in 1849, but the Byzantine general Belisarius. In the year 536 Belisarius, no barbarian, marched north to Rome along the Via Casilina, passing along the way a mountain, above the town of Casinum, where a decade or so earlier a Christian monk named Benedict had founded a monastery. But Belisarius met no opposition on that road, and that was a blessing Clark could not expect.

The Allied decisions that brought Mark Clark to that trailer behind the palace at Caserta grew out of the great events of the first half of 1943. In 1942, the Allies had still been struggling for sheer survival. By mid-1943, it was clear to the Allied leaders—and to many German generals as well—that Germany could no longer win the war. Three great victories had determined the outcome. In February the surrender of the German survivors at Stalingrad ended that monstrously bloody battle and ended, too, Hitler's hope of victory in the East. In the spring the Germans were forced by mounting losses of submarines to call off their U-boat campaign in the North Atlantic: Britain need no longer fear that she would be starved into submission. In North Africa, a series of victories that began with Lieutenant-General Bernard Montgomery's defeat of Rommel at El Alamein culminated in May with the surrender of a quarter of a million German and Italian soldiers at Tunis: the Allies need no longer fear that Rommel would cut the Suez Canal and drive into the Middle East.

With the ultimate outcome all but certain, the Allied leaders, and most of all Churchill and Stalin, could look beyond the immediate struggle to the shape of the postwar world and their position in it. The Western Allies had promised Stalin, whose people had borne almost the entire weight of battle since June of 1941, that they would invade the Continent in massive force across the English Channel. This invasion, known as Overlord, was now scheduled for the spring of 1944 and was supposed to take priority over all other goals in the assignment of Allied resources. Churchill's agreement to this strategy had always been less than wholehearted. He feared that a massive battle in northern France—the very site of the hideous slaughters of the First World War—would cost his small nation more manpower than it could afford. Churchill had always wanted to mount a series of attacks on what he persisted in calling, in defiance of topography, the "soft underbelly of Europe." If the Allies could gain a footing on the central part of the Continent, he reasoned, they would be better placed for the eventual contest with Soviet Russia for the

21

dominance of postwar Europe. In January, he had persuaded the reluctant Americans to invade Sicily after the conquest of North Africa.

The conquest of Sicily in July had the effect of knocking Mussolini off his perch and, soon after, Italy out of the war. On July 25, the Fascist Grand Council, disgusted with the course of what he had promised would be a cheap and easy war, voted Mussolini out of office. His successors, King Victor Emmanuel II and Marshal Pietro Badoglio, immediately started secret negotiations with the Allies through neutral Portugal in search of a way out of a war they had never wanted, at least not at the price they were now paying for it. In September the Italians signed an armistice with the Allies and joined them as "co-belligerents" against Germany.

Early in September Montgomery's Eighth Army had landed on the toe of Italy in a campaign that had the limited objective of capturing the great air base at Foggia, across the peninsula from Naples, from which Allied bombers could reach new targets in central Europe. Now Churchill was arguing for a strike at the great political and psychological prize of Rome. But the Americans were unwilling to risk the resources in men and machines needed for a landing near Rome. The result was compromise: the Allies would land on the mainland, but only at Salerno, south of Naples, and their forces would be diminished by two divisions sent to England for Overlord. So, even after a successful landing at Salerno, the Allies would have to attack Rome from the direction avoided from Hannibal's time on. On October 4, Roosevelt cabled Stalin that the Allies expected to take Rome "in a few weeks," but in fact their only hope for a relatively easy campaign was if the Germans decided not to mount any serious resistance below Rome.

The Fifth Army—"Mark Clark's Fifth Army," as he kept telling reporters to call it—had fought well at Salerno, and Clark had distinguished himself in his first combat command of the war. The German resistance was unexpectedly heavy; indeed, if Hitler had not refused a request for reinforcements, the defenders might have pushed the Allies off the beachhead. Refuse he did, the Allies prevailed at Salerno, and they moved north to occupy the great port city of Naples on October 1. But there were ominous signs in the nature of the German actions that Hitler was not going to follow his original strategy of falling back to a defense line in the north of

Italy. Clark's army would have to fight its way to Rome.

The terrain through which Clark must lead his men was forbidding in the extreme. From his headquarters at Caserta a string of mountains and hills stretched in jagged succession all the way to Rome, 190 miles to the northwest. These mountains, the Abruzzi, cover the entire Italian peninsula between Naples and Rome, and by land there is no way around them. The mountains are angular and rocky, and beyond each there is always another one. In the best of weather, this is difficult terrain for an attacker, and October's is far from the best of weather: that is when the winter rains begin, turning the land to mud and making movement of men and machines still more difficult. "Each hillside," Clark later wrote, "became a small but difficult military problem that could be solved only by careful preparation and almost inevitably by the spilling of blood." Two Germans with a machine gun dug in on one of those hillsides could stop many times their number. It was discouraging, he added, to take "one strong point after another, only to see, through the rain and the mud, still another hillside on which the enemy was entrenched in pillboxes and well-protected artillery emplacements." Yet it had to be done, and the only question in those early days of the campaign was which route to take.

Four major roads ran up the peninsula. There were also a number of minor roads, but those could be dismissed: especially in the rainy season, these roads could not carry the heavy equipment—the tanks and artillery and trucks—on which the Allies counted for the margin of victory. Of those four main roads, two lay on the other, eastern side of the peninsula; one ran along the Adriatic coast; and the other paralleled it a few miles inland. The Adriatic sector was the territory assigned to Montgomery's Eighth Army. Those routes could also be dismissed because, if the Allies had gotten up the coast along them, they would still have had to fight their way back across the peninsula, through mountain country, to reach Rome.

On the western side of the peninsula the main road forked just north of Caserta. The left fork, Route 7, the old Via Appia, ran along the coast of the Tyrrhenian Sea. This road was soon pinched against the coast by the mountains and then ran through the Pontine marshes, which the enemy could easily make impassable by flooding. Mark Clark judged that he could not go that way.

That left the right fork, where the road divided north of Caserta.

This was Route 6, the Roman Via Casilina, the route Belisarius took in 536. For about 75 miles north from Caserta this road led through difficult mountain country, but then the landscape opened out into the Liri Valley. From there the going figured to be comparatively easy all the way to Rome—if the Allies could get that far, for, as Clark wrote, "to reach the Liri Valley, we first had to drive the Germans off the Camino hill mass . . . that would lead us into the head of the valley where the Liri was joined by the Rapido River. It also would, unhappily, bring us under the guns of the Germans in high hills around a little town called Cassino."

Route 6 was the only way to go. But if this logic was clear to Mark Clark, it had to be equally clear to the Germans. There could be no surprises in the fighting to come. An enemy who was brave, skilled, and experienced would be waiting for Clark's army in those terrible mountains.

In the mornings Clark set out from the trailer behind the palace to visit "his" army. Sometimes he traveled in a Piper Cub that flew low enough to avoid enemy aircraft, but more often the general traveled by jeep. The Fifth Army had overrun the roads of Italy. All the roads in the area around Naples were clotted with the military traffic of the Allies, a never-ending stream of khaki-painted vehicles of all sizes and descriptions. When it rained, as it did almost every day that October, the roads turned to yellow mud and the great lumbering vehicles bogged down, like hobbled dinosaurs, till the mud dried out. Alongside the roads the Allies had put up their own hand-lettered signs; at some intersections there were dozens of such signs and it might take a traveler many minutes to decipher them all. Occasionally, someone had put up a philosophical message, on a series of boards 50 or so feet apart, in the Burma-Shave fashion: "If you leave/good clothes behind/you may need them/some other time."

The great bulk of the army shoved the Italian peasants carelessly out of its way. The peasants stood by the roads in dark, gloomy clumps watching the army roll heavily by, and, when it was gone, they ventured back to their homes and fields to salvage what was left. The war meant nothing to the Italian peasants. Started by a distant tyrant in Rome, continued now by foreigners from over the mountains and the seas, this war was no different from all the others inflicted on them over the centuries. Of this war, like all the others, the peasants knew only one thing: whoever won, whoever profited, they would suffer.

Wherever Mark Clark went, people were aware of him. At six feet two inches, with that great Roman nose and with his brash, youthful stride, Clark was not a man to be overlooked in a crowd. And he wanted to be noticed: he strode into a room in a manner that was meant to be noticed. He loved the attention he was getting from reporters and cameramen: fame had come only recently to Mark Clark. That fall the American press was full of copy, most of it admiring, about Clark. On September 19 the *New York Times* ran a particularly worshipful article under the title GENERAL MARK CLARK GETS THE TOUGH JOBS. The author, Milton Bracker, reported that Clark "flies his own plane," that his "voice can bark but it can purr, too," and went on to tell a sorry anecdote, patronizing even for its time, about a "Negro anti-aircraft crew" who petitioned, in dialect, to stay with Clark because, apparently, he "laughed at their jokes."

Clark was hogging the limelight, it often seemed, and no one was more prone to resent his attention-getting ways than the generals who found themselves under his command. In the delicately political layering of command in the Allied armies, Clark had been placed under a British commander, Alexander, and over a half dozen American and British generals. Because of his own rapid rise in rank, Clark commanded American colleagues who were older than he and who only yesterday had outranked him; one of these, Major-General Fred L. Walker, commander of the 36th Division, had once been Clark's instructor. Among the British generals were men who were far more experienced than their commander in the business of war. Clark's experience in battle was measured in weeks, and not many of them. Under him were officers who had been in combat off and on since 1939, and who in many cases had a generation earlier fought the four bloody years of what used to be called the Great War. Such men would be quick to resent the young charging commander of "Mark Clark's Fifth Army." Dealing with this collection of subordinates, as strong-willed and egotistic as he was himself and as eager as he was to reap glory from their brief moment in the spotlight of history, would have taxed the skills of the most experienced of diplomats, and diplomacy was not one of Mark Clark's natural endowments.

COLORADO MOUNTAIN COLLEGE
LRC–WEST CAMPUS
Glenwood Springs, Colo. 81601

The problems of managing a polyglot army did not end with Anglo-American diplomacy. The Fifth was one of the most diverse armies ever assembled. Only about one-third of its troops were American. About the same number were British. Among its one hundred thousand men at one time or another were units from New Zealand, India, France and North Africa, Poland, and even Brazil. Differences in language and custom multiplied the usual confusion and tension of war. Each nation had its own distinctive military ways, and the religion of some of the soldiers from India and North Africa imposed special dietary requirements. Because of the difference between American and British equipment, the army needed two completely separate supply lines for ammunition and spare parts. Such difficulties simply multiplied the problems of men and machines who already were wallowing around in seas of yellow mud. At times, indeed, it seemed that the terrain of south Italy was quite capable of defeating the Allies without any help from the Germans.

As if all that were not enough, Clark also had to deal with the Italian people his army had brought under Allied rule. The Allies were not sure how they viewed the Italians since the fall of Mussolini: no longer an enemy, but not yet an ally. On this question there were important differences between the two major Allies. The English had painful memories of Mussolini's stab in the back of June 1940—a lot of English soldiers had died because of that act of betrayal; and England itself was home to only a few Catholics and virtually no people of Italian origin. But across the Atlantic President Roosevelt was getting ready to run for reelection, for his fourth term, in November of 1944. He was as aware as anyone that his nation included many Italian-Americans and many more Roman Catholics, and that most of them normally voted Democratic. This basic political arithmetic would color Roosevelt's view of the Allied role in Italy. Throughout the war he had kept a line open to the Pope through his envoy in the neutral Vatican, and now, in September, Roosevelt suddenly proclaimed that the Allied invasion of Italy was a "crusade to save the Pope."

The encounter between the Allies and the Italians in the port city of Naples was a memorable meeting. Here was the American G.I.: setting foot for the first time on the continent of Europe, he was totally ignorant of the land and people around him; young, generous, naive, he viewed the Italians he saw with a mixture of kindness and contempt; his cigarettes and candy bars made him a wealthy man in that time and place. And the ragged, hungry Neapolitan street urchin: young but cynical beyond his years; descended from a people who had been surviving a procession of conquerors for two millennia; he saw that G.I. as his chance to survive.

The people of Naples were starving and their city had been ruined by Allied bombing and German demolition. In addition to destroying the port, the retreating Germans had killed many Italian civilians and had made a public spectacle of burning the contents of the Royal Society library. The Germans, who had been subsidizing their allies with food from conquered Europe, had cut off the supply when the Italians abandoned them, and the farms of southern Italy could not begin to feed the people of the city. The Allies in those first weeks did not bring in enough food to feed the Neapolitans as well as their own soldiers. But the Allied presence stoked the local economy in other ways. Allied engineers, working at astonishing speed, within days managed to get the port installations, demolished by the retreating Germans, working well enough to receive a vast stream of military supplies. About one-third of this stream never made it to the front; it was stolen on the docks and soon appeared for sale or barter on those streets of Naples. Also for sale on those streets were many of the women of Naples, who, whether by profession or out of desperation, prostituted themselves for a pack of cigarettes: they gave the Allied soldiers a moment of pleasure and a particularly virulent strain of gonorrhea that seemed at times to be felling more soldiers than the Germans.

The Allies would be fighting the Germans all over Italy, and the question was how much the Italians would suffer—how much their land would be trampled underfoot—in the course of the struggle. How much the Allies would destroy from the air, by bombing, was the form in which the question would most plague Mark Clark and the other Allied commanders. In 1943, the air generals of both the United States and Britain were offering the seductive prospect of *Victory Through Air Power* (the title of Alexander P. Seversky's best seller). This was strategic bombing, not the battlefield bombing so brilliantly demonstrated early in the war by the German Stukas. The theory of strategic bombing—and it was no more than theory—was that heavy and repeated bombing of the centers of production would so damage Germany's industrial base that its armies' capacity to

27

wage war would be at least seriously impaired. Failing that, perhaps the bombing would break the morale of the German people and they would force their leaders to seek peace—and this was said by the very people who in 1940 had boasted that the German terror bombing of England had only stiffened the English will to fight. That this strategy involved large-scale bombing of civilians had been accepted by all but a tiny minority of Allied public opinion. When the Germans had begun bombing civilians, in Guernica, then in Warsaw and Rotterdam, people in the West were horrified; but the ethics of war had hardened them since then. In July and August of 1943 the Royal Air Force had incinerated sixty thousand German civilians in a series of raids on Hamburg that were of only hypothetical military value. The ethical justification for such wholesale slaughter of noncombatants, if one was needed, was that the German people had put the Nazis in power and so shared the guilt of their crimes against humanity. (This reasoning would be grotesquely mirrored by Joseph Goebbels, the Nazi propaganda chief. Surveying the ruins of his nation in the closing days of the war, Goebbels said that "the German people had failed their Fuehrer and must be punished.")

Though they agreed on the principle of strategic bombing, the British and American air generals differed on how it should be carried out. The British practiced large-scale bombing by night, when German fighters and anti-aircraft fire found it hard to shoot down the bombers. This kind of bombing was admittedly so inaccurate that the smallest area the British could target was an entire city. In practice, their bombing was even less accurate: many if not most of their bombs missed the city at which they were aimed, and only a small minority actually hit anything of military or industrial value. At this stage of war the Americans had not yet been converted to indiscriminate bombing of cities. The American airmen advocated what they called "high-level precision bombing" by daylight: planes flying high enough to escape the German defenses would, by daylight, be able to hit their targets with far greater accuracy. The American press that summer was filled with admiring descriptions of this technique; when the Americans bombed railway yards in Rome, *Life* magazine wrote of their "astonishing accuracy . . . cleancut precision" compared to "ordinary [British] area bombing." This was largely nonsense, but it was widely believed, and in the fall of 1943 the American airmen were eager for opportunities to demonstrate the superiority of their way of bombing over that of their British rivals.

No one proposed for Italy the kind of bombing that was then being inflicted on Germany. The Italians, after all, had already surrendered, and, more important, their land was the museum of Western civilization. Here, in entire cities like Rome, Florence, and Venice, and in a thousand cathedrals and churches and monasteries, was embodied the progress of humanity from ancient Rome through the rise of Christianity to the Renaissance. This was the civilization the Nazis sought to wipe out; and the Allies did not propose deliberately to destroy its artifacts. Accordingly, Allied bombing in Italy had been restricted to clearly military targets: rail yards, port installations, the roads on which the enemy was bringing supplies from Germany. Still, it was clear enough that Italy could not hope to come through the battle completely unscathed. Already, in Sicily and in the early days of combat on the mainland, a distressing number of monuments and churches had been damaged or destroyed.

In the United States, cultural groups like the Council of Learned Societies had been pressing their government for many months to do something to minimize the destruction of the monuments of Europe. In August, after the campaign in Sicily and with the invasion of the mainland in prospect, the State Department set up something called the American Commission for the Protection and Salvage of Artistic and Historic Monuments; it soon came to be known as the Roberts Commission, after its chairman, Supreme Court Justice Owen J. Roberts. Cordell Hull, the secretary of state, sold the idea for its propaganda value rather than its intrinsic merit; when it was put that way, the Joint Chiefs of Staff dropped their earlier objections.

The commission's first goal was to provide the military with handbooks and maps showing the location of important monuments. The idea was to pinpoint for the military commanders those places that should be preserved "to the extent allowed by military operations." Next, the War Department created a program for Monuments, Fine Arts and Archives (MFAA), which was to be part of the prospective structure of Allied military government—AMGOT, in the vernacular—on the Continent. A single MFAA officer, Major Paul Gardner, arrived in the ruins of Naples in early October. Gardner's job was at best lonely and unpopular—MFAA officers were called "mousy Venus-fixers" by the troops—and it was made no easier when a British officer carrying all the maps for

ABOVE: Lieutenant-General Mark W. Clark attending a ceremony at a monastery near Salerno; Clark presented to Monsignor Francesco Cuzzo money raised by American soldiers to repair damage done by artillery fire aimed at the monastery in the belief the Germans were using it as an observation post. OPPOSITE, TOP: General Clark (left) with his commanding officer, General Harold Alexander. OPPOSITE, BOTTOM: Two views of General Frido von Senger und Etterlin, commander of the 14th Panzer Korps.

the Naples area on a motorcycle was captured by the Germans.

Mark Clark himself, no matter what that Roman princess might say or German propagandists might write, did not intend to go down in history as a barbarian of a conqueror. Naples was the first city on the Continent to be occupied by the Allies; Clark believed it was important to make a good impression there, and indiscriminate destruction would not further that impression. He cultivated his image as a warrior who cared about culture. In early October Clark had himself photographed receiving a "carved carnelian stone" from a Monsignor Francesco Guazzo. The gift—according to the caption under the photo in the *New York Times*—was in gratitude for the money American troops had raised to repair the damage their artillery had done to a monastery at Capaccio, a village in the hills near Salerno. "The Germans," the caption said, "had used the monastery as an observation post." It was an unusually civilized act in wartime, and Clark was happy to be in the picture.

The general concern about Italian monuments began, in late October, to focus on places that lay in the path of the probable Allied advance. E. C. Norris, a London art specialist serving in Naples as flight lieutenant, had sought out the provincial fine arts superintendent, whom he found home in bed with a leg wound, and from him Norris had learned that the valuables of the Naples museum and gallery had been sent to Monte Cassino. On October 20, Norris radioed the information to the Mediterranean Air Command in Algiers. He sent the message "in clear" (not in code) in the hopes the Germans would intercept it; Norris later believed it was his information that caused the Germans to move the treasures from Monte Cassino. On October 25, the air command radioed Fifth Army headquarters that "Italian museum authorities stress urgent importance of preservation from bombing of Abbey of Monte Cassino." Two days later the essence of the message was repeated, and on November 5 Alexander's headquarters informed Clark's headquarters that:

> From time to time details of artistic, historical and ecclesiastical centers which it is desired to preserve will be issued. These will be serially numbered: first two serials are:
> 1) Papal domain in Castel Gandolfo.
> 2) Ancient Benedictine Abbey of Monte Cassino.

5

The scene at the Abbey of Monte Cassino in those late October days was one of purposeful confusion. It looked more like a military construction site than a monastery. The cloisters rang with the tramping of military boots, and from the improvised carpentry shop was heard the whine of saws and the banging of hammers. The work force was an odd mixture of German soldiers, some still wearing tropical uniforms from the North African campaign; Benedictine monks in their black cowls; and raggedly dressed Italian men.

Each morning German army trucks—open-backed vehicles painted in camouflage colors and marked with the insignia of the Hermann Goering Division—drew up empty at the monastery gate. A steady stream of men carried crates through the cloisters and out the gate to the waiting trucks. Each evening the trucks left, loaded with people and treasures, on the road to Rome 80 miles away. Presiding over all this activity was Lieutenant-Colonel Julius Schlegel.

Schlegel seemed to be everywhere at once—in the archive with the monks and the carpenters, dashing through the cloisters, outside the gate where the trucks were being loaded, managing, ordering, cajoling. Schlegel was in his element. Transport was his business—in Vienna before the war, and now in the Hermann Goering Division —and by all accounts he was excellent at it.

For the monks the evacuation of their monastery was a shattering experience. On the evening of October 16, two days after Dr. Becker's first visit, Abbot Diamare had told them what was to happen. The monks were gathered in their most holy place, the crypt of Saint Benedict, a low-vaulted room under the basilica. The crypt was lit by candles; the electricity was no longer working. After they had sung the mass of Benedict and Scholastica, the old abbot told the monks that the family of Benedict would again be forced into exile. Again, because the Abbey of Monte Cassino had been destroyed and its inhabitants scattered three times over the centuries: by the Lombards, sometime between 577 and 589, in the first century of its existence; by the Saracens in 883; and by an earthquake in 1349. The

31

fourth destruction was now in prospect, the abbot said.

Leaving Monte Cassino, for the monks, meant leaving the only home they had or ever expected to have. When a man chose the Benedictine vocation, he vowed himself for life to a single monastery. These men had exchanged the world outside, the world in which they were born, for the isolated, self-sufficient community of Monte Cassino. They had intended to live all their remaining days in the never-changing, minutely ordered cycle of work and prayer laid down by the Rule of Benedict. Their lives were utterly predictable, or so they had thought; change, then, was far more upsetting to the monks than to those who lived in the world outside the monastery's walls.

Now, the abbot had told the monks, they were to be uprooted and taken to Rome, all but the handful who would stay with him. The treasures of the archive in which many of them worked, the familiar objects of beauty that they saw every day, this too would be taken away. No one could know, the old abbot said, whether the monastery would survive or whether any of them would live to see their home on the holy mountain again. Dismayed and reluctant, most of the monks nonetheless agreed with their abbot, and all of them cooperated actively in the evacuation that was already disrupting the fixed cycle of their days.

By now the commander of the Hermann Goering Division, General Conrath, had given his approval to the removal of the treasures. With the general's backing, Schlegel had arranged to use trucks that, after delivering supplies to the front to the south, were returning empty to the division's supply depot at Spoleto, north of Rome. From the soft drink factory—near the front, but Schlegel got to it before the Allies—he got lumber, tools, and nails, the materials needed to crate the treasures of Monte Cassino. And he persuaded his fellow officers to assign to him a handful of skilled German carpenters from units that were not at the front.

Even with the soldiers and the monks, Schlegel needed more labor. He was racing the clock of war. The use of the trucks might be taken away by his superiors at any time, and neither Schlegel nor anyone else knew when the Allied forces might appear in the valley below Monte Cassino. Already, when the wind was right, the sound of the guns at the Volturno River, 40 miles to the south, could be heard at the abbey. In his search for more hands, Schlegel hit upon a stratagem

32

that would meet his needs and also solve the abbey's most urgent problem.

The problem was the refugees, the Italian civilians who fled in waves to Monte Cassino each time the Allies bombed Cassino or the nearby villages in the plain below. About a thousand of them were now living in improvised shelters in the abbey's cloisters. They clustered in family groups around their few possessions, the women invariably in black, the children huddled close to them in the growing cold. Few able-bodied men were among them; the Germans had rounded up most such men and sent them to Germany as slave laborers. Nobody wanted these human leavings of the war. From the abbey's point of view, they were placing an intolerable strain on the supplies of food and water, and, living in filthy conditions, they were becoming a hazard to their own health and that of others. Yet the Rule of Benedict forbade the monks to deny hospitality to anyone who sought it. From Schlegel's point of view, the refugees were a mere nuisance; they and their improvised quarters were cluttering the passage from the archives to the trucks. He now saw a way to turn the liability of the refugees into an asset.

Schlegel had the refugees summoned to the central cloister and, through an interpreter, he told them they would either have to work on the evacuation or leave the abbey. Most of the refugees left, as he had anticipated—to the relief of the monks—but a few stayed on to work. Schlegel provided these workers with a daily ration of food and twenty cigarettes.

The massive job of evacuation centered on the library and archive, with their 70,000 documents. Many of these were hand-lettered parchment scrolls stored in large wooden drawers. They represented many centuries of careful labor by generations of monks. At the end of each scroll the monk recorded the date and his name and sometimes his further comments. One such notation read, in Latin: "The transcription of this volume was completed on May 19, 1676, by Father Bartholemeo. Inasmuch as Father Bartholemeo was promised absolution of one sin for each letter, he thanks God that the sum total of the letters exceeds the sum total of the sins, though by but a single unit."

The archive was presided over by Mauro Inguanez, a sharp-eyed bald monk in his fifties. From the beginning, both Becker and Schlegel had sensed this monk's hostility to them and to the idea of letting the Germans take away the treasures. Inguanez was Maltese, a British subject; his native island had been under German seige for three years. At the monks' emotional night meeting in the crypt, he argued against letting the treasures go. Still, once the majority of the monks had made the decision, Inguanez cooperated in the evacuation. Now he marked each drawer of scrolls with chalk as it was packed in a crate, which in turn was marked "M.C. Lib."

Another monk, Eusebio Grossetti, an artist, was assigned the responsibility for choosing those of the abbey's works of art that would be rescued. Schlegel noted with pleasure that the wooden Madonna he had admired in the abbot's waiting room was packed to be sent. Among the treasures that were rescued, Dr. Becker remembered some paintings by Italian old masters and a collection of gold and silver measuring devices inlaid with gems. When time and lumber were running short, they wrapped paintings and books in the abbey's equally valuable tapestries.

There was another aspect of the evacuation about which the Germans knew nothing. The Naples museum authorities were not the only ones to entrust their valuables to Monte Cassino. The numismatic museum of Syracuse had sent a crate containing its ancient coins, and the church of San Gennaro in Naples had sent three small lead-sealed wooden boxes. The monks had first become concerned about these valuables they were keeping when, in early September, Germans appeared at Monte Cassino to ask about the weather station that the Italian military had operated in the *torretta,* the tower that was the monastery's highest point, until Italy's surrender to the Allies. The three Italian airmen who ran the *osservatorio* went into hiding when the Germans came. The Germans left, but the monks feared they might return and take over the monastery for their purposes. Working at night, a small group of monks secreted parcels of coins and the three small boxes in the remote recesses of the monastery. Each monk knew only the location of what he had hidden. The only monk who knew all the hiding places was the abbot's secretary. Now, again at night, when the Germans were not in the abbey, the secretary was managing another covert operation. The monks were mixing the coins and the three boxes in with their personal property and smuggling them out on the trucks going to Rome.

The first trucks were ready to go less than a week from the day

Becker and Schlegel first came to Monte Cassino. The nuns from Cassino and the orphans in their care climbed into a truck and settled themselves around the crates of the abbey's possessions. The Benedictine abbess, who was partially paralyzed, had to be lifted carefully onto the back of the truck. The trucks were parked under the trees, though most of the leaves had fallen so the trees did not offer much concealment from the air. Two monks would accompany each truck going to the Benedictine monasteries in Rome.

The whole community of Monte Cassino—the monks, joined by German soldiers and refugees—turned out to see off the first trucks carrying people. At their head, standing in the road outside the gate, was the squat, stooped figure of Abbot Diamare. Beside him, much taller, was a well-built 40-year-old monk with a prominent nose and close-cropped graying hair: Martino Matronola, the abbot's secretary and chief assistant. The abbot gave his blessing to those who were departing. The trucks were ready to go.

At that moment Allied fighter-bombers appeared screaming overhead. They were bombing Cassino town, just below the abbey. The sound of the exploding bombs, of the anti-aircraft fire, above all the shriek of the motors as the planes pulled out of a bombing run—all this terrified the refugees waiting in the trucks. Schlegel shouted at them to stay where they were, but many of them scattered from the trucks in search of shelter. The old abbot and his fellow monks knelt under the trees as if in prayer and remained still until the bombing was over.

No bombs had fallen on Monte Cassino. No one was injured. The only casualty was an earthenware jug filled with olive oil that was shattered during the moment of panic. The trucks left for Rome. "Saint Benedict had helped," the German monk wrote years later.

Two monks carried the abbey's most precious possession to Rome during the early days of the evacuation. These were two silk-covered boxes, the size of small suitcases, in which were reliquaries that contained tiny fragments of the bones of saints Benedict and Scholastica. The major bones of the saints remained buried in the monastery. Saint Benedict had been buried under what later became the basilica; the chronicler relates that he had died standing erect, his arms raised in prayer. Saint Scholastica, who founded a nunnery in the valley below Monte Cassino, had been buried beside her brother. This was not the first time that the mortal remains of the abbey's patron saints had been disturbed. In the late seventh century, after the first destruction, monks found the saints' bones in the ruins and took them to an abbey at Fleury, near Orleans. The monks at Fleury returned the bones—but not all of them—to Monte Cassino in the next century.

Abbot Diamare and his secretary, Matronola, had carried the two silk-covered cases of relics to the German truck and carefully placed them aboard. The old abbot kept his hands on the relics until the truck drove away. Schlegel saw tears in the abbot's eyes. Schlegel later recalled that he had heard the abbot did not sleep until he was informed, some time the next day, that the relics had safely arrived in Rome and were in the hands of Benedictines there.

Dr. Becker helped Inguanez, the Maltese archivist monk, to take another set of human relics to Rome. These were two oblong metal boxes containing original manuscripts by the English poets John Keats and Percy Bysshe Shelley. An Italian diplomat had brought the boxes to Monte Cassino for safekeeping from the Keats-Shelley house in Rome, the four-story memento-filled stucco building next to the Spanish Stairs. When the Germans came to Monte Cassino, Inguanez had hidden the two boxes among his personal possessions. Becker took the monk and the boxes to Rome in his little Fiat. Instead of the direct route to Rome, which was under frequent Allied air attack, Becker chose to drive on a back road that snaked up into the mountains of the Abruzzi in the rugged center of the Italian peninsula. Along the way he stopped so Inguanez could talk to the managers of abbey farm properties about the food supply for the swollen population of Monte Cassino.

They halted for a rest on the heights looking down to the hill town of Avezzano. It was, Becker recalled, a warm, sunny day and they saw a wild, beautiful mountain panorama as yet untouched by the war. The German doctor and the Maltese monk talked over their differences. Inguanez said he especially hoped that no harm would come to Monte Cassino because of the English. He told Becker that when the Italian state took possession of the Monte Cassino archive in the nineteenth century, it was William Gladstone, the English prime minister, who persuaded the Italians to leave the archive in the custody of the monks. It would be tragic, said Inguanez, if the English were now to be responsible for the abbey's destruction.

The monk asked Becker bluntly if he were a Nazi. Becker replied

ABOVE: Abbot Gregorio Diamare (with cross) and Lieutenant-Colonel Julius Schlegel (left) during the evacuation of the abbey treasures. The monk between Schlegel and the abbot is Agostino Saccomanno. RIGHT: Abbot Diamare studies a map with Schlegel and, at right, his secretary, Martino Matronola.

ABOVE: German soldiers and Italian civilians packing the treasures of Monte Cassino for their journey to the Vatican. BELOW: Dr. Becker (right) with the monk Eusebio Grossetti in the workshop where crates are being assembled.

by telling him about the night in 1938 when he was beaten unconscious by a band of brown-shirted thugs. The young doctor then confided in the older man. He told him the source of his personal wartime torment, a secret unknown to any of his fellow officers: Becker was a British citizen. Born of an English mother and German father, he had grown up with dual citizenship. In 1939, with the storm clouds gathering, a British consular official in Berlin told Becker that if he was ever to leave, now was the time. Becker was almost through medical school, but the University of Edinburgh, to which he had applied, would not accept his German credits. Becker stayed, war came, and soon he was a soldier fighting his mother's people; fortunately she did not live to see that.

Now that he knew the young doctor was his fellow citizen, the monk Inguanez offered his help. Becker thought the monk was hinting that he could arrange through the Benedictines in Rome to smuggle the doctor across the lines. Becker was sorely tempted: a couple of days and he would be free of this dreadful war. But he had no way of knowing how the British would receive him. Would his dual citizenship make him a traitor in their eyes? Besides, his wife and daughter were in Berlin. Who knew what vengeance the Nazi state might take on the family of a deserter? Becker could not expose them to that risk. Reluctantly he refused the monk's offer. They got back in his little car and went on to Rome.

The evacuation of Monte Cassino was completed in the first days of November, less than three weeks after Dr. Becker's first visit to the abbot. Julius Schlegel, the bluff, hearty Nazi from Vienna, could be proud of the operation he had improvised with the men and materials he was able to find. More than a hundred truckloads had been carried to Rome or the supply depot at Spoleto and not a single one had been lost or even damaged on the way. The work force Schlegel had put together had moved all the treasures of the Naples museum, had crated and moved most of the archive and library of Monte Cassino, and had taken to Rome most of the monks and some of the refugees. In three weeks, in the middle of a losing war, in another country, it was quite a feat.

When the work was nearing its end, Dr. Becker suggested that the abbey might present a ceremonial scroll to General Conrath, commander of the Hermann Goering Division. After he had led a mass in the basilica, attended by German soldiers and officers, and recorded by a German cameraman, Abbot Diamare formally presented a scroll for the general and two other scrolls to Schlegel and Becker. The scrolls were written on parchment in Lombard script with letters illuminated by Eusebio Grossetti, the artist monk. The text, signed by Abbot Diamare, praised the Germans in Latin—*tribuno militum Julio Schlegel,* and *Maximiliano Becker medecinae doctori*—for rescuing the monks and treasures of the Abbey of Monte Cassino.

6

The little medieval town of Roccasecca is tucked in at the head of the Liri Valley. Rome lies 75 miles to the northwest across fairly open country. From the town, the Liri River runs down the valley, between high mountain walls, to join with the Rapido below the crest of Monte Cassino, 15 miles away. In November 1943, Panzer General Frido von Senger und Etterlin had his headquarters in an old palazzo in Roccasecca.

From his headquarters Senger could gaze down the Liri Valley, past Cassino, and to the tangle of mountains and valleys through which lay the road from Naples to Rome. The enemy—the Allied Fifth Army commanded by the American general Mark Clark—was fighting his way up that road. Now, in mid-November, the enemy had reached the village of San Pietro, just south of the valley.

Senger, more than any other man, was responsible for stopping Clark's advancing army. Senger commanded the 14th Panzer Korps, five divisions totaling close to seventy-five thousand men spread out on a front that stretched from the western coast 50 miles into the wild heart of the Abruzzi mountains. If the Allies were to be stopped on the road to Rome, this is where it would have to be done, and these men commanded by Senger would have to do it. It was a task to which Senger brought great professional skill—and profound misgivings.

Senger, in retrospect, stands out as one of the most extraordinary of Hitler's generals. His face once seen was not easily forgotten: his high forehead, under black hair receding at 53, bisected by a prominent vein, and his great beak of a nose between deep-sunk dark eyes, gave him in profile the look of a hawk. In repose his face was austere, but when he smiled, as he often did, the effect was attractive; and his hands with their long fingers, with which he gestured eloquently, were those of a pianist. His daughter remembered especially the way her father carried his trim, athletic frame: "He was quite different from the Prussian image. You would have to see him move, with that gentle grace, not at all stiff—more French really than Prussian." Indeed, Senger was more at home talking history or music with a Frenchman or an Englishman or an Italian—in each case in the other person's language—than he was discussing current events with his fellow officers. If Senger looked and acted more like an intellectual than one of Hitler's generals, it was because he had set out on an intellectual career but had been diverted by the consequences of an earlier war.

A child of the petty aristocracy of southern Germany, Senger had been one of only six German students chosen to attend Oxford in 1912 as a Rhodes scholar. His education at St. John's College was interrupted by the First World War, in which he served his nation with distinction as an infantry officer. After the war, when his family lost its land and money in the inflation of the early 1920s, Senger chose the safe harbor of a military career. He decided to make that career in the cavalry, not because he thought it had a future in warfare, but just because he and his wife loved horses. They had met during the war, when she was in the Bavarian Red Cross. Senger's wife enjoyed riding and hunting, and he approved; "It is narrow-minded," he wrote, "to think that women should not pursue all the sporting activities that attract men." The years between the wars, so turbulent for Germany, were pleasant and uneventful for the Sengers. They moved from post to post accompanied by their three horses. Senger stayed out of politics, even military politics; though known for his brilliance, he did not belong to the inner circles and did not seem headed for the highest level of command. But while the Sengers were enjoying their insulated life, Hitler had come to power, and then came 1939. "He had to go or stay," his daughter said, "and he believed that in spite of Hitler he should remain with his people." Once again Senger stayed with his country in war.

Now, after four years, Senger knew this war was lost, like the first one. An Italian general would recall after the war that in the summer of 1943, when they were both serving in Sicily, he had quoted to Senger Clausewitz's observation that when defeat was certain a nation should negotiate the best peace it could get. Senger had nodded but added that he was sure Hitler had not read Clausewitz—a statement that in Nazi eyes would have been defeatist if not outright treasonous.

Senger had good personal reason to know the war was lost. His own career had spanned the full arc of Germany's wartime experience, from the easy victories of the early days to the colossal defeat that, more than any other, had made the end inevitable. In 1940, Senger had commanded a motorized brigade during the quick conquest of France. He had raced in hours past battlefields where, two decades earlier, he had fought for months; he recalled passing the mass grave, in Belgium, where in 1917 he had searched for his brother's remains. In June 1940, Senger had bested the great Erwin Rommel himself in a race to capture the port of Cherbourg. Occupation duty in defeated France was pleasant for Senger. He set himself up in a castle in Normandy and made sure he had plenty of good food and champagne; at home with the ways and language of the French, Senger made friends with the local rural aristocracy, many of whom in those early days looked as favorably on Germans, particularly a fellow aristocrat, as Senger did on the French. Senger then spent two years in the very cushiest of wartime assignments. He was stationed in Turin as chief liaison officer to the Franco-Italian Armistice Commission. The fighting was far away, his duties were light, and Senger loved Italy and the Italians.

In the autumn of 1942 Senger was suddenly transferred to the real war, the war in the East, where two bloodthirsty tyrants were committing their peoples to the carnage at a rate never before equaled. There was no champagne or good conversation in this slaughterhouse. Senger remembered nights spent half-freezing in peasant huts and washing his face in snow. His only happy moments were when, once in a while, he could get classical music on his service radio. In the dreadful winter of 1942–43, Senger took part in the decisive battle of Stalingrad. He commanded a division that tried unsuccessfully to reach the trapped army of Field Marshal Paulus. After the shattering defeat of Stalingrad, Senger had no illusions about the outcome of the war: there was no chance, now, that Germany could win. Nor did Senger even want a Germany led by Adolf Hitler to win the war. So he wrote after the war, when so many Germans discovered they had been against Hitler all along, but in Senger's case the testimony of fellow officers seemed to confirm his anti-Nazi opinions, though not necessarily his desire for Germany's defeat. According to one of his aides, Senger hoped that the German army could somehow make peace with the Western Allies, but he did not join those of his colleagues who were trying to remove the obstacle to that outcome. Senger knew by 1943 that some of his fellow officers, including a few who were his friends, were conspiring to rid Germany of Hitler; he stayed aloof from their plans, and so he was not one of the martyrs of the plot against Hitler.

Whatever his misgivings, Senger went on fighting, not only with bravery, but with the formidable professional skills honed in eight years of war. In the battle for Italy Senger's skills would cost thousands of men their lives, for the general who said he did not want to win fought with far greater ability than his antagonists, who had no misgivings about their cause. In his wartime diary, Senger asked the obvious question: "I wonder what will be the verdict of history concerning those of us who are discerning, unbiased, and strong enough to realize that defeat is inevitable and who nevertheless continue to fight and to contribute to the bloodshed." Senger found his answer in a great Catholic philosopher who, as it happened, was born on a hill just above his headquarters at Roccasecca. "According to the creed of Thomas Aquinas," he wrote, "no man can be blamed for the crimes of others insofar as he has no influence over them. However, the power is not in the hands of the generals but of Hitler and the German people who have voted him into power and who to this day are following him blindly and devotedly on the course he has selected." That answer was good enough for Senger and for all but the heroic few who paid for their dissent with their lives.

Senger had been given his present command, by far his largest and most important, despite an act of disobedience that could have cost

41

him his career, if not his head. It had happened two months earlier on Corsica, where Senger had been sent to direct the evacuation of eighteen thousand German soldiers. It was a risky assignment. This was just after Italy had dropped out of the war, and the German and Italian forces, on Corsica as elsewhere, did not know what to make of each other. It addition to the problematic Italians, Senger had faced French partisan forces of unknown strength, and had to get his men safely across 70 miles of water when the enemy controlled both the air and the sea. Senger had moved swiftly to take control of the port of Bastia, and in the process took prisoner a number of Italian soldiers, including about two hundred officers. Senger had then received an order from Hitler, furious at his former ally's treachery, that all Italian officers taken prisoner were to be shot. That was something Senger simply could not do. He had called his commander, Field Marshal Albert Kesselring, commander of German forces in southern Italy, on the radio-telephone and told him of his intended disobedience. Kesselring said nothing. The Italians were not shot, and Senger successfully evacuated his troops to the Italian mainland.

Senger left the island at night on a small ship with the last German soldiers, and the next day had a coincidental reunion with his son, who, like his father, had earlier been in combat near Stalingrad. The German high command hesitated whether to court-martial Senger for disobeying Hitler's order. Instead, Senger was commended for his skill in directing the evacuation and given his present command of the crucial part of the front south of Rome.

Senger was well aware of the great Benedictine monastery that lay 15 miles southeast of his headquarters. Each time he drove down the Liri Valley in his open Volkswagen jeep to visit his soldiers in the frontlines, he would pass by Monte Cassino, high above the road to his left. Senger knew that Mark Clark's army would inevitably fight its way out of the mountains to the south, into the Liri Valley, and there under the abbey the critical battle would be fought. The knowledge that the ancient monastery might be caught in that battle was particularly painful to Senger. He had intimate connections to the Benedictine order. This Rhodes scholar and continental bon vivant was also a devout Roman Catholic. As a young man he had joined a lay group committed to the Benedictine philosophy and had taken part in many trips to Beuron and other Benedictine monasteries in Germany. The Benedictine primate in Rome, Baron Stotzingen, was a family friend with whom Senger had spent many hours: like Senger, he came from the petty nobility of south Germany. Senger had visited Monte Cassino and chatted with the abbot; this worldly, intellectual soldier enjoyed the company of monks who were, like Senger, more worldly and intellectual than most of their kind. That the decisions he must make in fighting the coming battles might bring destruction down on the mother abbey of the Benedictines was not the least of the conflicts that raged beneath Senger's outwardly cheerful manner.

Until recently it had not seemed that the Germans would have to fight in the neighborhood of the abbey. The decision was Hitler's—he had taken personal command of the Italian campaign on September 12—and he had made it after weeks of hesitation. Hitler had not been able to choose between two strategies argued by two of his field marshals, Erwin Rommel and Albert Kesselring. Rommel was, of course, the dashing leader of the Afrika Korps, Germany's foremost war hero; Kesselring, while lacking Rommel's glamor, had built a solid reputation for competence in the four years of war. These two men, bitter rivals, had shared command in Italy since the German defeat in North Africa: Rommel in the north, Kesselring in the south. Each had argued his case with Hitler. Surprisingly, the dashing Rommel advocated the more cautious strategy. He advised Hitler to abandon Rome and the south, and to fight only on a line across the Po Valley in the north; this line, said Rommel, would be closer to sources of supply in Germany and would not run the risk of being turned by Allied landings to the north. Kesselring, the optimist, wanted to fight in the mountains of the south; this was easier country to defend, he argued. Germany should not give up the symbol of Rome to the enemy, and Rommel's northern line would give the enemy bomber bases closer to the German heartland. Had Rommel prevailed, Monte Cassino would certainly have been out of the combat zone and out of danger.

At first Hitler leaned toward Rommel's strategy; he seemed eager to wash his hands of the Italians. At one point, in fact, the order appointing Rommel to supreme command in Italy was actually written, but then it was shelved. Rommel was no longer a persuasive advocate. He was not the man he had been a year earlier. Rocked by his defeat in Africa, he no longer believed Germany could win the war. He detested the Italians on whose lack of support he blamed the disastrous outcome in Africa, and he had already made himself hated in return by drafting 250,000 Italian men for slave labor in Germany. His health was poor. Sour and arrogant, Rommel made a bad impression on Hitler. By contrast, Kesselring—"smiling Albert"—was expert at not telling Hitler what Hitler didn't want to hear. Kesselring's optimistic strategy appealed to Hitler's natural instinct not to give up any meter of territory, and certainly not Rome with all its symbolic meaning. Kesselring got along well with the Italians, in contrast to Rommel, and so had a better chance of gaining their cooperation. And he had contained the Allied landing at Salerno, south of Naples, better than Hitler had expected.

Hitler made up his mind in early October. On the 4th, he ordered resistance south of Rome instead of the planned retreat to the north, and on the 15th, in response to a message from Mussolini also urging him to fight for the capital, he said: "We are in Rome now and I think we shall stay in Rome." On the 24th, about the same time that Senger was taking command of the 14th Panzer Korps, Hitler put Kesselring in command of the Italian campaign. Hitler's decision meant that Monte Cassino must inevitably be in the frontline of the coming battle for the mountains south of Rome.

In the first weeks of his new assignment Senger spent much of his time getting acquainted with his men and with the terrain in which they would be fighting. In the mornings he would set out in his Volkswagen jeep from the old palazzo in Roccasecca to inspect one or another part of the wildly varied landscape that made up his 50-mile front. To his right, as he faced the advancing Allies, an enclave of coastal plain lay behind the Aurunci range: this was semitropical country where oranges grew even in winter. To his left, up the slopes above his headquarters, were the rugged, virtually uninhabitable peaks of the Abruzzi. Those sectors were both sideshows: Senger knew the enemy would come along the road to Rome that lay directly in front of him.

Wherever he went on his daily inspection tours, the wiry, athletic Senger loved to climb the hills on foot and feel the chill wind of early winter while he talked to his men face to face. He would drive as far as the jeep could take him, then, accompanied by a single aide, he would start off up the mountain, 6-foot walking stick in hand, in a rolling, loping gait. He would walk in unannounced at frontline positions and check the way the local commander had arranged his defenses. Senger's manner as he talked to the men was cheerful, even jovial, especially by contrast to some of his grim fellow generals, but he kept on asking questions till he had the information he wanted. He would stay for lunch at a field kitchen to taste for himself the quality of the food his men were getting. Senger talked to men of all ranks, but those who most interested him were the battalion commanders, men of 25 to 30 years of age, whose performance in combat, he believed, was the single most important ingredient of victory.

In the evening, after his day at the frontlines, Senger would dine with his staff officers—they too were new to him—at the old palazzo. Later he would retire to his room, which he had made homelike with "some fine old pictures and cretonne-covered furniture," and read or listen to classical music on his service radio. On his arrival in Roccasecca, he had been pleased and surprised to find in an adjoining house a library with books "in several languages." He discovered the reason for the books when, on one of his walks, he encountered an old lady whose "dessicated face, solid shoes and walking-stick proclaimed her to be of Anglo-Saxon stock." Despite this formidably English description, the old lady turned out to be American by birth, educated in France and Germany, and married to an Italian: her varied background accounted for the variety of her library.

In general, Senger was pleased with the men under his command, most of whom, unlike their commander, still believed in Hitler, the war, and the possibility of victory. The only exception was the 3rd Panzer Grenadiers, which in the fighting at Salerno had reported a suspiciously high number of men "missing." This division had a large proportion of *volksdeutschen,* men born in Poland of German ancestry. These men were taken by the military on probation and, though they had been through heavy fighting in the East, could not be promoted till their probation was over. Senger considered their second-class performance as soldiers to be a natural response to their treatment as second-class citizens. Besides, the soldiers knew the Allies welcomed deserters and treated prisoners well, while on the Russian front deserting was even more dangerous than staying to fight. The other four divisions, however, were all experienced in battle and led by competent officers. Senger thought he could count on them.

The German soldiers would need all of their reserves of competence and courage to do battle in this terrible terrain. There could hardly be a worse place for men to fight than these mountains of central Italy. In this flinty land, it was almost impossible to dig in, and nothing could destroy morale faster than the lack of some minimal shelter from enemy fire and the elements. The stone hillsides so magnified and repeated the sound of exploding shells that there was no interval of silence between one burst and the next, and the same hillsides also multiplied the effect of artillery explosions in the form of deadly stone fragments flying in all directions. And the winter that was now closing in would make everything worse.

But Senger knew this terrain worked primarily to his advantage, for, if it was hard for his men, it was harder still for the attackers. Senger's counterpart, Mark Clark, had several great advantages: his soldiers had more heavy equipment, the Allies had absolute control of the air, and they could afford to waste ammunition while the Germans had to ration their supplies. Against Clark, Senger had the advantage of the terrain and of his excellent combat soldiers. He had another asset—himself. Senger brought to the battle a brilliant intellect and eight years of experience in two wars. He was above all a professional soldier. For Frido von Senger, as for Mark Clark, the battle in Italy was the supreme moment of his career. Whatever doubts he may have had, then or later, about the cause for which he fought, the evidence is that Senger welcomed and relished the opportunity to display his skill in the ultimate test of leading an army in combat.

7

The Benedictine monk was in tears as he gazed out the back of the truck at the community he was leaving, perhaps forever. The great stone shape of Monte Cassino was bright in the noonday sun.

Before the gate stood Abbot Diamare and a handful of monks, black figures somber against the light yellow stone of the monastery. They were waving a grave farewell to one of their own, Tommaso Leccisotti, who was on the truck leaving for Rome.

Leccisotti was unhappy and frightened. Unhappy because the home he had never expected to leave was now retreating rapidly into the distance, and frightened at the heavy responsibilities that his abbot had laid on his slender shoulders. Three days earlier, after the emotional night meeting by candlelight in the crypt, when the monks had sadly accepted the Germans' offer to evacuate both their treasures and themselves, the abbot had summoned Leccisotti to his office. Leccisotti—a slight, bespectacled scholar in his forties—had been one of the minority that opposed the evacuation; if he had to leave, he preferred to go to a quiet place over on the Adriatic coast, not to Rome, where he had heard things were going badly. But the old abbot told him he was going to Rome, and he was going there as the abbot's emissary. In Rome Leccisotti was to tell the abbot primate of the Benedictine order about the plight of the monks and the danger to the monastery. He was to inform the Vatican of their situation in the hope that the Pope could and would do something to save the abbey from destruction. Leccisotti's job was to save his monastery, and it could only be done in Rome.

With the little monk in the truck starting out for Rome was the visible symbol of his mission: the two narrow silk-covered boxes containing the relics of Saints Benedict and Scholastica. The old abbot, weeping, had placed the holy relics in the truck himself and commended them to Leccisotti's care, while a German propaganda unit filmed the scene. Leccisotti was aware that whether the relics —and he and his four fellow passengers—would arrive safely in Rome was far from certain. The roads of Italy were subject to frequent Allied air attack, and a Hermann Goering Division truck, at noon on the road to Rome, was the most logical of targets. And, in fact, at Frosinone, halfway to Rome, a siren sent them all scrambling out of the truck. A fellow monk clutched Leccisotti's arm in fear, but it proved to be a false alarm, and by late afternoon they were in the outskirts of the capital. Neither the German driver nor any of the passengers knew their way around the streets of the city, so they wandered for some time before finding their destination, the Collegio de San Anselmo in the southern part of Rome. Leccisotti was relieved to have at least gotten the holy relics safely to Benedictine hands. He walked through the great brick entrance and was soon greeted by the Benedictine primate, Fidelis von Stotzingen. The monk took out the letter his abbot had given him and began to read:

> Make the Abbot Primate and the Abbot President [of the Benedictine monastery of San Paolo Fuori le Mura, also in Rome] understand our sad situation. We have been obliged to leave the monastery. We entrust ourselves to their charity. The community is formed of circa eighty monks between professed monks, novices, lay brothers and aspiring monks who cannot return to their families because they are in occupied zones where it is forbidden to go. There are also three students in the same situation. . . . Inform the Holy See of everything. . . . Our Benedictine nuns will also go to Rome, there are about thirty of them. . . . Please have the goodness to keep for us the things which we send. The haste in which we are making our preparations, and the huge quantity of things we have to try to save, does not permit us unfortunately to do it with the necessary calm and order. . . .

Now Leccisotti learned that circumstances in Rome were worse even than he had heard at Monte Cassino and that the feeding of another hundred-plus mouths would place a heavy burden on the Benedictine communities in the capital. Life had gotten much more difficult since the Germans came six weeks earlier. Food rations had been drastically reduced, and all too often people found, after standing in line for hours, that even the reduced ration was not available. Romans were dependent on a black market in which prices were astronomical. Meat could not be found at any price, and even pasta and potatoes were outlandishly expensive. The only people who got eggs and fresh fruits were those with connections among the farmers in the countryside around the city, and even then they paid the equivalent of 40 cents for an egg and 56 cents for a lemon. Most people did without. The Germans had also greatly reduced public services of all kinds. Cooking gas was cut off except for a few hours a day. The electricity was rationed by zones: each part of Rome was left without power two nights a week. Worst of all, at least for the male population, the Germans were rounding men up for forced labor. It was common practice for the Germans to raid restaurants or cafés or even churches and to seize thirty or forty men at random for their slave labor battalions.

Leccisotti learned firsthand what life in Rome was like the next day when he set off to carry out his abbot's simple order: "Inform the Holy See of everything." The Vatican was on the other side of Rome, across the Tiber, 5 miles from the Benedictine monastery of San Paolo, where Leccisotti was staying. Service on the green wooden trolleys was sporadic at best, and many stops had been eliminated, but eventually Leccisotti was able to make his way to the Vatican. In St. Peter's Square the monk in his black habit passed the symbol of the German presence: two helmeted paratroopers in green and brown camouflage dress carrying guns, slouched in the colonnade near the white line the Germans had painted to mark the exact boundary between the Italy they occupied and the independent state of Vatican City.

The scholar monk knew nothing about the byzantine ways of the Vatican bureaucracy, and he found himself wandering like a country bumpkin down ornate halls in search of someone who would hear his story. At last he was admitted to the office of Cardinal Maglione, the papal secretary of state. Leccisotti gave the cardinal his two messages from the abbot of Monte Cassino. The first essential, urgent message was a plea to the Pope to use what influence he could with both the Allies and the Germans to save the mother abbey of the Benedictines from destruction. Leccisotti also explained how the Germans had come to Monte Cassino and were evacuating its treasures and those of Naples to a destination unknown to the monks. He asked the cardinal if the Vatican could find out where the treasures were being taken in those trucks that were leaving Monte Cassino every day.

Cardinal Maglione told the monk that he would inform the Pope at their next meeting, two days later.

Pope Pius XII was born Eugenio Pacelli in 1876. His family were Roman aristocrats; his father was a Vatican attorney. Most of Eugenio Pacelli's career as a priest was spent in the Vatican's diplomatic service, and most of that in Germany. In 1933, as papal nuncio, he negotiated a concordat with the new government of Adolf Hitler, four years after the then Pope had negotiated a similar treaty with Mussolini. Pacelli was elected Pope in the spring of 1939, only months before the German invasion of Poland that started the war. The war was the central fact of his papacy. All Pius' diplomatic skill was devoted to trying to assure the survival of the church he led both during the war and in whatever world might emerge afterward. In the early years, when the Axis was winning, this meant accommodating the church to a Europe ruled by Hitler. Now, with an Allied victory ever more probable, the Pope's attention seemed to have turned to the postwar world: he seemed more worried about Stalin than Hitler, concerned, above all, over the possibility of a Communist Italy.

In the immediate, however, the Vatican and the Pope himself were at the mercy of the Germans symbolized by the paratroopers in St. Peter's Square. As one German officer said, "Now the Pope is nearer to Himmler than to heaven [*himmel*]." Any time they wanted to the Germans could take over the Vatican in a matter of minutes. In fact, just six weeks earlier, on September 12, Hitler had summoned SS general Kurt Wolff and ordered him to make plans "to occupy Vatican City as soon as possible, secure its files and art treasures, and take the Pope and the Curia to the North. I do not want him to fall into the hands of the Allies or be under their political pressure and influence. . . . I shall arrange for the Pope to be brought either to Germany or to neutral Lichtenstein, depending on political and military developments." The Pope knew about the plan to take him prisoner: its gist had been broadcast by both the BBC and the Italian Fascist radio. Now, in late October, Pius was going to great lengths to avoid provoking the Germans; though whether Hitler would refrain from putting his plan into effect no doubt depended less on anything the Pope did than on Hitler's own fear of the possible reaction among German Catholics.

Pius had shown on October 16 just how far he was willing to go to avoid antagonizing the Germans. On that date—it happened to be two days after Dr. Becker's first visit to Monte Cassino—the SS had gotten around to some unfinished business. Mussolini, despite much anti-Semitic bluster, had refused to turn over the Jews of Italy and Italian-occupied France to the SS for extermination. Now, with the Germans in control of Italy, this oversight could be remedied. On the night of the sixteenth, SS troops poured out of trucks and motorcycles into the Jewish quarter of Rome. They caught about a thousand Jews, who by the following week were entering the gas chamber at

Auschwitz. The Allies' representatives hoped that this action, happening literally next door to the Vatican, would cause the Pope at last to speak out. There could be no doubt in Pius' mind about the meaning of the Final Solution: he had received ample eyewitness reports from Vatican representatives in Eastern Europe. Now the American chargé d'affaires, Harold Tittmann, asked the Vatican for the second time—the first had been in July 1942, long before the German occupation—to make a statement about the extermination of the Jews. Cardinal Maglione refused, adding that there was "not sufficient proof of the rumors going around." When Tittmann saw the Pope himself three days later, at their regular meeting, Pius said nothing about the SS roundup, but instead told Tittmann he was worried about "little Communist bands stationed in the environs of Rome." As if to underline the point, the Vatican radio on October 29 said: "The Holy See confirms that German troops have respected the Roman Curia and Vatican City and welcomes the assurances given by the German ambassador as to the future."

As for the Allies, whose armies were now moving slowly up the Italian peninsula, the Pope's most urgent concern was about damage to his home town and capital. Allied planes had bombed Rome twice briefly during the summer, and, though they had not bombed the city since then, they were regularly bombing targets on the outskirts.

It was against this background that Pope Pius XII received the plea for help from the abbot of Monte Cassino.

Four days after his first visit Leccisotti was summoned to the Vatican by Monsignor Giovanni Battista Montini.*

On each of the intervening days the little Benedictine had made the long, uncertain journey by trolley to plead the cause of Monte Cassino, and on one such visit he had left a long memorandum detailing the plight of his monastery. Between trips to the Vatican, Leccisotti had scurried around Rome on other errands. One day he went to see the Italian fine arts officials in downtown Rome in the hope they would know where the Germans were taking the things they were trucking out of Monte Cassino; but the officials knew as little as the monks. Each day German trucks were arriving in Rome from Monte Cassino carrying monks, nuns, and students who some-

---

*In 1958 Montini succeeded Pius as Pope Paul VI.

ABOVE: Italian civilians who took refuge in the monastery in October 1943. OPPOSITE, TOP: Refugees loading their possessions on a truck of the Hermann Goering Division. OPPOSITE, BOTTOM: Abbot Diamare, with Matronola at his left, waves farewell to monks leaving on a German truck for Rome. The officer behind Matronola is Schlegel.

how had to be housed. Secreted among the monks' personal possessions were such valuables as the coin collection from Syracuse. At
Leccisotti's request, some of the trucks were also carrying food for
their human cargoes. One truck brought the report that the Germans
were believed to be taking the treasures to Spoleto, north of Rome.
Another brought the encouraging news that the officer managing the
evacuation, Colonel Schlegel, had said the monastery would not be
fortified by the Germans.

Now, at the Vatican, the monk did not know what to expect when
he entered the office and seated himself across the desk from Monsignor Montini. Leccisotti had heard varying opinions when he spoke
to Vatican officials about his monastery. A monsignor told Leccisotti
he thought any intervention by the Vatican might produce a contrary
effect by "irritating" German officials in Berlin. Another Vatican
figure, also a monsignor, was dubious about asking the Germans for
a declaration that they would not fortify the monastery; if they were
to violate that declaration in any way, he reasoned, the Allies would
feel free to do what they pleased. Still, this man added, rather
strangely, the Vatican could not be "indifferent" to the fate of Monte
Cassino, given world opinion. None of this encouraged Leccisotti
about the success of his mission.

Between constant phone calls, the suave, aristocratic Montini gave
the monk the Vatican's answer. Yes, the Pope would appeal to the
belligerents: to the Germans not to fortify the abbey, to the Allies
not to destroy it. Leccisotti had accomplished the mission for which
his abbot had sent him to Rome.

The following day, October 25, Harold Tittmann, the American
chargé, was called in by Monsignor Montini. Tittmann didn't have
far to go. Since December 1941, when Italy declared war on the
United States, the American had been confined to the 100-acre neutral territory of Vatican City. Under the Italians, Tittmann had been
allowed a weekly trip by car with police escort to the beach at
Fregeni, but with the Germans in Rome such excursions were only
a memory. So when Montini summoned him, Tittmann left his
apartment in Santa Marta, the building once used as a residence hall
for pilgrims, and walked across a courtyard to the Vatican office
building. It was a short walk even for a man with only one leg;
Tittmann had lost his right leg in a plane crash in the First World
War. For two years Tittmann had been making this walk for his

weekly meeting with Montini. The meetings were often void of any real content and always highly formal; Montini and his fellow officials were careful to avoid any show of favoritism to either of the belligerents.

This time Montini handed the American a note from the Vatican secretary of state, Cardinal Maglione. The note, which as usual was in French, pointed out that the combat zone was approaching Monte Cassino, spoke of the historic importance of the abbey, and asked the American authorities to give its preservation "all possible consideration." Similar messages, Montini said, were being delivered to the British and German representatives. It was the Vatican's first formal communication to the Allies about Monte Cassino, although the monastery had come up several times in Tittmann's conversations with Vatican officials, and in June Cardinal Maglione had even cited Hannibal's experience while describing how hard it was to attack Rome via Monte Cassino.

The American translated the Vatican's message and sent it on its roundabout way to the State Department in Washington. Cooped up in the Vatican, surrounded by enemy territory, Tittmann had no direct link to his government. His messages had to go with a Vatican courier overland to neutral Switzerland, where they were delivered to the American minister in Berne. The minister forwarded Tittmann's message either by radio or by mail via Spain or Portugal. Even by radio a message would take ten or fifteen days from Rome to Washington, and since the Germans could easily detain the courier and read what he was carrying, Tittmann never was able to send any intelligence that he gathered in the Vatican.

In the case of the Monte Cassino messages, the Vatican radioed a copy of the text directly to the apostolic delegate in Washington. He delivered a copy to the State Department that same day, long before Tittmann's copy arrived via Switzerland.

8

While Schlegel was managing the evacuation of the treasures, Dr. Becker was worrying about where those treasures were in fact going. His concern centered on Colonel Jacobi, the former Berlin policeman who at the very beginning had suggested that some paintings be diverted for the Hermann Goering Division.

Jacobi now came out in the open. In his house trailer, while he and Becker were discussing the evacuation, the former cop took a paper from a file folder and handed it to the doctor, saying, "Why don't you read through this letter—of course the matter is confidential— and tell me what you think of it."

It was a carbon copy of a letter from Jacobi to one von Brauchitsch, adjutant to Hermann Goering himself. The letter described the evacuation of the Abbey of Monte Cassino and mentioned that it included the art of the museum at Naples. The Hermann Goering Division, the letter said, wanted to offer a gift to the Reichsmarshal. The adjutant was urged to send an art expert to Italy, as soon as possible, to select some paintings and other art objects.

Now at last Becker understood what had been going on around him. Goering's birthday, his fifty-first, was coming up on January 12, about two months away. It would be a great gala affair at Karinhall, one of Goering's several estates. In earlier Januarys Nazi chieftains and sympathizers had made birthday gifts to Goering of the art that he loved to collect, to loot, or even, if absolutely necessary, to buy. Mussolini himself, in 1942, sent an altarpiece in which Goering had expressed an interest. It was only natural that officers of his own Hermann Goering Division would want to please their patron with a birthday gift from the masterpieces of Naples.

Only natural, Becker thought bitterly, and completely degrading to himself and his mission. All his work, and for that matter Schlegel's, would be discredited. If even a few paintings were taken, the world would see what they were doing not as a humanitarian rescue but just one more sleazy Nazi theft. Becker himself would appear to the monks of Monte Cassino as an accomplice in that theft. To

Jacobi, the doctor only said: "I do not think it is right." There was little more he could say. Becker could not openly oppose what he now knew was going on. Jacobi and Schlegel outranked him, and if he went to their superiors, the likely result would be that he would be reprimanded—or worse—and the rescue might even be stopped.

Becker had already found out at Monte Cassino that some of the monks were suspicious of the Germans' sudden desire to save the treasures of their abbey. A day or so earlier the German monk, Munding, had sought out Becker and asked him to join him in the refectory for a glass of wine. Over a carafe of the abbey's fine Frascati, Munding bluntly asked the doctor why no monks were allowed to accompany the trucks headed—supposedly—for the German supply depot at Spoleto. When a truck left for Rome, it carried one or more monks who would send back word that the cargo had safely reached its destination. But the other trucks, with the Naples treasure and the state-owned archives—no one knew whether those trucks were really going to Spoleto or what was happening to their cargoes.

Abbot Diamare and the archivişt, Inguanez, were disturbed and suspicious, and Munding himself was in a particularly embarrassing position. He, a German national, had strongly supported the rescue during the first discussions in the abbot's workroom. Was he helping loot the monastery? The best way to dispel suspicion, Munding told Becker, was for the Germans to let the monk ride a truck to Spoleto and report back to the abbot. Becker took the monk's request first to Schlegel, next to Jacobi, but both his superiors refused: no monks would be allowed to go to Spoleto.

Now, after learning from the letter to Goering that his and the monks' worst suspicions were all too well founded, Dr. Becker took another tack. It occurred to him after he left Jacobi's trailer that publicizing the rescue would not only bring credit to the Hermann Goering Division, and so please his superiors, but could also serve to discourage any looting of the treasures. He brought up the idea with Schlegel, who was strongly in its favor.

An incident both men had witnessed provided another powerful reason for publicizing the rescue. One day about twenty German military police had suddenly appeared at the gate of the abbey. The captain in charge of the unit explained that an Allied broadcast had accused the Hermann Goering Division of looting Monte Cassino. Field Marshal Kesselring, commander of German forces in the south of Italy, had sent the military police to find out if the report was true, and if it was to arrest the looters. After talking to the monks, the captain had been satisfied and had left without making any arrests.

Schlegel then went to General Conrath and argued that publicity about the rescue was urgently needed to counter what the enemy was saying about their division. The general agreed, and the next day a combat correspondent, one Sergeant Weber, arrived at Monte Cassino to interview Becker and Schlegel for a radio program called "Zeitfunk." The sergeant arranged to have the bells of the basilica rung as an introduction. Then he interviewed the doctor.

Becker, speaking to the German radio audience, emphasized that the treasurers of Monte Cassino were being saved for the Italian people. The treasure—all of it—would be turned over to the Italians as soon as possible. It was the Hermann Goering Division's contribution to European culture.

The radio reporter was followed by a film crew from a propaganda unit in Rome. Their cameras recorded the busy scene in the abbey: the soldiers, monks, and civilians packing the crates, carrying the crates through the cloisters, loading the trucks, the trucks lumbering off toward Rome.

Becker was pleased. The rescue he had conceived, and the ultimate destination of the treasure, were now public record. German authorities in Rome and even Berlin knew about it. This widespread knowledge would make it difficult, if not impossible, to loot the treasure without being caught. But there was something else Becker still had to do. He wanted to see for himself what was happening at the supply depot where the trucks were going. He resolved to take the first opportunity to go to Spoleto.

9

Not everyone, nor everything of value, left the Abbey of Monte Cassino on Schlegel's caravan of army trucks.

A large part of the library was left behind on the instruction of Inguanez, the archivist. Dr. Becker believed this was because of the Maltese monk's "unalterable mistrust" of the Germans. Both Becker and Schlegel remembered the beautiful wooden carvings in the choir of the basilica that were too large to move. And of course the most precious treasure of the Benedictines could not be moved, the monastery itself. The cloisters with their colonnades and the statues of Benedict and Scholastica, the basilica with its chapels and crypts, and the many lovely frescoes and mosaics that adorned them—all that would stay.

Schlegel recalled that the raven of Monte Cassino was left behind. The raven was a handsome, blue-black bird, who liked to perch on the statue of Saint Benedict in the cloister and who said "Niko" when asked his name. Niko was the last in a series of ravens going back to an illustrious sixth-century bird. In the chronicle of Benedict's life, the saint was about to eat a piece of bread poisoned by a jealous priest when a raven, the first Niko, swooped down and took the bread from his hand, saving the saint's life.

Abbot Gregorio Diamare had stuck to his decision to share whatever fate the war might have in store for his monastery. To stay with him and share that fate he had chosen ten monks, all much younger except one 79-year-old lay brother, and a handful of lay employees of the abbey. Among the monks was Martino Matronola, the abbot's tall, powerful secretary. About one hundred and fifty refugees also stayed.

The two trucks carrying the last monks to leave were scheduled for November 3. On the eve, All Saint's Day, the remaining community of Monte Cassino—those who were to leave and those who were to stay—gathered in the crypt before the burial place of Benedict. They sang the last high mass. The next morning at the monastery gates the abbot embraced each of the departing monks. The last trucks moved out on the road to Rome. An old monk, weeping, was heard to say, "I will never see my monastery again."

The great abbey was half empty. The remaining monks had already chosen their shelter—two corridors under the *collegio* where they kept a small natural science museum for their students. Some monks had already moved into the shelter, but Abbot Diamare stayed in his cell in the monks' quarters on the other side of the monastery. His secretary, Matronola, stayed in the adjoining cell.

On the day after the last truck left, two of the monks who stayed at Monte Cassino—Eusebio Grossetti, the artist, and Matronola—began to keep a diary. All but a few pages of the diary survived the war. After the war Matronola reconstructed the missing entries from memory. The "I" in the diary refers to Matronola.

FROM THE MONKS' DIARY:

NOVEMBER 4–8

Lieutenant-Colonel Schlegel came to take his leave for the last time. The abbot gave him a bottle of our forty-year-old wine. At our insistent request, he left a document signed by him in which it was declared that the monastery was under military protection and that it was absolutely prohibited to requisition anything without an order from the Division. This was put up on the gate, where there was already a sign saying that soldiers visiting the monastery must be accompanied by a monk.

The captain who had come on the third returned; he reported that the abbot's desire for a military guard had been granted. About the food we requested, vague promises.

The evening of the eighth two soldiers from the Graeser Division arrived for the protection of the monastery. . . .

During the night the usual bombardment and a few planes flying over.

NOVEMBER 19

Much activity in general, but not even a beginning towards resolving our local crisis. Misery and hunger grow every day. God continues to test these poor people; perhaps we are still too far from a sincere and Christian repentance.

Today and yesterday sacred tapestries belonging to the Benedictine nuns were brought from Cassino to Monte Cassino.

Their nunnery was totally ransacked by German soldiers and above all by looters from the area.

In the afternoon a German chaplain came with an old book (1868) and some sacred vessels of rare value from Santa Elia. He said the churches there had been abandoned by their priests.

10

The Hermann Goering Division had taken for its supply depot the Villa Colle-Ferreto, a huge castlelike country mansion in a pine forest outside Spoleto, 70 miles north of Rome. This was where the trucks returning from the front south of Rome had unloaded the treasures of Monte Cassino.

One day in late November Dr. Becker strode through the entrance of that country estate. He was accompanied by the officer in charge of the supply depot, a Captain Claus. Becker had heard at division headquarters in Teano that Goering's representative, the art expert requested by Becker's fellow officer Jacobi, had arrived in Spoleto. If anyone planned to loot the treasure, now was when it would happen. Becker had driven to Spoleto in his little Fiat convertible, a journey of 150 miles. In normal times the trip would have taken no more than five hours. But in the chaos of wartime Italy, with the roads under frequent Allied air attack, it took Becker, traveling at night, ten hours to get to Spoleto. Anticipating a confrontation with Goering's man, the young doctor was irritable and tense.

Becker looked around the big hall-like room on the ground floor of the mansion. Several large paintings were learning against a wall; at a glance Becker saw they could only be from the Naples collection. In the middle of the room he saw a jumble of crates that had been broken open: those crates had been sealed when he saw them at Monte Cassino. Packing material was strewn all over the floor. Several German soldiers were standing around.

So this was it, Becker thought savagely. He had walked right into the middle of the looting he had been trying to prevent. This spectacle before him—the crates broken open, the priceless paintings against the wall—was the result of all his efforts since he had first gone to Monte Cassino more than a month ago. And not just his efforts, those of the Benedictine monks, German soldiers, and Italian civilians who had packed and trucked the treasures to this place. For this he had given his solemn pledge to the old abbot that the cargo would be safe in the hands of this division. So they could be stolen for Hermann Goering!

In a fury Becker roared at the officer in charge: "There's some unbelievably shitty business going on here!" The soldiers in the room looked around at the sound of his angry voice. Becker demanded to see the person responsible for what was happening in the room.

A small, slim man in a corporal's uniform came forward and told Becker that he had been sent to Spoleto, by a "high source in Berlin," to look over the paintings and pick out a few. Many years later, in 1967, Becker met Walter Andreas Hofer, Goering's art expert, and thought he recognized in him the man he had seen in corporal's uniform in Spoleto. According to Becker, Hofer would neither confirm nor deny that he was the Spoleto "corporal."

Becker calmed down somewhat. He told the corporal that the paintings, and everything else that had been brought from Monte Cassino—the archive, the other works of art—all was the property of the Italian state. It was only temporarily in German hands. The officers of the Hermann Goering Division had pledged their word of honor that this treasure—all of it—would be turned over to the Italians. The delivery had already been arranged by the German high command in Rome. For all these reasons, what the corporal was doing was a criminal act and would be punished as such.

The corporal repeated that he had been ordered to select some paintings. "All right, then carry out your orders," Becker said. "But no painting, nor anything else from the salvage property is going to leave the depot without written orders from the high command." If anything was taken, Becker said, he would report it directly to Field Marshal Kesselring.

60

The captain in charge of the depot then told Becker that some representatives of the Kuntstschutz, the German art protection bureau, had come to inspect the treasure in early November. He assured Becker that nothing—so far— had been taken from the depot.

Becker wondered, as he drove his Fiat south toward Rome and the front, whether his threat to the corporal would be enough to stop the looting. Not likely, he thought. He was, after all, only an unknown captain, and his antagonists spoke in the name of the man who ranked second only to Hitler himself. But Becker found a touch of sardonic humor in something he had seen at the depot. Among the paintings taken out of their crates he had recognized Peter Brueghel the Elder's *Parable of the Blind*. The painting shows six blind men, linked with staffs, groping across a deserted village, gaunt faces turned up to a hostile sky; the first man has already fallen and the second is stumbling over him and falling in his turn. It occurred to Becker that the man in corporal's uniform might have chosen the Brueghel for Goering as a silent comment on the current situation of Germany.

11

FROM THE MONKS' DIARY:

NOVEMBER 21

This evening there came a Red Cross soldier, a fine young man who offered to take our news to Rome. So the abbot wrote a letter to the Prior and Dom Eusebio a card to his family.

The Germans are beginning to blow up the houses in the outskirts of Cassino and in Cassino itself. The first to go was the second house on the left on the via San Angelo, after the funicular bridge. The mines that blew up the villa of T. Varrone, behind the railroad station, were tremendous and colossal. Suddenly, I saw a tall column of thick yellowish material rising several hundred meters high and immediately after I heard a tremendous explosion. The column thrown up by the explosion looked like the monument to Lenin which is in Moscow, with the hillside as its pedestal. After the smoke cleared, the hillside seemed completely bare and strewn with stone fragments.

During the day the usual activity. At night great flashes of light from the direction of the front.

NOVEMBER 22

A parish priest from Acerra [near Naples] arrived. . . . He told us he had fled in danger of being shot by the Germans and told us about the humiliation the Germans inflicted on his bishop. At Terelle [a hamlet 5 miles north of Monte Cassino] three men were killed trying to flee from being taken by the Germans. One was a boy of ten to twelve.

NOVEMBER 24

Signor Aceti came from Rome with several letters from monks concerned about our fate, among whom there had spread—we don't know how—the report that the *torretta* [of the monastery] had been hit by shellfire. We gave him a letter in reply in which we reassured our brothers in Rome.

General Fries, commander of the new [German] division, came. The abbot gave him a medal of Saint Benedict and asked him to warn us if it became necessary to blow up the church in Cassino, because he wanted to save some things that were still there. . . . The general, who is Protestant, replied that it would happen not because of hatred of the church but only through military necessity and promised that on his return through Cassino he would find out from the sappers what orders they had been given.

Abbot Diamare's repeated denials never caught up with the report that the abbey had been hit by shellfire.

Tommaso Leccisotti, the monk sent to Rome by the abbot, had

heard the report a day before it reached the monks at Monte Cassino. On the 23rd, Leccisotti noted in his diary that he had heard "disastrous news" about Monte Cassino; he did not record just what the news was or who told it to him. That same day the Benedictine made his way across Rome to the Vatican and passed on his news to the secretary of state.

The following day Leccisotti recorded hearing "reassuring news" about Monte Cassino: presumably this was from the Signor Aceti who had taken the rumor to Monte Cassino and then returned to Rome with the abbot's denial. Another letter from the abbot saying "Monte Cassino is still intact" reached Rome on December 17. But it was not till January 3 that Leccisotti reported to the Vatican that the news he had brought six weeks earlier was in error. Baron Ernst von Weizsaecker, the German ambassador, had told the Vatican on December 23 that Monte Cassino was still undamaged. But the Vatican never transmitted the information to the Allies.

The Vatican authorities took Leccisotti's first report at face value, and on December 7—a poorly chosen date—Monsignor Montini delivered to Tittmann, the American chargé, a message reading:

> The Secretariat of State of His Holiness hasten to inform the Legation of the United States of America that, according to reports from various sources, the abbey [of Monte Cassino] is said to have been seriously damaged by artillery fire directed against the German positions on the mountain called "Rocca Janula." [Rocca Janula is a 600-foot hill below the abbey and above Cassino town.]

The message crossed the Atlantic to Washington, and on December 24, it came back from the War Department in a cable to Eisenhower's headquarters with this added observation:

> The note from Vatican requested that since the Pope attaches great importance to the preservation of this abbey, that the proper authorities be reminded of this.

Two weeks later, on January 6, Mark Clark's Fifth Army replied:

This headquarters became aware of the desirability of preserving Abbey of Monte Cassino through Mediterranean Air Command message A347 dated October 27 and suitable instructions were issued to the appropriate commanders. There are many German gun positions and installations in the vicinity of Cassino. These have been taken under fire and it is possible that erratic bursts may have hit the Abbey. If so, the damage is unintentional and unavoidable. Every effort will continue to be made to avoid damaging the Abbey in spite of the fact that it occupies commanding terrain which might well serve as an excellent observation post for the enemy.

Another twelve days would go by before the gist of this report from the Fifth Army—that any damage was "unintentional"—would be sent back to Tittmann for the Vatican. By then the news that had originally been false—that the abbey had been hit by shellfire—had become reality.

12

FROM THE MONKS' DIARY:

NOVEMBER 25

Quite an active day, full of wind and rain.

Around noon came a lieutenant of aviation who insisted on going up to the meteorological observatory to see the Gaeta mountains. Dom Eusebio, who accompanied him, tried to convince him that it was not an observation post. He went away after visiting the Basilica.

In the afternoon a group of women known to our tenants and

servants arrived accompanied by some armed soldiers. They had been arrested in Cassino for having taken—according to what others said—some utensils; two soldiers took them away on the pretext of evacuating them. The soldiers' real motive was quite different: among them was a young girl. At the insistence and tears of the women that they be taken first to Monte Cassino, one of the soldiers was moved, and got the other one, who was more ferocious, to bring them up here. I was called to the gate, where I saw among the soldiers and the weeping women a fat soldier wrapped in an officer's overcoat who had brought out from the infirmary a girl who had taken refuge there. . . . I gathered what was going on. As long as it was a matter of requisitioning donkeys, patience! Now it was a question of honor. I shouted for the chief of the gendarmes. He was behind the soldiers and waiting for our orders. I signaled to him. The chief jumped on the back of the soldier who was passing himself off as an officer and stripped off his coat to see if he really was one; when he had uncovered his imposture, he knocked the soldier to the ground with his fists. . . . The soldier was seen leaving greatly subdued without his victim. The chief gendarme was a professional boxer.

Things were quiet again at the gate, when the aviation lieutenant reappeared. He wanted absolutely to speak to the abbot. I escorted him and acted as interpreter. The lieutenant demanded that an aviation soldier be stationed in our observatory to observe—the clouds. The abbot replied that such an observation post would change the situation of the monastery, that it would be in open contradiction to the propaganda the Germans were giving out concerning the monastery. When the officer insisted, the abbot said we could not permit it, that if it were done we would be forced to inform the Holy See. At that the lieutenant dropped his request and asked only to be allowed to spend the night.

13

Baron von Tieschowitz invited the neutral press to the Quirinale Palace in Rome on November 25. He wanted to tell the world what the German army was doing to protect the art treasures of Italy and in particular those of Monte Cassino. Correspondents from the handful of neutral nations—notably Switzerland, Sweden, Spain, and Portugal—were the only conduit through which the Germans could send a public message to the other side of the battlefield.

Bernhard von Tieschowitz had been in Italy less than a month, but he was an old hand at the wartime politics of art in Nazi-occupied Europe. He was a tall, elegant man of 40, an art historian by profession. According to an OSS informant who knew him before the war, Tieschowitz was "no Nazi"; his stepmother, in fact, was "not Aryan."

Before coming to Rome, Tieschowitz had been stationed in Paris as the civilian representative of the German army Kunstschutz, the Bureau for the Protection of Art in Occupied Countries. Part of the work of the Kunstschutz in France was to identify and confiscate Jewish-owned art collections; the looted art was then sent to Germany, where much of it was sold, and some found its way into the hands of Hermann Goering. Tieschowitz did what he could under the circumstances: he put a tiny mark on each piece of looted art that passed through his hands and kept a record of where it was sent, in the hope that one day it could be restored to its rightful owner.

Tieschowitz had been sent to Rome to set up a Kunstschutz for Italy, now that Germany's onetime ally was in effect an occupied country. In the strange world of Roman politics at that time, Tieschowitz found himself dealing with Italian officials who did not know who were their superiors. Mussolini's puppet republic in the north? The king's supposed government behind the Allied lines in the south? One thing was certain, though: effective power was in the hands of the Germans. So the Italian fine arts officials took their problems to Tieschowitz. Now that the war had come to Italian soil, these officials were trying, pretty much on their own, and often in disobedience to the orders of Mussolini's men, to bring the nation's art treasures to Rome for safekeeping on the neutral soil of the Vatican. But they had no access to either vehicles or fuel. Their greatest concern, they told Tieschowitz on his arrival, was about the treasures of Monte Cassino. The Hermann Goering Division had removed the treasures from the abbey, and since then the Italians had heard nothing of their whereabouts. Could Tieschowitz rescue these treasures?

Tieschowitz now assured the correspondents assembled in the Quirinale Palace that the Monte Cassino treasures were only being held temporarily by the Germans to protect them from attack from the air. Contrary to what the correspondents might have heard from the enemy press, which in fact had reported the moving of the treasures, the Hermann Goering Division was not looting Monte Cassino. Soon—as soon as possible, but transport and fuel were both scarce—the treasures would be turned over to the Vatican.

Tieschowitz's stress on the German army's role in protecting Italian art represented a major change in German propaganda. Until then, German press accounts of the war in Italy had concentrated on accusing the Allies of looting. One such account reported that a "Colonel James Morrison" had been captured in Sicily by the Germans with a Titian painting wrapped around his body. More generally, Allied actions concerning Italian art were interpreted as camouflage for looting for the benefit of President Roosevelt, "Wall Street brokers," and—a favorite target because he was Jewish—Secretary of the Treasury Henry Morgenthau.

That was the line of the German Ministry of Propaganda. Now, however, the German army had taken control over publicity about its activities, and evidently the army leadership preferred to stress its own efforts to protect Italian art. And the action for which the Germans were heaping the most lavish praise on themselves was the outcome of an initiative taken by an obscure doctor in the Hermann Goering Division: the rescue of the treasures of Monte Cassino.

Tieschowitz himself knew that the facts were considerably different from the picture he was painting for the neutral correspondents. When he had heard about the Monte Cassino affair from the Italian officials, Tieschowitz had arranged for the two responsible officers of the Hermann Goering Division to be summoned to Rome. He'd demanded to know where the treasures were and when they would be handed over to the Vatican. The answer of the Hermann Goering officers, Tieschowitz said, was: "We didn't get that away from the priests just so we could give it back to the church. This stuff belongs to Germany!" The two officers then mentioned the forthcoming birthday of "the Fat One," meaning, of course, Goering. Tieschowitz, who said he was shocked, recalled that he told the Hermann Goering Division officers that he had orders to the contrary and would do all in his power to get the treasures intact to the Vatican. To this the officers had replied: "You're upsetting our whole applecart!"*

After that confrontation, Tieschowitz had gone to see Field Marshal Kesselring at his headquarters in Monte Soratte, 25 miles north of Rome. It was on November 12. According to Tieschowitz, Kesselring was "incensed" at the behavior of the Hermann Goering Division and promised to back Tieschowitz in his efforts to get the treasures into the hands of the Vatican; even though Kesselring was the commander in chief, he could not command the obedience of a division that had a direct line to Berlin. Kesselring also signed a poster Tieschowitz had put before him: the poster would be used to put ruins and religious monuments off limits to the German military. The next day Tieschowitz showed the poster to the Italian officials and told them he had been informed that the Monte Cassino treasure was in "good condition."

In the next few days articles reporting what Tieschowitz had said in his press conference in Rome appeared in Swiss and Swedish newspapers. Tieschowitz left Rome on November 29th, and never returned. When he left, the treasure of Monte Cassino was still at Spoleto and still in the hands of the Hermann Goering Division.

*After the war, Tieschowitz said he was sure one of the two officers was Schlegel and he thought the other was Jacobi.

14

FROM THE MONKS' DIARY:

NOVEMBER 28–DECEMBER 2

During these days the tenant farmers began moving their possessions into the monastery and placing them on the main stairs. Later they settled themselves in San Giuseppe and in the section beneath the *collegio* known as the *conigliera* [rabbit warren]. . . .

In the monastery life goes on quite peacefully, as in the preceding days. The abbot works in his study, usually on his private files, assisted by me. The aerial incursions in the zone don't make us go to the refuge, because we trust that the monastery will be safe. We watch the artillery action in the plain below without too much apprehension.

DECEMBER 8

A lieutenant artist, Gugliemo Vessel [Wilhelm Wessel], came to make some sketches of the front (Monte Camino, Trocchio, Sambucaro) as artistic documentation. He made four pastels that were not bad. It seems the Allies are approaching: they are certainly at Monte Camino and perhaps also at Cocuruzzo; they have also advanced in other places.

That afternoon, from the abbot's room, where we had gathered for a cup of tea, we watched the hellfire on Monte Camino and Monte Maggiore.

15

Everything was ready by the time the trucks were due to come rolling down the bank of the Tiber. It was late on the morning of December 8, a cold but sunny day in Rome.

A crowd of several dozen people had assembled in front of the Castel Sant' Angelo, the massive brick Vatican-owned castle on the west bank of the Tiber. This was where the ceremonial presentation of the Monte Cassino treasures was to take place. The press was ready to record the sights and sounds of the event: there were German photographers with both newsreel and still cameras and an Italian Fascist radio reporter in a blackshirt under an army uniform with his microphone.

The Germans had asked that the ceremony be conducted with a "certain solemnity," in order, as an Italian official noted in his daily report, to counteract British propaganda, and to "show how solicitous they are to save manuscripts and works of art from the dangers of battle." Accordingly, the Italian fine arts officials had asked their senior employees to attend with their families. These were the civilian men and women—well-dressed by the standards of Rome in that hard winter—who were now standing in front of the gate of the Castel Sant' Angelo. Some of their smaller children had climbed up on the statues of angels, designed by Bernini, that lined the sides of the bridge across the Tiber. Above them all, surveying the entire scene, a bronze archangel Michael stood on top of the Castel Sant' Angelo.

Lieutenant-Colonel Julius Schlegel was there for the Hermann Goering Division. He was handsomely outfitted in dress uniform and winter greatcoat. It was a big day for the division and for the Nazi from Vienna. Schlegel was there to take credit for organizing the evacuation of the treasure of Monte Cassino, which was justified, and to take credit for the original idea, which was not.

Overshadowing Schlegel, by size and by rank, was the bulky figure of Major-General Kurt Maelzer, the German commander of Rome. Maelzer was a man of 55, thick of mind as well as body, known as a brute and a drunkard. He liked to call himself the "King of Rome."

ABOVE: At the presentation in Rome of the treasures of Monte Cassino to the Vatican for safekeeping, Major-General Kurt Maelzer holds a scroll in which Abbot Diamare thanks the Hermann Goering Division for the rescue of the treasures. Schlegel is at center. BELOW: German soldiers display a painting from Monte Cassino in front of Castel Sant' Angelo.

ABOVE: General von Senger studies a map with his commander (left), General Heinrich von Vietinghoff. RIGHT: General von Vietinghoff.

He had just arrived in the city, but he made sure he was present at this event commemorating the role of the German army in preserving Italian culture. The people back home in Germany would see it, and him, at the movies in the weekly newsreel *Die Deutsche Wochenschau.*

Now the line of trucks came down from the north on the far bank of the Tiber. There were fourteen of them, big canvas-backed Blitz trucks bearing the insignia of the Hermann Goering Division. The cameras caught the trucks as they lumbered across the bridge, past the Bernini statues, where they stopped, still in the sun, before the gate of the Castel Sant' Angelo. Julius Schlegel ceremoniously read a proclamation into the microphone of the Italian Fascist radio reporter. Schlegel shook hands with a man in clerical garb representing the Vatican; both men turned to let the camera record their smiles. General Maelzer looked on grinning fatly.

German soldiers began to unload the trucks under the watchful eyes of the camera. They were unloading the drawers full of precious scrolls whose packing Schlegel had organized at Monte Cassino six weeks earlier. At the gate of the castle, the soldiers handed the heavy wooden drawers over to Italian workmen, who carried them down a ramp onto the neutral soil of the Vatican. The soldiers and workmen moved a total of 387 cases into Vatican custody.

The cameras recorded the details of the ceremony: a German soldier, looking like a bewildered teen-ager, holding up a scroll. . . . Four grim-faced soldiers, battle-ready in helmets, incongruously posing alongside a painting from the abbey in front of the sentry box of the Castel Sant' Angelo. . . . Soldiers carefully unloading the big globe from the Monte Cassino library. . . .

These surroundings—the bridge with its giant Bernini angels, the grim, windowless Castel Sant' Angelo, etched by the sharp winter sun —made an incomparable backdrop for still another spectacle in the city that is the theater of the world. That thought was going through the mind of Emilio Re, an archivist with the Italian Ministry of Education who had been involved in the complex negotiations with the Germans and the Vatican that had led to the day's events. He was sure he knew why they had their cameras there to record the deed. It was because of the worldwide reaction to the Germans' deliberate burning of the Naples archives on September 29. If it were not for the Germans' embarrassment over what had happened in Naples, the

Monte Cassino archive might well be in Germany by now, he thought. The Naples archives had died so that others might live.

The show was over by noon, the crowd scattered, the cameras gone. It had been a good day for German propaganda. Now that the Allied armies had landed on the Continent, the Germans were posing as the defenders of European civilization against the invaders. It was not often that the German military—still less the division named after the number two Nazi—had a chance to show themselves in that protective role. So they made the most of the rare occasion.

However, not all the treasures from Monte Cassino, nor everyone involved in saving them, were present that day in front of the Castel Sant' Angelo. The art treasure from Naples was not on the trucks. It was still in the Hermann Goering supply depot at Spoleto, 70 miles away. And the man whose idea originated the evacuation of the treasures, Dr. Maximilian J. Becker, was not there for the ceremony. No one had told him about it.

16

FROM THE MONKS' DIARY:

DECEMBER 9

No visitors today except three soldiers who were working in the vicinity of the monastery. The chief of the *Feldgendarmi* went to Villa Santa Lucia to speak with his captain about the placing of artillery in the immediate vicinity of the monastery. . . .

Today, meanwhile, Italian workers told us they had unloaded heavy munitions into the caves next to the main road at Kilometer VIII below the *collegio*.

From 11:30 on there was one visitor after another, among them Lieutenant-Colonel of Artillery Pollack, commander of the zone. The abbot told him about the military works undertaken in the vicinity and made him understand that the Germans would be showing an ugly face to the world after all the great propaganda they had made about saving Monte Cassino. The colonel promised to report to General Fries and gave the abbot his usual good wishes. I showed him several places where the military were working.

The Allied artillery is closer, and there is a continual roar of aircraft despite the cloudy, misty weather.

17

The work that the monks were witnessing around them on their mountaintop and in the plain below was the Germans' preparation for their last stand south of Rome. Monte Cassino is the final natural barrier on the way north; beyond it the widening Liri Valley provides an easy road to the capital. The purpose of the Germans' stubborn defense in the mountains to the south, conducted with great skill by General von Senger, was to delay the advancing Allies while they prepared to use the Monte Cassino barrier to its fullest effect.

The German position at Monte Cassino was part of what was called the Gustav Line. In the early weeks of December, German engineers were managing the extensive preparations for battle on that line. Their laborers were whatever Italian men they could find by whatever methods were needed. Sometimes they could hire laborers for food or tobacco; and sometimes German soldiers just rounded men up at the point of a gun: how they got the workers didn't matter as long as the work got done in time.

The Gustav Line stretched from the Tyrrhenian Sea at the port of Minturno along the Garigliano River to the Liri Valley, across the valley to Cassino town, along the 5-mile promontory of Monte Cassino, then up into the wild Abruzzi mountains. The focal point of this line of defense was the hill on which stood the abbey. It is a place of such intrinsic strength that the teachers at the Italian war college used Monte Cassino as an example of a position made impregnable by nature. The land drops off from the monastery in all directions. In front of the monastery is the steep hill below which lies the town of Cassino. On the two adjacent sides, as on the sides of a ship's prow, the drop is almost equally steep. The approach from the north, toward the rear of the monastery, is just as difficult. The slopes that lead up to the ridge on top of the Monte Cassino promontory are precipitous and rugged. What few roads and trails there are wind up in hairpin turns. Once up on the ridge an attacker finds that there is still no clear path to the monastery hill. He must advance through broken, rocky country, and, as he approaches the monastery, he finds himself on a narrow rib of land with deep ravines on both sides.

The Germans were adding to the enormous defensive advantages nature had provided. They made good use of the many natural caves in the limestone of the mountains, caves that the Italian peasants used as shelter for their animals and themselves. The Germans would deepen the cave and install living quarters. With a machine gun at the entrance, a platoon could live in the cave and take shelter there when the enemy artillery was firing. Elsewhere the Germans used prefabricated steel bunkers; during the construction work the steel shell provided shelter for the men excavating the bunker's place in a hillside. They dug out emplacements for machine guns and covered them with shields of steel; the machine guns were located so their fields would interlock. They placed their mortars where they could drop their shells on the few trails that led up the mountainside. Wherever an enemy might come the Germans sowed mines that could kill a man who stepped on them, or, failing that, blow off his leg or his genitals.

The Germans built fortified places around the abbey's hill and on the ridge behind it. One was at Monte Venere, a knob on the hill below the abbey on which stood the trestle of the ruined funicular to Cassino. Here the Germans established a mortar battery and an observation post that overlooked Cassino, the highway, and the valley. The men who manned this position could take shelter in a cave in the rear of the knob that was almost impossible to hit with artillery fire from below. The Germans found and occupied two natural caves in the hill immediately below the foundations of the monastery. Behind the abbey, they put an observation post on the highest point of the ridge, a knoll named Monte Calvario that was about two thousand yards from the monastery. They fortified stone farmhouses by building inner rooms protected with heavy logs and crushed stone. One of these fortified farmhouses was at Albaneta, a farm beyond Monte Calvario, and others were in the hamlets on the slope of the ridge facing the monastery. In a deep ravine immediately behind the abbey, the Germans found and occupied *il fortino,* a small fort built by the Italian military in 1820.

Down on the plain below Monte Cassino the Germans were turning the town of Cassino into a fortress by wrecking it. The Germans knew from their bitter experience at Stalingrad that rubble makes a better defensive position than intact buildings. They were making the main road and the streets of the town impassable for tanks. Should the Allies try to bypass the town, they would have to deal with the river system—the Liri, and the Rapido that becomes the Gari and joins the Liri to form the Garigliano, which crosses the valley and flows down to the Mediterranean 15 miles away. The Germans prepared for an attack from across the river by clearing its banks to provide them with a clear field of fire and by destroying its bridges. They destroyed the river dams and diverted the Rapido, thereby turning much of the plain into a swamp in which tanks would bog down. By the time the Germans had finished building the Gustav Line, there was no way the Allies could go that would not encounter formidable natural and manmade defenses.

General von Senger passed all this construction activity when he drove down the valley from his headquarters on his frequent visits to the front in the mountains to the south of Cassino. Down there Senger's soldiers were fighting for time. They would fight at each turn of the road through the mountains till the Fifth Army pushed them back with its overwhelming firepower. The Germans would then retreat to prepared positions at the next turn. The Allies would have to clear the mined road, repair the destroyed bridges, and bring up their artillery to push the Germans back again. Soldiers on both sides fought and tried to survive in the freezing rain of one of Italy's worst winters. In this climate, Senger worried less about the battle itself than he did about the effect that lack of any decent nighttime accommodations was having on his troops' morale. Morale was all the more important because in the mountains men fought in small isolated groups that could not easily be supervised by their commanders.

On one of his visits to the front Senger was, he later wrote, "astounded and dismayed" when he experienced a "bombardment of an intensity such as I had not seen since the big battles of the First World War." He was seeing firsthand the Allies' ability to pour enormous material resources into the war in Italy, even though it was a secondary front, while the Germans had to ration their use of ammunition to a small fraction—a fifth or a tenth—of that fired by their enemies. Senger was also gaining a new respect for the Americans. In Sicily he had found the Americans' attack "lacking in spirit," but here in the mountains Senger saw them "swift in attack" and concluded they were now hardened to combat.

In early December the Germans were driven off Monte Camino, one of the two mountains—the other was Monte Sammucro—guarding the road north. These two mountains were, in Senger's opinion, the key to the entrance to the Liri Valley. Senger was in no doubt about the intentions of his opponent, the American Mark Clark. Once the Anglo-Americans captured these two mountains, they would come down in the valley and the battle would then take place on the Gustav Line. With this prospect in mind, Senger asked for a ruling on the status of the Abbey of Monte Cassino. As the request was worded by Senger's superior, General Heinrich von Vietinghoff, in his message of December 7 to Kesselring, it did not hold out much hope that the abbey could be spared:

> 10th Army Headquarters requests that a decision be reached as soon as possible as to the treatment of Abbey of Monte Cassino during preparation of and in case of occupation of "G" position [the Gustav Line]. According to view of Army, preservation of extraterritoriality of monastery is not possible. . . . Of necessity it lies directly in the main line of defense. In this case, it would

signify a very great danger, because along with renunciation of good observation posts and positions of concealment on our part, the Anglo-Americans almost certainly would not bother about any sort of agreement at the decisive moment but would without scruple place themselves in occupation of this point that in certain circumstances might be decisive.

The subject of Monte Cassino had been on Kesselring's desk for more than a month. When the Vatican, in response to the plea from the abbot, had asked the Allies to spare the monastery, a message was also sent to the Germans asking them not to fortify it. The German embassy's response, as relayed on November 7 by D'Arcy Osborne, the British minister at the Vatican, was that the abbey "will not be occupied by regular German troops." This did not satisfy Osborne, who a few days earlier had told the Foreign Office that he had heard the Germans had already occupied Monte Cassino and "sent the monks away." He asked the Vatican to find out what the Germans meant by "regular" troops. If the Germans did in fact use the abbey, Osborne told the Vatican, "the Allies will be obliged to take whatever countermeasures, aerial or otherwise, that their own military interests may require." But on December 7, Osborne reported to London that "the Germans have now definitely said the abbey will not be used for military purposes."

Kesselring sent his instructions down to Senger at his headquarters in the Liri Valley on December 11:

Commander-in-Chief Southwest [Kesselring] states that the Roman Catholic Church was simply promised that the Abbey of Monte Cassino would not be occupied by German troops. . . . This means only that the building itself must be spared.

18

FROM THE MONKS' DIARY:

DECEMBER 12

This evening a German captain came, sent by the Supreme Command of the South with an important communication for the abbot. He was accompanied by an interpreter. I was present at the discussion which took place in the guest hall of the *collegio.* The captain first said that the Vatican had sent a message to the German Command asking if the monastery had been hit by shellfire. The Holy Father—this is what he said—feared that the presence of the three gendarmes might constitute in some way a military objective: therefore the German Command asked the abbot to permit the withdrawal of the gendarmes. In order to safeguard the monastery from damage caused by the belligerents, the Supreme Command of the South was establishing a zone of 300 meters [333 yards] around the monastery that was forbidden to any military personnel; the main road and the other roads leading to the monastery would be closed; the gendarmes would be posted outside the 300-meter limit to make everyone respect this international zone. On his way back the captain would give orders to that effect to the division. The fact that this action had been taken could be communicated to the other side by means of the Holy See.

The abbot answered that till now not a single shell had hit the monastery and that the monks were all unharmed; he then informed the captain of his concern about the motor vehicles that appeared on the mountaintop carrying visitors or material of war, for example the ammunition placed at Kilometer VIII and the work at the trestle. The captain in a curt, formal tone assured the abbot that the munitions would soon be moved and that any visit or travel would from now on be forbidden to all military personnel and machines. About the gendarmes the abbot stated his opinion that, since he had requested them only for the protection of the monastery and they had given good service for just that purpose, he saw no reason they should not stay in the room by the gate. The captain insisted that they should be put outside the 300-meter limit. When he was taking his leave the captain asked if, since he was in the abbey, he could visit the Basilica. The abbot agreed and invited him for a cup of tea.

We were happy with this communication and gave thanks to God and Saint Benedict. But the gendarmes were furious with us, accusing us of having written to Rome and causing them discomfort, making them move to a cave because they had served us: they promised to take reprisals against us in any way in their power. There was no sense in what they were saying. God save us from such sulkers.

DECEMBER 13

Today we began closing the door to visitors. We feel rather bad about it, but it is necessary.

Towards ten o'clock Chaplain Meyer arrived, sent by General Fries to ask for clarification of yesterday's communications. The general wanted to know if the abbot had officially communicated to the Holy See the news of a bombardment of Monte Cassino. The abbot assured him he had not done so because the abbey had never been hit. The chaplain then asked the abbot what he thought about the matter of the gendarmes. The abbot repeated what he told the captain yesterday. The chaplain gave orders that, barring orders to the contrary, the gendarmes could for the time being stay where they were. . . .

Tomorrow we shall put up some provisional signs.

DECEMBER 14

Because the command of the division had not sent soldiers to measure the 300 meters and put up signs, we measured the ground, at the suggestion of the gendarmes themselves, and put up signs at the limits. The road was blocked halfway between the *Madonnina* of mosaic made by dom Eusebio and Kilometer VII with this sign: "Durchfahrt u. Durchgang fur alle Wehrmacht angehoerige verboten. O.K. Sud." [Driving or passing through forbidden to all Wehrmacht personnel.] A few vehicles passed on the way to Albaneta, but they will be the last.

It is certain that the positions prepared in many places will have to be removed, either because they are within the 300-meter limit or because there will be no access to them [because of the limit]. On the road a gendarme acts as a sentinel barring any approach to Monte Cassino.

DECEMBER 15

In the plain the Germans broke the dams on the river and the water is flowing towards Cassino. They blew up the wall around the orphanage.

This morning I measured the distance from the monastery wall to the trestle of the funicular: it is precisely 300 meters. We put up a wooden sign on the side of the trestle, right opposite the observation post built by the Germans; on it is written "Montecassino—Neutralzone." There are still munitions in the cave at Kilometer VIII. The abbot officially charged the marshal of the gendarmes with telling his commanding officer that the munitions are still there and that the work is still going on, despite their promises and despite the neutral zone.

DECEMBER 17

We finished the work of measuring and putting up signs at the 300-meter limit of the neutral zone. . . . No more Germans are to be seen in this zone, nor at Monte Cassino.

Tomorrow the truck will go down at five o'clock to grind the tenants' grain in an old mill on the plain. The harvesting of olives continues, not far from the monastery. People have begun to come back to Monte Cassino, or rather to the zone. The Germans themselves encouraged them, saying it would not be destroyed because it was an international zone. Especially at night people take refuge in the buildings near the monastery and then during the day they take to the woods to avoid being taken away by the Germans.

DECEMBER 18

Chaplain Meyer came this morning on behalf of General Fries. He renewed the general's request that we reduce to the very minimum the number of tenants and servants at Monte Cassino. We told him the munitions were still in place. He expressed surprise because the general had ordered that they be taken away: he assured us it would soon be done. He brought letters from Rome and a calendar for the new year. Dom Eusebio received news of his family. The most comforting news was that the library and archive had been returned to the monks and were now deposited at the Vatican: this had happened on the eighth of December, the *festa dell' Immacolata.*

Four shells landed on [the mountain of] Monte Cassino. One fell in the garden, below the large cornice of the *conigliera,* in the direction of, and only a few meters from, the munitions cave; this one came a little after noon. Despite the signs indicating the neutral zone, they are still working on the cave and the observation post at the trestle.

This is really scorched earth, and the reports we hear of the results of this resort to violence are piteous. May God shorten these terrible days.

DECEMBER 19

About 10:30 two photographers came from the German Propaganda Office in Rome: they took some photographs of the monastery because "in case it was destroyed, they could use the pictures to show the barbarity of the Anglo-Americans." We offered them lunch.

In the afternoon about 3:15, while we were saying the rosary in the chapel of the *collegio,* there was an aerial attack: the explosions were very powerful and close, shaking the whole building; we went on praying. After vespers we realized that Monte Cassino was saved by a miracle, because the closest of the bombs fell hardly six meters from the Novitiate, tearing up everything; the whole hillside from Monte Cassino down to Cassino was hit; but the road is still usable. The planes, from what eyewitnesses reported, went to great lengths to avoid hitting the monastery; the Anglo-Americans evidently were trying to hit the cave below the Novitiate. We got off with only a few broken windows. We thanked God and Saint Benedict for our escape. The caves are still full of munitions, and there is still construction at the trestle. Despite our efforts we obtain nothing. Today, during the above-mentioned attack, a bomb hit only a few meters from some munitions, and the peril was very great because the caves contain large-caliber ammunition for mortars.

19

The two American generals drove up the mountain road to the frontlines. To avoid attracting the unwelcome attention of the Germans dug into the hills around them, the generals went in two jeeps and were accompanied by a minimum of aides. One of the generals was Mark Clark, commander of the Allies' Fifth Army. The other was Clark's close friend from West Point days, the commander of all Allied forces in the Mediterranean theater, General Dwight D. Eisenhower.

That day, December 19, the visibility was unusually good. For once it was not raining, and, when they got out of their jeeps at the turn in the road, Clark and Eisenhower could see for miles ahead. Before them, Route 6 wound down into a plain. This was the Liri Valley, for two months the objective of Clark's army. On their right, as they gazed down the road, was the snowcapped peak of Monte Cairo. To their left, blocking access to the plain, was a huge isolated hill called Monte Trocchio. In the center of the generals' field of vision, rising immediately above the valley plain, was the ridge of Monte Cassino. On the prow of the ridge, 10 miles away but easily visible in the December sunlight, the yellowish-white bulk of the Abbey of Monte Cassino stood out from the bare landscape around it. Clark and Eisenhower were seeing the monastery for the first time.

Clark thought that day, so he later recalled, that the way ahead looked relatively easy. Once the Allies had fought their way down onto that plain, they could use their heavy equipment on its level terrain and the road to Rome would be open to them. Certainly it could not be as bad as the dreadful mountains through which his soldiers had been fighting for the past two months. The way ahead had better be easier, for Clark's army was far behind schedule: by now it was supposed to be up at the other end of the Liri Valley. That same day Winston Churchill, who bore much of the responsibility for the way the war was being fought in Italy, was saying: "The stagnation of the whole campaign on the Italian front is becoming scandalous."

Behind the two generals, on the slope of Monte Sammucro, was the village of San Pietro Infine, or rather what was left of it. Not long ago San Pietro had been one of those pretty Italian hill villages loved by painters: houses of masonry painted in pale pinks and yellows that looked like patches of flowers against the backdrop of the mountain. The people were poor, but they scratched out a living from their plots of fertile ground and the olive groves on the rocky hillsides. Now the people were scattered and destitute and their village was a ruin: the wreckage of their homes was wet and cold and stinking from the decaying corpses of soldiers and civilians and animals.

The American 143rd Infantry had just taken the ruins of San Pietro after a week-long battle.* It had been a hideous struggle. The Germans held the high ground, so it was uphill all the way, and all the forces of nature seemed to conspire against the Allied soldiers. Mud alone was an opponent as formidable as the Germans. So pervasive and crippling was the mud that those old enough to remember compared it to the mud of Flanders fields in the earlier war. Mud mired the Allies' heavy vehicles, and everything the soldiers needed—water, food, ammunition—had to be carried up hillsides on the backs of mules and men. Mud made soldiers climbing under fire slip and fall and sometimes die. Ernie Pyle, the American correspondent who lived with and wrote about the soldiers, had this to say about that December:

> Our troops were living in almost inconceivable misery. The fertile black valleys were knee-deep in mud. Thousands of men had not been dry for weeks. Other thousands lay at night in the high mountains with the temperature below freezing and the thin snow sifting over them. They dug into the stones and slept in little chasms and behind rocks and in half-caves. They lived like men of prehistoric times, and a club would have become them more than a machine gun. How they survived the dreadful winter at all was beyond us who had the opportunity of drier beds in the warmer valleys.

In the mountains of Italy the Americans and the British had rediscovered the mule. Only mules were strong, hardy, and sure-footed enough to carry supplies from the roads, where vehicles were

*John Huston made *The Battle of San Pietro,* one of the best film documentaries of war, during that week.

mired in mud, up into the hills where the men were fighting. The Allies combed Italy for mules, and they searched their own ranks and the Italian civilian population for men skilled in the obsolescent trade of mule skinning. A mule could carry 160 pounds, but some of that was for his own use: 19 pounds of food and eight to twelve gallons of water per day. The mules were pitifully vulnerable to enemy fire. They did not know how to hide, and, panicked by shellfire, they often jumped to their death off the narrow mountain trails. Recurring shortages of shoe nails and pack equipment would keep the mules out of action, and at times their sharp hooves would cut military telephone lines laid across or along their trails. But the mountain war could hardly have been fought without the mules.

Because of strategic decisions made far away from the reality of those wintry mountains, the Fifth Army had been required to do too much—the conquest of Rome—with far too little, and the soldiers, as always, were paying the price. In the field the Allied commanders were increasingly concerned about the soldiers' ability to endure and carry on the struggle. The British were particularly worried about their continuing losses of men. They had been at war much longer, their small nation had lost many more of its men, and the insistent reminders in Italy of the First World War—the mud of Flanders fields—evoked memories far more alarming to them than to their American allies. Mark Clark, in fact, thought that the British commanders under him had been hanging back and letting the Americans carry the weight of the fighting and the dying.

So both the Americans and the British, but especially the British, hoped even against the accumulating evidence that their great superiority in firepower would save them from spending too many of their soldiers' lives on the ground. Their control of the air was all but complete. Bombers based now in Foggia in the south of Italy ranged up and down the peninsula, rarely challenged by what was left of the Luftwaffe, dropping their bombs on the enemy supply lines coming down from Germany. The British had hoped that bombing alone would drive the Germans out of southern Italy, and the RAF's great enthusiast, Air Marshal Sir Arthur Harris—"Bomber Harris"—was saying that December that the war could be won in the air: enough bombing of the European mainland would make the planned cross-channel invasion unnecessary.

But the bombing in Italy did not prevent the Germans in the

mountains from getting enough supplies to carry on the battle. On the ground the Allies' artillery was firing off enormous barrages against the German positions in the Camino mountains. In two days of combat in the mountains around San Pietro, 925 Allied guns fired 206,929 rounds weighing 4,066 tons. Even this massive series of explosions did not dislodge the Germans. Later on, Clark learned that a group of Germans in an underground bunker had played cards throughout the attack. They hadn't even moved from their table.

The two American commanders gazing down the road ahead that day were aware of the special significance of the monastery they were seeing for the first time. Clark's headquarters had received the first message on October 25 asking that Monte Cassino be protected within the possibilities of military necessity. Eisenhower had repeated the gist of the message to General Alexander, Clark's superior, on November 4, and the next day Eisenhower reported:

> Consistent with military necessity all precautions to safeguard works of arts and monuments are being taken. Naval, ground and air commanders have been so instructed and understand fully the importance of preventing unnecessary or avoidable damage. AMG [Allied Military Government] officers qualified to advise commander are available. Information as to location and identity of works of art is on hand and is being disseminated.

Herbert L. Matthews, the influential *New York Times* correspondent, who knew Italy well from prewar years, had taken the issue of Monte Cassino, and Italian art treasures in general, directly to Eisenhower. Matthews wrote Eisenhower on November 17 that he thought much of the destruction that had already taken place could have been avoided without military risk. As an example, he wrote, "Our only mistake on the Rome raid (on which I flew) was to make the bombing run in such a way that we were bound to hit the Basilica of San Lorenzo, and that got us some grievous publicity." Matthews urged that commanders on the post be briefed about what to avoid if possible. Eisenhower's chief of staff, General Walter Bedell Smith, wrote the correspondent a reassuring but noncommittal reply.

But Eisenhower and Clark did not aim the guns themselves, and what Matthews and another correspondent learned on the ground in

ABOVE: A British truck mired in the Liri Valley mud. BELOW: An American tank bogged down in the Rapido Valley. OPPOSITE, TOP: A soldier of the Indian Division leads pack mules up path to the Monte Cassino ridge. OPPOSITE, BOTTOM: A bone-weary American soldier of the 36th Division sips coffee.

the mountains south of Rome was quite different from the official pronouncements. Will Lang, of *Time* magazine, talked to the commander of the Fifth Army artillery, which now had Monte Cassino within its range. Matthews talked to the divisional intelligence officer. The artillery commander had gotten no instructions about Monte Cassino. The intelligence officer had never heard of the place.

20

Dr. Becker's efforts to prevent any looting of the Abbey of Monte Cassino treasures caught up with him in late December. About two weeks after the ceremonial presentation at the Castel Sant' Angelo, he was ordered to report immediately to Lieutenant-Colonel Alexander Roscher, a doctor and the chief medical officer of the Hermann Goering Division.

Becker reported to his chief at a field hospital in Genzano, near Rome. The young doctor knew immediately that he was in trouble. He soon found out why. The chief medical officer was furious, and it was about the Monte Cassino affair. In a harsh, angry voice, the powerfully built chief accused Becker of meddling in affairs of the Hermann Goering Division that were none of his business as a medical officer; of "extracurricular activities" with Italians and monks; of making unauthorized trips to Spoleto; of leaving his unit without permission. For all this, the medical chief said, he could have Becker court-martialed.

Becker was silent. He thought back over his recent actions, wondering which of them had gotten him into this jam. Someone obviously had complained about him, but who? After his return from Spoleto, he had gone immediately to Schlegel and told him he had seen the corporal from Berlin, Goering's representative, breaking into the crates of paintings at the supply depot. The Austrian seemed to agree that any looting would discredit the work they had done together, but he told Becker he was sure the idea of a present for Goering had now been abandoned. He advised him to talk with Jacobi, the supply officer, before going any further with his complaints about Spoleto.

Becker's confrontation with Jacobi had been unpleasant. Jacobi had insisted on the Hermann Goering Division's right to a reward for the work the rescue had taken. It had been a much bigger job than he had been led to believe at the beginning; Becker had told him he would need one or two trucks, but the job had occupied fifteen. The division was not a welfare institution, Jacobi reminded the doctor; they were at war and in a difficult combat situation besides. Becker had repeated his threat to go to Field Marshal Kesselring if anything was stolen at Spoleto. Jacobi replied that he would take the whole business up with the commander of the division, General Conrath. Perhaps, Becker thought, Jacobi had complained to the general about the doctor's meddling, and that was why he was now facing a court-martial.

The chief medical officer, apparently angered still further by Becker's silence, now shouted at him: "Don't you hear me? Speak! Explain yourself!"

Becker defended himself as best he could. General Conrath knew what he had been doing at Monte Cassino and, he thought, approved of the rescue operation. Becker's unit was not in combat at the time, and whenever he left the men he made arrangements with a fellow doctor to cover for him. He was ready to justify himself before a court-martial. "What I did," the young doctor concluded, "I did for European civilization."

At that the chief medical officer's face turned crimson, he jumped to his feet, and he roared at Becker: "If you want to do something for civilization, you're in the wrong place here in Italy. You can do that in Russia. I will see to it that you are transferred to the Eastern front immediately!" He stormed out of the office slamming the door behind him.

A few days later Dr. Becker was ordered to report to a Luftwaffe unit near Bologna, far to the north. His role in the affair of Monte Cassino was at an end.

FROM THE MONKS' DIARY:

DECEMBER 22

The abbot wrote a letter to General Fries about the shells and bombs that have fallen near the stores of munitions: he asked the general to give formal, explicit orders for the removal of the munitions and the observance of the 300-meter zone set by the Supreme Command. The abbot also wrote a letter to the Abbot Primate in Rome to advise him (in terms that would not prejudice our situation) of the danger caused by the construction, etc., around the abbey; and asked the Abbot Primate to make these facts known higher up.

This morning we settled more or less on what would we do for the liturgical celebration of Christmas. We shall do the best we can.

DECEMBER 24

The evening service began at two o'clock in the Crypt. The Crypt was full of the faithful. . . . Right at the end of the service General von Senger und Etterlin, commander of the 14th Panzer Korps, a practicing Catholic, arrived; he wanted to take part in the service; he said he would return tomorrow morning.

DECEMBER 25

Christmas in wartime. The abbot celebrated the conventual mass in the Crypt, before the singing of terce [fourth of the eight daily hours]; during the mass we sang several things. General von Senger arrived. We had saved a place for him in the Crypt. We offered him lunch. He spoke to me about the battle of the Garigliano. I took advantage of the opportunity to tell him about the contents of the letter the abbot had sent to General Fries (on the 22nd). I told him we had faith that the protective zone would be respected. He gave me no answer.

22

General von Senger was returning in his battered Volkswagen jeep from an early morning visit to the frontlines south of Cassino when he stopped to attend services at Monte Cassino. For the men at the front, December 25 was just another day of freezing, fighting, dying. The German commander was trying to extricate his soldiers from a potential trap in the mountains to the south. The Allies had captured the two mountains, Camino and Sammucro, that were the key to the German position. Now some German units were in danger of being caught with their backs to the Garigliano River, which they could not cross because other Germans had flooded the plain and blown up the bridges. Just like the French in 1504, Senger thought.

The parallel to that earlier conflict was much on Senger's mind in those days. In 1504, the French were fighting the Spanish for control of the Italian peninsula. The French were pushing down from Rome and trying to break through the Spanish at Monte Cassino—like the Allies in 1943, except in the reverse direction. But the Spanish had trapped the French against the Garigliano and destroyed them just as Senger feared might now happen to his men. That, perhaps, was what caused Senger to describe the earlier battle in his conversation at lunch with the monks on Christmas Day. Another event in that same struggle in 1504 was of far more interest to the monks than the fate of the French soldiers. The Spanish commander, Francesco Gonzago de Cado, had noticed that the monastery on the mountain-top would make an excellent fortress. Not wanting to let the French have it, he ordered its destruction. But that night Saint Benedict appeared to him in a vision, and in the morning the Spanish commander canceled his order.

Senger's Christmas visit was not his first to Monte Cassino—he had come by and met Abbot Diamare in the summer—but it was his first as commander in the area. He had stayed away, so he later wrote, to underline the German policy of keeping all military personnel out of the abbey. He made a point that day of not looking out the abbey windows that offered an excellent view of the combat zone below. Senger wrote—in contrast to the monks' recollections—that when he asked them, the monks had said they had no complaints about the behavior of either the Germans or the Anglo-Americans.

There was, in fact, nothing reassuring Senger could tell the monk Matronola when the monks expressed the hope that the 300-meter zone would be respected. The day after he visited the abbey, Senger's headquarters issued an order to the 44th Infantry Division: "Evacuate civilians as soon as possible, and make no use of abbey buildings, but make defenses right up to the abbey wall if necessary."

23

FROM THE MONKS' DIARY:

DECEMBER 28

[The refugees] were trying to hide in safe places as much as possible.

Meanwhile quite terrible things were happening. In brutal fashion the German soldiers were using whips and clubs to drive these poor people as if they were packhorses. They shoved and struck in the face a poor widow with a child who had written permission to enter the monastery. They beat Luciano over the back because he wanted to take some of his things with him, and they did the same to several women.

Two of Anna Pittiglio's daughters clung desperately to dom Agostino to escape being taken away, and I barely avoided being in a similar situation.

I protested to some of the most brutal soldiers, and to the lieutenant in charge of the evacuation. These inhuman soldiers try to prevent the people from taking their things and then the soldiers at their leisure search through their baggage. At San Onofrio they were eating [the refugees' food] and stealing [their goods].

The family of dom Francesco Falconio was hidden in our baking house. Many people were in the monastery and all around. But the Germans did not go into the monastery.

After many quite anguishing scenes and much resistance we were successful in that we managed to save all of our people except one poor woman who was at San Onofrio and did not escape their roundup in the zone. Our gendarmes, and two others, came at evening and gave the "all-clear" signal, then we saw people of all sorts emerge.

Dr. Matronola [the monk's cousin] was there. . . . We had put all the sick people in the infirmary. Many people were sleeping on the stairs.

I would dearly have loved to have saved one person, Ubaldo Dematteis, the [Italian] soldier from the observatory. But since he was burdened with a family and was almost betrothed to a girl, I would have failed if I had tried to do too much.

Much artillery action during the night. We learned that some people were loudly complaining that we had not told them that the gendarmes were coming, without realizing that only by acting as we did were we able to save almost all of our people.

DECEMBER 29

The day was more calm. But in the morning, when the lieutenant in charge yesterday, who had slept the night at Monte Cassino, was about to leave, one of the gendarmes came with a request for a list of the monks and one of the peasants.

The two gendarmes assigned to the monastery then protested about what had happened yesterday and reprimanded the lieutenant for having spent the night in the monastery against all orders, and told him never to do it again.

We succeeded in putting Dr. Matronola and our nurse Gennarino on the list of those to stay; this was a real stroke of luck.

That afternoon a colonel from the new Division came instead of the general. He was accompanied by a captain of gendarmerie and an interpreter. The abbot received the colonel and the others in the guest hall of the *collegio*. The colonel courteously asked that we reduce the number of our tenants and their dependents to the fewest possible, that is to very few people. The abbot pointed out that, in addition to the tenants, and against the will of the monks, there had come a large number of strangers for whom we were not responsible and that it would be hard for us to make a choice among the tenants given the many requirements of the monastery's land and buildings. The captain was rather curt.

The abbot told the colonel that the protective zone established by the German High Command was not being respected. The colonel gave him formal assurance that the munitions would soon be removed, the construction stopped, and vehicle traffic barred.

This evening the brother of one of the employees at the funicular came to get his father at Albaneta and take him to Rome. He has some kind of pass. We gave him letters for Rome. The abbot wrote the Abbot Primate about our situation and about the belligerents' continuing infringements on the supposedly neutral zone. We hope the boy will be able to reach Rome.

The munitions are still in the caves: they have again promised that work will be stopped and the munitions removed—but seeing is believing.

24

By now Tommaso Leccisotti could consider himself an old hand at navigating the city of Rome and the corridors of the Vatican. In the two months he had been in Rome as the emissary of Abbot Diamare, the tiny bespectacled monk had made the 5-mile journey from the monastery at San Paolo to the Vatican more than a dozen times. Much of the rest of his time had been spent scurrying around Rome on behalf of the refugees from Monte Cassino. Leccisotti was even advising more recently arrived monks on how things were done at the Vatican.

The monk made the journey confidently when, on December 29, he was summoned by order of Monsignor Montini. At the Vatican a priest read him a statement by the German ambassador concerning Monte Cassino. The ambassador, Baron von Weizsaecker, repeated that "the abbey is not occupied by German troops," and added that a guard was posted outside the gate to prevent the military from entering. Most of Weizsaecker's statement was devoted to the question of the civilians—150 of them by German count—in the abbey. These people presented a "certain danger" if the front came closer to Monte Cassino. Should the enemy see the civilians coming and going in the area, Weizsaecker said, they might mistake them for German soldiers, and that might provoke the bombing of the abbey. The German thought the civilians should be removed. As for the monks, they could stay if they chose, but the Germans could not guarantee their safety. (Ten days later, on January 8, the Vatican communicated part of the German statement to the Allies. But all that reached Washington, on January 20, was Weizsaecker's meaningless concluding statement that "insofar as the German military authorities are concerned everything possible is being done to preserve the Abbey of Monte Cassino from war damage both at the present time and in the future.")

Leccisotti, listening to the priest, thought he heard an offer to the Vatican to "ascertain"—the Italian is *constatare*—what the Germans were doing at Monte Cassino. This sounded like an opportunity to send a neutral observer who could then give the Allies disinterested information on the military situation at the abbey. In fact, no such offer appears in the text of Weizsaecker's message as later published by the Vatican, though he could have made the offer orally.

In any event, Leccisotti was not pleased but frightened by what he thought the German was suggesting, and, after consulting with the abbot of San Paolo, he decided to keep the offer a secret. Evidently he thought that a neutral observer at Monte Cassino would discover what Leccisotti already knew: that the Germans were violating the

300-meter zone. Once the Allies also learned this, Leccisotti feared, they would feel free to attack the abbey.

Leccisotti never informed the monks at Monte Cassino of the German offer, if such it was, so Abbot Diamare never had the chance to make his own decision about it. The Vatican never acted on it either. Thus the opportunity, if there was one, to verify the German claim that they were not using the abbey slipped away unnoticed.

25

FROM THE MONKS' DIARY:

DECEMBER 30

False alarm this morning. A soldier arrived on a motorcycle, and people began fleeing, thinking it was another roundup. Instead he brought, at long last, the official order to be posted at the limits of the international zone:

SPERRGEBIET

DAS BETRETEN DES KLOSTERGEBIETES

IM UMKREIS VON 300 M.

IST FUR MILITAERPERSONEN

VERBOTEN

DAS GLEICHEN DAS ERRICHTEN VON MILITAERLISHCEN ANLAGEN

O.N. 30.12.43 DAS DIVISION KOMMAND*

It will be posted for New Year's Day.

---

*Trespass on the grounds of the abbey within a radius of 300 meters is forbidden to all military personnel. The same applies to the erection of military facilities.

In the late afternoon dom Falconio served *frittelle,* sweets and wine for the usual celebration in the Curia Diocesana. A day of complete calm, even from our troublemakers. But towards evening some shells landed quite close.

A terrible year has ended; but Divine Providence has not failed us even in our gravest moments. It is a year that will be memorable in the history of our abbey as well as the history of our poor country, lost and vilified, surrounded by enemies and without any true friends. God forgive us our errors and reward us for the days of our deserved and dreadful ordeal.

26

Times Square was almost as brightly lit as it had been before the war. Here at least the lights were beginning to go on again. The people crowding the streets of New York for the traditional New Year's Eve celebration were in a festive mood, and the street lights —lit up after two years of blackouts—reflected their mood. "The whole picture had changed," Meyer Berger wrote in the *New York Times,* "from dark foreboding to the certainty of victory."

Few Americans had ever really expected their nation to suffer defeat, but now, two years after Pearl Harbor, victory seemed sure, and in Europe the end was in sight. Everyone knew the cross-channel invasion was coming, and General Eisenhower himself had said: "We will win the European war in 1944." *Newsweek* said the war might be over in four months.

Everywhere the Allies were pushing the Germans back, beating them on land, at sea, and in the air. In the east, the Russians were about to cross what had been the border of Poland until Stalin seized a large chunk of that country as part of his August 1939 deal with Hitler. The war was going well everywhere, except perhaps in Italy. The murderous battle being fought in the mountains south of Rome was the one dark spot on the war map as seen by the American public. Assessing the cost, *Time* asked in a headline "What Price Success?" and pointed out that Tito's partisans were tying down more German divisions in Yugoslavia than the Allies were in Italy. The Germans in Italy, it seemed, did not know that Germany had lost the war.

On Broadway, around the corner from the crowds in Times Square, *Life with Father* was in its fifth year, *Arsenic and Old Lace* in its third. Tommy Dorsey was playing live at the Paramount, brother Jimmy was at the Roxy with Kitty Kallen, and the star of *Tarzan's Desert Mystery* was still Johnny Weissmuller. Radio City Music Hall was showing Greer Garson and Walter Pidgeon in *Madame Curie*. The number one draw at the box office was Betty Grable, whose legs adorned American barracks all over the world; her June wedding to Harry James, leader of the nations's most popular swing band, had been the merger of the year.

The Mills Brothers' version of "Paper Doll" led in record sales that week, but in Italy, American soldiers were tuning their sets to the German Radio Belgrade to hear "Lili Marlene," the song that was uniquely popular on both sides of the lines.

One show on Broadway, the Rodgers and Hammerstein musical *Oklahoma,* seemed to have a special meaning for the young Americans in uniform who were pouring through the port of New York. They were on their way to board troopships that would take them to England for the coming invasion: 3.8 million Americans were overseas already, and a million more would go over in the next few months. Years later Agnes de Mille, choreographer of *Oklahoma,* would remember the rapt faces of young soldiers standing in the back of the orchestra watching the mythic America enacted on stage on their last night before they sailed to the real war.

In London the mood of people was one of weary confidence. The British were enduring their fifth wartime New Year. Life was still much harder for them than it had ever been for the Americans. London was blacked out for fifteen hours a day, and rationing was severe. But the worst at last was over. In 1940 and 1941 the British had stood alone on the edge of the abyss, and even a year earlier the U-boats still threatened to starve them out. Now signs of life and hope were appearing. The flower girls were back in Piccadilly, the hurdy-gurdies in Soho. Two years' growth of moss and fern had softened the harsh outlines of the ruins left by the German blitz. When the crowds waiting in front of London theaters and restaurants looked up to a sky full of warplanes, the traffic was in the opposite direction: RAF and American bombers headed for Germany. The men in uniform who crowded the streets and pubs were there not to defend England but to invade the Continent. "Expectation reaches its utmost peak with the opening of 1944," the *Times* of London editorialized on New Year's Day. "This is the time of opportunity when all the endurance of the years of adversity is about to be rewarded."

The city of Berlin was as somber as New York was cheerful and London confident. Americans had never been bombed; the people of Berlin had just undergone their ninety-ninth raid by Allied bombers. Thousands of Berliners were dead; more thousands were homeless or living in buildings without fuel or windows. On New Year's Day, Adolf Hitler put out a bleak proclamation to the nation he had led into war. He said: "The year 1943 brought us our heaviest reverses. Our oldest ally fell away first of all, fell away as a result of long and carefully planned betrayal. . . ." The coming year did not look any better: "The year 1944 will make great and heavy demands on all Germans." Hitler devoted much of his proclamation to blaming the British for what had happened and telling them that they would eventually lose out to the Bolsheviks and the Americans.

But the bombing campaign in which the Allied air generals placed so much faith showed no sign of driving Germany out of the war. German war production was rising, not falling. The battered German civilian population was not demanding an end to the conflict that was causing their country's devastation. Quite the contrary, according to Allen Dulles, the OSS man in neutral Switzerland. In an "appraisal of stiffening morale" radioed to Washington, the American agent said that "German morale has somewhat recovered from the tailspin it took last autumn. . . . The morale of the fighting forces, particularly of the younger Nazis, appears to be unimpaired." About the war from the air, Dulles observed: "The bombings have so far failed to break German civilian morale. In general, the bombed-out people seem to become fanatical; probably the majority feel that since they have lost everything, they might as well fight on to the bitter end."

27

FROM THE MONKS' DIARY:

JANUARY 5

The saddest of sad days.

The interpreter for the new Division arrived about 8:30. He asked to speak to the abbot, and he informed him of very painful orders. He declared that by decision of the Supreme Command of the South, the 300-meter zone no longer existed; that all civilians without any exception must be evacuated; German trucks would come for that purpose. He invited the abbot and the monks to leave the monastery, and offered to have them transported to Rome; if we remained we would do so at our own risk. Finally he said it was the German Command's intention to buy the monastery's animals.

Asked if the monastery itself would be used for purposes of war, the interpreter envoy answered that the abbey itself would still be respected by the German military authorities and that nothing that was a military objective would be placed within it.

The abbot took note of what had been said, and reserved his answer till after the civilians had been evacuated.

Few words but full of sorrowful reality. Meanwhile three German trucks came and even before one o'clock they had taken away almost all our tenants and many of our workers. They left, but only for the time being, sick people from three families, patients in our infirmary downstairs, and that only because after an unfriendly discussion they saw that it was impossible to transport them given their number and the gravity of their special illnesses. They said they would come get them with a special vehicle.

It is useless to try to say what this day meant to our little community . . . and all this was accompanied by artillery fire that was heavy until the afternoon. The day was cold and gray.

The German interpreter stayed all day at Monte Cassino and will spend the night. . . . Nothing is left to us but to commend ourselves to God and Saint Benedict. Men with their selfishness and their bad faith want to betray us.

JANUARY 6

A day as terrible as yesterday. It was hardly morning when the abbot summoned me to give his answer to the interpreter. I said that, given the importance of the matter, it would be better for him to answer in person. He did so. The interpreter came to the guest room of the *collegio,* and with him was an officer who had come to buy our animals. The abbot, in the presence of all us monks and dom Falconio, asked the interpreter to transmit to the military authorities that had sent him the following statement:

First of all he protested what had been done and stated his surprise at the German military authorities' reversal of their position towards the abbey, having on December 12, through a high-ranking officer, guaranteed our situation in the theater of war. . . . One day—the abbot continued—the whole world would learn the truth about what happened at Monte Cassino. He and the monks, remaining as custodians of the sepulchre of Saint Benedict, would not be moved from Monte Cassino except by force.

As to the animals, the abbey did not intend to engage in business; but since the monks were now unable to care for the animals, because the monastery's workers had all been evacuated, we would concede the animals to the German Command,

99

and they could make a generous offering to Saint Benedict, with a written receipt.

A very emotional day. The gendarmes came for the final evacuation. They were more agreeable than the day before. They asked me in confidence for some sheep for their consumption. I gave them four or five, they left an offering with me. Mindful of Our Lord's precept of returning good for evil, I also gave them half a lamb. The gendarmes told me in confidence that, after themselves, no one would come to Monte Cassino to evacuate the civilians and that they would leave the sick people in the infirmary in view of their grave condition. I said we did not want to compromise ourselves with the German Command if they were one day discovered. The gendarmes said we need not worry. I told the unfortunate people that they could stay, but at their own responsibility concerning the imminent danger of battle. They are very happy: the parents said they were ready to stay, since they were sure their children would be killed on the road if they left; they put themselves under the protection of Saint Benedict. . . .

During the entire evacuation we tried to persuade the people to leave, saying that here they would be in the battle zone; but some of them spoke against us, believing it was we who were sending them away. Some preferred to take refuge in the brush, but we did not allow anyone to stay in the monastery except those who were authorized.

Towards evening they came to take our animals: they took 14 cows, 35 sheep, and about 10 lambs: they had already taken our donkeys without a word about compensation. In all, they gave us 30,000 lire, not even the price of a pair of cows.

The situation of those who remain is that we have no contact with the outside world and no one is allowed in.

After all our situation is very precarious and we do not know, from one moment to the next, what will happen to us monks. One cannot reason with these people.

It seems the front is now close. . . . The Germans' urgency about the evacuation shows that they have given, or are giving, ground. The gendarmes have taken down the signs on the main road marking the neutral zone. In fact, the zone never existed, despite the official communications made to us. The marshal told me that, according to my request, he had given orders to allow no one in the monastery and that the area within the orchard fence, including the adjacent buildings, was a protected zone forbidden to the military.

It seems that the family of dom Falconio was able to reach Rome and to tell them [the monks there] about our new and grave situation. It is the only human ray of hope left to us.

JANUARY 8

Dom Eusebio finished preparing the cemetery at Sant' Agata with names, crosses, etc. The body from yesterday was buried, and a little one who was brought this morning.

JANUARY 9

This morning Germans from the "SS" Division came with a truck and took 88 sheep against a payment of 10,500 lire; now our flocks are almost all gone. But we brought inside the monastery some 30 sheep for breeding; the best milk cows, goats, pigs, chickens, donkeys: a real Noah's Ark.

We have begun to see the Germans invading the ground around the monastery. The 300-meter limit had become a nuisance to them. The ban on visits continues.

We are all depressed by not knowing what the next day will bring.

JANUARY 10

Today one of our patients died: Lucia Verecchia, 13 years old, daughter of Orazio, our cook. The father's Christian behavior is admirable. The body was viewed wrapped in a sheet in the Chapel of the Crucifixion, in the *torretta*. Dom Eusebio made her coffin: he has become our official grave-digger.

The Germans now surround us. They have even made lodgings in the cave under the main wing of the monastery. . . . We are still in anguish about our future, and still there is no ray of hope. . . . It seems that there are German batteries behind us, in the plain, so that now the screams of the two belligerents' artillery shells meet above the monastery: not so bad as long as it is only the sound.

JANUARY 11

This evening, at nine o'clock, the first Anglo-American shell hit the monastery. The situation has really changed, and it is the fault of the Germans, who would not give up a half-kilometer square of land and their more or less touristic coming and going at Monte Cassino. Before this shell, two others landed at San Guiseppe about 8:45. At the sight of those two, we left the infirmary—our usual evening observation post—and went to the refuge, and no sooner had we entered than we heard a formidable explosion. According to dom Oderosio, who was still outside, the explosion was in the entrance cloister and it hit right in the middle. Two more very loud ones followed, we did not know where, but surely quite near. Tomorrow we will inspect the damage.

JANUARY 12

The cloister was partly smashed. This is how men sculpt in stone their modern civilization! Almost all the windows of the cloister were riddled. We saw with horror the remains of the portico where we had passed only a few moments before the explosion. A special protection by Saint Benedict.

Two German officers came in the afternoon who are living in the cave under the windows of our cells [the cave was about 50 yards down from the corner of the seminary, on the east side of the monastery]. Dom Eusebio had a friendly conversation with them and showed them around the cloister and the church.

28

Hermann Goering's birthday was a major occasion on the Nazi calendar. Goering celebrated his birthday at Karinhall, his country estate 45 miles southeast of Berlin. The sprawling building at Karinhall, one of eight Goering residences, was filled with the art he had grabbed all over Nazi-occupied Europe. The shelves of the library were lined with rare volumes stolen from Jewish owners now mostly dead; one salon was hung in Gothic tapestries; French, Greek, and Italian statuary stood or reclined on the lawns; above the canopy of Goering's bed was a life-sized nude painting of Europa.

On January 12, 1944, his fifty-first birthday, Goering added to his already enormous quantity of loot. On that date he collected the annual tribute due the second-ranking figure in the Nazi Empire. In German government ministries huge sums were withheld from employees' salaries to buy Goering gifts he himself would select. Major figures invited to the birthday party at Karinhall were told by Goering what gifts he expected them to bring him.

Albert Speer, Germany's war production chief, recalled Goering's 1944 birthday party as a "ghostly celebration taking place against a background of collapse and ruin." The table in the luxurious dining room was magnificently set, and the flunkies were outfitted in white livery; but the meal itself was austere compared to the birthday fare in years that were fatter for the Nazis. The toastmaster lavished praises on the man he called "one of the greatest Germans," but Speer thought his words "contrasted grotesquely with the actual situation." That situation, in Speer's view, was that Germany was losing the war, and that Goering himself had largely withdrawn from participation in the effort that absorbed the rest of the Nazi leadership.

But, if the food was austere, the birthday gifts were still lavish. Goering's tribute was spread out on a gift table in the library, under the shelves of stolen books. Here were cigars from Holland, gold bars from the Balkans, paintings and sculptures, and, from Albert Speer, a more than life-sized marble bust of Hitler—that was what Goering had asked him for. On the table, also, was a gift from Goering's architect, a set of building plans to double the size of Karinhall. After the war Goering planned to run cut-rate tourist trains to Karinhall so the residents of Berlin could see his collections.

There was no gift on the table from the Hermann Goering Division, then fighting in Italy. It was not for want of trying. In fact, at the time of the birthday party, the division's intended gifts for its patron were on display in another of Karinhall's many rooms. What had happened, as best the story could be pieced together years later, was this:

In late December 1943, Goering's art director, Walter Andreas Hofer, was summoned to the headquarters of the Hermann Goering Division, at Reinickendorf, near Berlin. There, according to Hofer, officers of the division told him they had brought from Italy some paintings and other art objects which they wanted to give to Goering as a surprise birthday present.

Hofer took the cases from Italy back to Karinhall and set to work getting their contents ready for his chief's approaching birthday. It soon became obvious that the Hermann Goering Division had sent gifts of extraordinary value. Among the many paintings were world-famous masterpieces by Brueghel and Titian, and Raphael's *Madonna of the Divine Love;* the archeological objects from Herculaneum and Pompeii were of equal distinction. The officers of the Hermann Goering Division had every reason to think that their patron, who in earlier years had demanded gifts of Italian art, would be delighted with the treasures they had sent him. But—for reasons never explained— Goering told his art director that he would not allow such things to be presented to him as gifts. Instead, he ordered that the Italian master-pieces be set aside as a temporary exhibit at Karinhall. That is where they were at the time of Goering's birthday party on January 12. Some time later, though, Goering showed the Naples art to Albert Speer along with another treasure, his hoard of French soap and perfume.

That something was missing from the Naples treasures had become evident in Rome a week earlier, on January 4, when the Hermann Goering Division had finally given up possession of the materials it had evacuated from Monte Cassino two months earlier. On that day the division's trucks brought 600 cases from its supply depot at Spoleto and turned them over to the Italian authorities in a second filmed and publicized celebration of the German military's regard for the arts. Included in the cargo were 172 cases from the Naples collections. The Italian fine arts officials receiving the treasures checked against their records and found that the Naples collection had gone to Monte Cassino in 187 cases—15 more than they were now receiving. When they asked the Germans about the discrepancy, they were told that two trucks had been delayed by "machine gun fire." The Italians waited all night, but no more trucks arrived.

One German would later claim he had been absent from the January 4 presentation—Lieutenant-Colonel Julius Schlegel. Schlegel, who had managed the evacuation of the treasures from Monte Cassino, had presided with great gusto at the first ceremonial presentation a month earlier at the Castel Sant' Angelo. Schlegel later wrote that when he was asked to arrange the second presentation, he "begged to be excused in view of the fact that I had been informed that a few of the cases were no longer intact." Yet German photographs plainly show Schlegel at the occasion.

Dr. Maximilian Becker, the young captain whose initiative had launched the evacuation of treasures at Monte Cassino, was also absent at the January 4 ceremony. Becker had missed the December 8 ceremony because no one had told him about it. By January 4, Becker had been transferred out of Italy, because, he was told, he had meddled in the affairs of the Hermann Goering Division. At the time of the presentation Becker was on leave with his family in Tecklenburg. He was not sent, as threatened, to the Eastern front.

29

FROM THE MONKS' DIARY:

JANUARY 13

Pietro did not get up this morning: he has a severe pain in his throat. So now of the seventeen people left with us, only four are able-bodied, plus three children who are not sick. The ordeal is great, but God can always help us.

The poor sheep, left without a shepherd, got through the door today and wandered through the cloisters, famished.

JANUARY 14

Rifle and machine gun fire towards Pastenelle. It seems that Cervaro has fallen.

This afternoon an officer came who had been here on the 12th and he kept his promise to bring some oranges for our sick people; he brought half a sack; we thanked him. He was a good young man of 23. . . . The officer told us that within days the front would be in Cassino and then Monte Cassino would be an inferno, just as had happened to other mountains all around us. So we should take measures while there was still time, whether it was for the sick or for our food supplies. In answer to dom Eusebio's question, he said that the closest caves were used only for quarters; the combat positions were farther away.

JANUARY 15

About 12:30 in the night we were awakened by a tremendous explosion nearby. The Allies are in the environs of Monte Cassino. . . . It is frightening to cross the cloisters while the shells are whistling over the monastery. . . . The German artillery is behind Monte Cassino now and its racket prevents us from sleeping.

At 7:30 in the morning, while we were having breakfast, some Allied shells hit between the funicular and the trestle. Dom Eusebio, who had finished and was about to leave, waited behind the door for the reverberations to end, and it was good for him that he did so because at that moment a very loud explosion and a puff of smoke notified us that a shell had exploded in the Prior's Cloister. Dom Eusebio's fear was great, and so was that of all of us in the monastery. The damages were serious.

JANUARY 17

One of the Viola family, which lives at La Valletta, where there are also some Germans, came today. He said they had met a good captain and a good sergeant who call the old ones papa and mama. The sergeant supposedly said that soon there would be contact with the Anglo-Americans and that everyone should get out of the way. The captain has an observation post in a shack from which the firing is directed. The soldiers living at the *fortino* [within the 300-meter zone] supposedly said they were going to have to leave because the place was a "neutral zone." And a donkey was seen entering the cave below our cells unloaded and coming out with a load. Does this mean we obtained some results in Rome? This evening we saw a gleam of light—but it is a doubtful thing. We are waiting with anxiety for surer evidence.

30

Leccisotti's letter was gloomy enough. He had heard in Rome that the abbot would be invited to leave Monte Cassino, but Leccisotti advised him to refuse. Despite the danger, he wrote, someone had to stay in the monastery. Unfortunately, the abbot and the other monks at Monte Cassino were now really and truly caught in the battle.

The monk reported no efforts in Rome on behalf of Monte Cassino, no signs of hope in any direction. The principal help that can come to the monks at Monte Cassino, he wrote them, was from God.

Less and less news reached Monte Cassino now from the outside world, deepening its isolation. And less and less news reached Rome from or about Monte Cassino. Aside from whatever the Germans might communicate, the only news from Monte Cassino was carried by the occasional Italian traveler who brought letters, or rumors that might or might not be reliable—like the false report that the abbey had been hit by shellfire in November.

Though they could not contact the abbot directly, officials in the Vatican had heard some reports about what the Germans were doing there at the abbey. On January 8, the Vatican secretary of state informed the German embassy that the protected status of Monte Cassino was endangered because the Germans were conducting military operations "in the immediate vicinity of the monastery"—a reference to the Germans' repeated violations of the 300-meter zone —"and, still more serious, because munitions were stored in the monastery itself." This apparently was a garbled version of the information, which had reached Leccisotti a week earlier in a letter from Monte Cassino, that the Germans had stored munitions in the two caves immediately below (but not in) the monastery.

In its reply of January 12, the German embassy ignored the first —accurate—claim by the Vatican, and instead gratefully concentrated its indignation on the second: "The Embassy of the Reich has expressly explained on several occasions, first of all with the Note of November 7, that the Abbey of Monte Cassino was not occupied by German troops, nor would it be used for military purposes. Despite this, the Secretary of State thinks it could be used by the Germans as a munitions depot." Given that his government's reputation for veracity was even lower, and with ample reason, than that of other governments, the ambassador's conclusion had a distinctly comic ring: "The German Embassy has taken note with surprise of the fact that doubt has been cast on its formal assurances."

The Vatican made no further appeals to the Allies that month about Monte Cassino. The Pope's priorities were the same in January as they had been in October: to avoid giving the Germans a pretext to occupy the Vatican, to do what could be done to persuade the Allies to spare the city of Rome, and to maneuver a favorable position for the church in postwar Italy and Europe. Nor was Monte Cassino the only monastery seeking his help. The monks at the two small Benedictine monasteries at Subiaco, where the saint preached before he came to Monte Cassino, had asked the Vatican to intervene on their behalf with the belligerents. So had the Cistercian monks at Casamari, up the Liri Valley from Monte Cassino. Under these circumstances, it was unlikely that the Vatican would make a special effort on the behalf even of the mother abbey of the Benedictines.

31

FROM THE MONKS' DIARY:

JANUARY 18

At noon a shell hit in the Fossa [the ravine behind the abbey]. It killed a woman and wounded several others, among them a girl of 20 months. She was brought to Monte Cassino to be treated; the brain tissue was coming out the hole made by the fragment. The Anglo-Americans are firing on the Fossa because they see movement there.

During supper mail arrived from Rome with many letters from dom Tommaso [Leccisotti] etc. They are informed about our situation, but their hands are tied. Only God can save us. One day perhaps we will find out the reason for things that seem somewhat mysterious.

JANUARY 20

Aerial bombardment of the center of Cassino in the afternoon. In the evening the lieutenant from the cave came and gave us to understand that soon we would be under the Anglo-Americans.

Around seven o'clock hellish firing started on the plain, which looked as if it were erupting all over; an awful noise shook the whole monastery. I watched the battle for some time from the monks' corridor: the firing did not come as much as halfway up the mountain. This was the first great battle for Cassino and the line of defense. We watched as well as we could and then in great fear we went to the refuge; we knew the Allies were making a great effort to break through.

The Rapido has its source in the high Abruzzi. It earns its name plunging down steep mountain valleys, runs along the east side of the Monte Cassino ridge, then cuts across the Liri Valley plain. In the plain it joins the Liri, coming down from the direction of Rome, and the combined stream, known as the Garigliano, flows southwest to the Tyrrhenian Sea 15 miles away. Anyone going north to Rome, as the Allies were trying to do in January 1944, must cross that river system.

The American attempt to cross the river is known as the Battle of the Rapido. It was the most painful defeat that the Americans suffered in the war in Europe, and it is always associated with the name of Mark Clark.

The attack across the Rapido was conceived by Clark in conjunction with a landing that was to take place a few days later on the beaches near Rome, between two small towns named Anzio and Nettuno. At the very least, Clark reasoned, the attack on the Rapido would prevent the Germans from moving troops north from the Liri Valley to oppose the landing. Better, it might induce the Germans to move troops in the other direction, away from the landing area. Better yet, if the crossing was successful, it would break the Gustav Line and open the road north to the Allies' armored vehicles. Then the Fifth Army could drive north to join the beachhead—and Mark Clark could lead his soldiers marching into Rome.

The Rapido crossing was to be preceded by British attacks at two points on the Garigliano, downstream from the Americans. The first of these attacks, on the coast where the Garigliano reaches the sea, was a diversion intended to draw the Germans away from their defenses in the Liri Valley. The second British attack, at the southwest edge of the valley—on the left as the Allies looked up the valley toward Rome—was intended to capture the heights overlooking the Rapido and thus protect the Americans' flank when they made the main crossing.

The first British attack on the night of January 17 caught the Germans by surprise. The British quickly captured the town of

Minturno, near the mouth of the Garigliano, and they established a large, secure beachhead on the north side of the river.

Within hours of the British crossing, General von Senger drove in his battered Volkswagen jeep to the headquarters of the 94th Division, the force defending the German position. Standing on a hill behind the lines, Senger interrogated the officers on the scene in his cultivated but determined way until he knew what was going on. The German commander had to make a quick and difficult decision. The 94th Division obviously could not contain the British attack. It was a division of uncertain quality, newly assigned to Senger, which was why he had put it in what seemed to be a secondary area. Yet the British had to be stopped, for if they were allowed to move north they could go around the coastal mountains and take the Liri Valley from the rear. It seemed that the German ability to hold the Gustav Line —and thus to hold Rome itself—would depend on what Senger did in the next few hours.

Now Senger's months of careful preparation paid off. Ever since assuming command of this front in October he had been spending his days touring his sector studying his terrain and his troops. He had, he later recalled, climbed "every hill that offered a clear view," and he had spoken to his soldiers face to face, evaluating their strengths and their weaknesses. He had done what he could to maintain their morale, and he had placed them where they could perform within their abilities against the moves he expected from the Anglo-Americans. German intelligence these days provided him with virtually no useful information, so Senger was forced to rely on his own instinct and experience in calculating what his opponent would do. By January, Senger knew his men and his mountains better then anyone else on either side, and that knowledge informed his actions at the moment of decision.

Senger needed more troops to stop the British. The nearest units were those holding the Gustav Line in the Liri Valley, 15 miles away. But Senger was certain that the Anglo-Americans had yet to make their main move and, if so, moving his troops down the river was exactly what Mark Clark hoped he would do. There was just one other possible source of help: the two divisions that Field Marshal Kesselring was holding in reserve near Rome against a possible enemy landing on the coast.

Heedless of military protocol, which required him to go through his immediate superior, Senger telephoned Kesselring at his head-quarters near Rome and asked him for the loan of the two divisions. If the two divisions moved south immediately, Senger told his chief, they could catch the British at a vulnerable moment, when their attack had spent itself, and drive them back down the coast. Senger said he thought he could return the two divisions to Kesselring within a few days. Kesselring promised him a prompt answer and hung up. As he waited for Kesselring's decision, Senger was far from optimistic. If he were in the chief's shoes, he reflected, he would probably decide it was more important to hold back the two divisions for the enemy landing.

But Senger was in luck. Kesselring, ever mindful of Hitler's dislike of giving up any territory, was determined to hold the Gustav Line, and that meant the British must be stopped on the coast. There was something else Senger did not know. A few days earlier the chief of German military intelligence, Admiral Wilhelm Canaris—a shadowy figure who a year later would be executed for plotting against Hitler—had visited Kesselring in Rome. In answer to Kesselring's question about the enemy's intentions, Canaris had said: "There is not the slightest sign that a new landing will be undertaken in the near future." Thus encouraged, Kesselring, who in any event had the instincts of the true gambler, decided he would take the risk. He called Senger back and told him he could have the two divisions. Within three days the British had been stopped on the coast without weakening Senger's forces in the Liri Valley.

Senger therefore was ready when the British launched their second attack farther up the river, at the village of San Ambrogio. They crossed the river at night, in fog, against a current strong enough to snap the moorings on their boats. Only a single company of men got across, and then the British commander called off the attack. Thus, when the Americans in turn made their crossing, the Germans would hold the high ground on both sides of them: on their left, the heights the British had failed to take, and on their right the massive ridge of Monte Cassino. Waiting for the Americans on the far side of the river were Senger's best troops: he had put them there in anticipation of the main attack.

At first glance, the river winding across the level farmland of the Liri plain did not seem like an imposing obstacle. But the appearance was deceiving, especially under the circumstances the Americans faced that January. The river's banks were 5- to 10-foot steep slopes slippery with mud. The Rapido was too deep to wade, and its 50-foot width was difficult to negotiate against a freezing current moving at a relatively fast 8 miles an hour. The ground on the American side, though level, was a swamp. January was flood season anyway, and the Germans had improved on nature by diverting part of the river current into the plain. Tanks and trucks bogged down hopelessly in the swampy ground. The attack would have to be made by soldiers carrying all their equipment through mud and German minefields. All their preparations would have to be made at night. There was no place to hide in daylight. The Germans had cut down the trees and brush on the American side to give themselves a clear field of fire. Their artillery, guided by observation posts on the heights on either side, made it suicidal to approach the river except in pitch darkness.

Once the Americans got across the Rapido—if they got across—they would find the Germans well prepared. The infantry was well dug in trenches and bunkers near the river, and behind them was a line of five machine gun posts spread over half a mile. The ruins of the village of Sant' Angelo were heavily fortified. The Germans had placed four self-propelled guns on a 40-foot bluff that overlooked the river where the Americans were to cross. Heavier artillery was behind the bluff. The riverbank was mined and strung with barbed wire.

The task of crossing the Rapido was assigned by Clark to the 36th Division, a Texas National Guard division whose members wore a sky-blue patch with the letter *T*. Two infantry regiments, the 141st and the 143rd, would make crossings immediately upstream and downstream from the village of Sant' Angelo. The attack was scheduled for January 20. The night before the crossing the combat engineers would bring up, as close as possible to the river, the supplies needed: the boats and the materials from which bridges would be constructed. The infantry would have to carry the supplies the rest of the way, about a thousand yards, along with their own equipment. The engineers would sweep corridors through the minefields and mark them for the infantry. The first wave of infantrymen would cross in boats, either inflatable rubber or wooden. Once they had secured the opposite bank, the engineers would lay a footbridge, a kind of catwalk supported by inflated pontoons. When the troops crossing on this bridge had pushed the Germans well away from the bank, the engineers would put across a Bailey bridge: a bridge made of parts looking like an erector set, capable of carrying vehicles. Then the American tanks could cross the river, smash the Gustav Line— and on to Rome.

Such was the theory. The mood among the Americans at the scene was one of foreboding. The commander of the 36th Division, Major-General Fred L. Walker, remembered the day on the Marne a quarter-century earlier when the battalion he commanded had destroyed the Germans trying to cross the river. Now it seemed to Walker that the positions were reversed and his men were about to be butchered by the Germans. The British failure to take the heights to his left deepened Walker's gloom. But Clark insisted that the Rapido attack go ahead as scheduled, even though the German position on the heights was bound to reduce whatever chance it had to succeed. On the eve of the attack Walker wrote in his diary:

> Tonight the 36th Division will attempt to cross the Rapido River opposite Sant' Angelo. . . . We might succeed but I do not see how we can. The mission assigned is poorly timed. The crossing is dominated by heights on both sides of the valley where German artillery observers are ready to bring down heavy artillery concentrations on our men. The river is the principal obstacle of the German main line of resistance. I do not know of a case in military history where an attempt to cross a river that is incorporated in the main line of resistance has succeeded. So I am prepared for defeat. . . . Clark sent me his best wishes, said he was worried about our success. I think he is worried about the fact that he made an unwise decision when he gave us the job of crossing the river under such unfavorable tactical conditions. However, if we get some breaks we may succeed.

In practice everything went wrong at the Rapido. When darkness fell at 6:00 P.M. on the 20th, the men of the 141st Infantry regiment left the improvised shelters in which they had spent the daylight hours and started toward the dump where their boats were stored. They were carrying rifles with fixed bayonets. Soon they were groping around in fog through muddy fields. When they reached the boats, they found that half of them had been damaged or destroyed by German shellfire. They picked up the remaining boats and moved on, heavily burdened, toward the river. German shells began to fall among them, and they scattered. As they did so, they left the safety of the marked corridors and stumbled into minefields where many men were killed or injured.

The first soldiers of the 141st reached the river bank at 9:00 P.M., two hours behind schedule, and tried to launch their boats and paddle across. But some of the boats sank immediately because German shells had put holes in them; others capsized; still others got away from the men and rapidly drifted off downstream. Only about one hundred men managed to get to the other bank. The engineers were supposed to lay four footbridges for the infantry. But half their equipment was destroyed or dispersed, and by 4:00 A.M. the engineers had managed to lay only one footbridge, and that one was slippery and unsteady. By 6:30, with dawn at hand, only about four hundred men had crossed the Rapido. Quite a few others had simply vanished during the night and would later turn up at the rear saying they had gotten lost. The attack was halted at dawn. Soon after daybreak German fire cut the phone wires laid across the river; all the radios on the other side were already lost or out of commission. The handful of Americans on the far bank was completely isolated. Only the sound of their rifle fire gave proof that anyone was still alive over there.

The attack by the 143rd Infantry upstream went just as badly. By dawn, another small group of American soldiers was trapped on the far bank with no prospect of advancing and very little of getting back across alive. That morning, by telephone, Mark Clark ordered the 36th Division to attack the Rapido again—this time by daylight. This meant that men who were by now badly demoralized would have to attack under circumstances still more adverse than those under which they had just been defeated. "I expect this attack to be a fizzle just as was the one last night," Walker wrote in his diary—and he was right. A few more infantrymen got across the river, but the Bailey bridge for vehicles was never built, and without tanks the crossing was doomed. By the morning of the 22nd, two days after it had begun, it was all over. The few Americans on the other side either managed to swim back or were dead or prisoners. "Yesterday two regiments of this division were wrecked on the west bank of Rapido," Walker wrote. The American losses in dead, wounded, and missing totaled 1,681.

So ended the battle of the Rapido. It was fought in vain. The supposed purpose of the Rapido—to draw German troops away from the Rome area—had been accomplished four days earlier by the British crossing at the mouth of the Garigliano. The American attack scarcely disturbed the Germans. The troops holding the far bank repelled the attack without calling for help on nearby units, much less asking for help from Rome. In fact, while the Americans were attacking, the Germans sent troops to Anzio from the Liri Valley front. After the battle, the Germans sent back a captured bird with a mocking message: "Herewith a messenger pigeon is returned. We have enough to eat, and what is more we look forward with pleasure to your next attempt." On the Allied side, the fiasco at the Rapido produced enduring bitterness and recrimination. Clark blamed the British for not making a determined enough attempt to capture the heights on the left of the valley. Walker blamed Clark for wasting his men's lives in a hopeless undertaking. The survivors in the 36th Division blamed Clark for sending them across the river while the Germans were looking down at them from the heights of Monte Cassino.*

For Adolf Hitler, the Rapido was a victory at a time when victories were rare indeed. For General von Senger, the battle was little more than an opportunity to use his superb professional skills. He had done his duty at minimum cost in lives to the men under his command. A local victory did not change Senger's bleak view of the larger struggle: the war was still lost. Some day—next week, next month, whenever—Senger's troops would once more be in retreat. A few days after the Rapido, Senger moved his headquarters from Roccasecca to Castelmassimo, which was farther from the front. This was a move Senger felt he could not make during a losing battle for fear of its depressing effect on his men's morale. He might privately view the war as hopeless, but according to Senger's standards he would be failing in his duty to his men if he ever let them suspect by any act of his that their commander believed they were giving their lives in a lost cause.

---

*After the war, veterans of the 36th Division demanded and got a congressional investigation of Clark's conduct of the battle. Clark was exonerated, but the public reminder of the disaster at the Rapido did his reputation no good.

33

FROM THE MONKS' DIARY:

At five o'clock we heard knocking at our door. Much questioning. They told us the gatekeeper's little boy was dying. Dom Agostino went right away. When he came back he said the boy had died in half an hour.

The firing kept on but at a reduced pace. An evil surprise greeted us in the morning: during the night an Anglo-American shell had penetrated the Basilica; later with the light we will examine the damage, which is bound to be serious in a church like ours.

After the conventual mass we went into the church. It didn't seem the same. A cloud of dust covered everything; the confessionals were smashed and so were some marbles. The most important damage was done to the great painting by Luca Giordano; it was torn and disfigured, on its left side as you face it. The shell entered through the last window and hurled itself on the painting. The stained-glass window was also ruined, but that is not a great loss. The fragments damaged several paintings and marbles. We decided to leave everything as it was because we must pick up the pieces with a certain amount of planning in order to salvage the most we can. Almost all the windows are gone and with yesterday's bombardment a part of the stained glass in the Crypt fell. From now on entering the church is forbidden.

Dom Eusebio had to make a coffin for the boy who died this morning. We tried to persuade the abbot to be more cautious and to stay in the refuge for lunch and supper and part of the divine office.

JANUARY 22

This morning everyone said mass in the *torretta,* but I as usual went to celebrate it in the Crypt. We found several broken windows in the *torretta,* also in the Cell of Saint Benedict. Conventual mass in the Cell.

The Anglo-Americans are relatively silent compared to the Germans, who instead of explosions produce screeching sounds that are prolonged and made louder by echoes. It is exasperating music: who knows how long it will last!

JANUARY 23

This morning 144 Anglo-American planes passed overhead: some bombed the area between Pignataro and Roccasecca, the others went on.

This evening a German soldier who had come to look for his comrade who was staying at the monastery told us that there had been a naval and aerial landing near Rome. He advised us to remove the wheels of the abbot's car so the Anglo-Americans will not take it. In short they [Germans] have decided to flee from here.

JANUARY 24

Now we are set up in the refuge. . . . Hellish firing started at around 9:30 [P.M.] and continued intense until about 11:30. Several shells fell on the monastery. One on the *collegio* [at northwest corner], where it smashed the roof; two on the Novitiate, one at exactly 11:30 on the Bramante Cloister, where it blew into pieces a column standing near the observatory. Fragments flew all over the place, and one flew into the Physics study, where fra Giacomo was sleeping: it grazed his head, but did no harm, it only scared him. . . . The most courageous among us are the lay brothers who go all over the monastery; they do not think too much about the danger.

PART TWO
DECISION

The French were fighting up in the high mountains, about 10 miles inland from the Americans down in the Liri plain. In the long painful advance north from Naples, the two divisions that made up the French Expeditionary Corps had comprised the right flank of the Fifth Army. Now, in mid-January, the French were in the grim Abruzzi mountains around the narrow gorge of the upper Rapido, and they were up against the inland part of the German Gustav Line. Below them, toward the sea, was the lower Rapido Valley, which lay alongside the Monte Cassino ridge and joined with the Liri Valley in front of the jutting hill on which stood the abbey. Before the French, as they looked up the Italian peninsula, stood the peak of Monte Cifalco, a snow-covered, cliff-ringed mountain that faced out over the Liri plain.

The French commander, General Alphonse Juin, knew how he intended to go about conquering the Germans ahead of him. Juin was a distinctive figure as he rode around the Italian front on his little pony, a cigar between his teeth. He was a short, stocky man, with the rosy cheeks of a Breton peasant, whose headgear immediately announced his nationality: he wore either the kepi or a blue beret adorned with his general's stars. At 56, Juin was one of France's most illustrious soldiers. His right arm was paralyzed from a wound in the First World War; he had fought skillfully but in vain during the French debacle of 1940. Appointed by Marshal Pétain as Vichy's commander in North Africa, he had joined the Allies after their landing and had helped raise the troops that came to Italy in November and December of 1943.

From Juin's perspective, a direct attack on the powerful German positions in the Liri plain and on the Monte Cassino ridge would simply waste the lives of Allied soldiers to no result. In this terrain, where the Allies' great superiority in equipment could not be brought into play, war had to be fought by maneuver, not by frontal assault. Juin had said as much to his commander, the American Mark Clark, when they were riding in a jeep together outside Naples back in October. But Juin had sensed, accurately, that Clark was paying little attention. Who, after all, was likely to listen to the French after their performance in 1940? Juin recalled that no one had even come to meet him when he landed in Italy.

Juin wanted to bypass the Liri and the Monte Cassino ridge entirely. His plan was to swing far to the right, through the heart of the Abruzzi, behind Monte Cifalco. His objective was the town of Atina, about 7 miles up a gorge from the Rapido Valley. Atina was an important German communications and artillery center, and from it a valley led down into the Liri plain far behind the German positions at Cassino and on the Monte Cassino ridge. From Atina, the French could push down that valley and come out on the plain behind the Germans. This maneuver would unhinge the entire Gustav Line, and the German position at Cassino and on the Monte Cassino ridge would fall without a battle.

Juin's route would take the French soldiers through forbidding country. These were bleak mountains and ravines, without roads, where even the Italians seldom ventured during the bitter months of winter. But the very difficulty of the terrain was what made Juin want to go there. Kesselring, the German commander, was known to be a firm believer in taking advantage of the terrain, and Kesselring surely expected his primary antagonists, the Anglo-Americans, to go where they could use their vastly superior armor. So he would concentrate his limited resources in and around the Liri plain. Up here, in the high Abruzzi, was where Kesselring would skimp on both fortifications and men. Juin would be hitting the Germans at their weakest point.

In striking inland, moreover, Juin would be using his greatest asset —his men. Most of his officers were French, but most of the soldiers in those two divisions were North Africans, men from the three French possessions of Morocco, Algeria, and Tunisia. These men had grown up and trained in the harsh interior of the Atlas Mountains, where the land is as forbidding and the winter as bitter as it is in the Abruzzi. Mountain living and fighting were natural to them; country that others saw as a handicap the North Africans considered to be an ally. Another important fact was that where it was so difficult to supply men in the lines, the North Africans were able to get along with small supplies of food and water. In their brief time in Italy these men in the brown-and-white-striped *galabia* had earned a terrifying reputation; they fought at night with knives and they treated the Italian civilians as harshly as they did any Germans who fell into their hands. The French officers who led them were highly motivated men who were fighting to win back their homeland and erase the dishonor of 1940. Together, Juin was sure, his men and his officers could beat the Germans. Although Clark would not make the main effort in the high mountains, he agreed to a limited offensive, and on January 21 Juin launched the French attack.

General von Senger, looking at these same mountains from the other side of the lines, saw the situation much as did his French antagonist. In his three months in Italy, Senger's quick, adaptable mind had grasped the peculiar nature of warfare in these mountains. He had realized that war here was unlike any of his previous experience. Battles here could not be fought, like those of the First World War, by ill-trained men herded in great mobs into the trenches. Nor was this a war to be dominated, like the 1940 German campaign in France, by tanks and air power. In these mountains the quality and experience of the individual soldier was all-important. Men fought in small units, often less than a hundred, sometimes a handful, and they fought in isolation from their superior officers and from each other. Often it would take three hours to reach another unit only 500 yards away. The men who faced death in the mountains were cold and wet and lonely. The din of artillery, magnified and prolonged by echoes, was nerve-racking. Just climbing up and down these steep hillsides while heavily loaded was an ordeal for men, like most Germans, accustomed to level terrain.

Senger had few men under his command who were qualified for this sort of combat. He had recently received the 5th Mountain Division, but it had proved to be a disappointment. This division, of supposedly mountain-trained Austrians, had gotten itself transferred from the Russian front to Italy, apparently because its commander had connections to Hitler himself. Perhaps they had come with visions of "sunny Italy," Senger thought, but what they had experienced there—in combat against the North Africans—had been so horrifying that men of the 5th Division wrote in letters home that rather than stay in Italy they would crawl back to Russia on their hands and knees.

Senger had devoted much of his effort to compensating for his soldiers' lack of experience in mountain warfare. He trained them in digging into rocky positions with crowbars and explosives in place

ABOVE AND OPPOSITE, TOP: Colonial soldiers of the French Expeditionary Corps. OPPOSITE, BOTTOM: General Alphonse Juin (left), commander of the French forces in Italy, with American major-general John P. Lucas.

of the spades they had first been issued. He tried to teach the supply soldiers how to manage the mules—"not like horses"—that were the indispensable carriers of supplies to the front. Senger was distressed to find, on his frequent trips into the mountains, that the "hot food" that was supposed to be delivered once a day was rarely hot when it reached the cold, wet soldiers. So he moved the field kitchens closer to the lines and had the food containers insulated with straw. The evacuation of the wounded posed a particularly painful problem to an army that was running short of men. If a wounded man had to be carried out on a stretcher by four of his comrades, five men were lost to the battle, out of a unit that might number fifty or fewer. In brief training courses organized by Senger, the Germans learned that a single man could lower a wounded comrade with ropes and move him on an improvised sled. Still, German commanders when retreating at the front often had to choose between abandoning valuable, irreplaceable weapons—or wounded men. "The tragic part," Senger wrote in his diary, "was that in most cases the troops were not held responsible [by the German high command] for the loss of the wounded whereas they were held responsible for lost weapons."

The French attack menaced the whole Gustav Line, and it posed an immediate threat to the German observation post on Monte Cifalco, the 3,015-foot mountain that stood at the end of the Rapido Valley. From the valley floor, Cifalco looked like just one among many mountains, but from its upper slopes there was an extraordinary view. An observer up there could see the entire Rapido Valley, Cassino town and the Liri plain below it, the area behind Monte Trocchio, and the entire eastern flank of the Monte Cassino ridge. Every Allied position anywhere on the plain was visible from Cifalco; from here the Germans could call down accurate artillery fire on anything that moved below. This was the most important of the German observation posts in the area—far more important than the posts on the Monte Cassino ridge. Senger himself often climbed up to the observation post and, through its high-powered lens, watched the attacking Allies from the rear. Later he would call the artillery fire directed from Cifalco the single most important factor in the Germans' successful defense of their positions around Cassino.

In the first days of Juin's attack, the French gained a position on the foothills of Monte Cifalco. But then an order from Mark Clark removed the French threat both to Cifalco and to the German positions in the mountains behind it.

The Anzio landing had enormously increased the pressures on Mark Clark and on his superior, General Harold Alexander, the overall Allied commander in Italy. The landing itself had been a success. On January 22, the Allies landed two divisions, one American, one British, on the beaches 34 miles south of Rome. It came as a complete surprise to the Germans; the first German to learn of the landing was a corporal who happened to be in Anzio to supervise local suppliers of timber. Because Kesselring had sent his two reserve divisions south four days earlier to help Senger contain the British attack across the Garigliano, he now had no troops immediately available to counter the landing. But the Allied commander at Anzio, Major-General John P. Lucas, chose—in a much-disputed decision—to dig in rather than advance on Rome. Within a couple of days Kesselring had managed to scrape together enough troops to contain the Allies in the beachhead. The purpose of the Anzio landing had been to help the Allies in the Liri Valley, 70 miles away, by exploding the German positions from the rear. But now the soldiers on the beach at Anzio were in danger of being driven into the sea. Because of Anzio, it was now impossible to do what some advocated —wait till spring and better weather to attack the German Gustav Line. It was up to Mark Clark to do something to relieve the beachhead.

That something, in Clark's view, could only be another major attack on the German positions in the Liri plain. His army's disaster at the Rapido had convinced Clark that no advance up the Liri Valley was possible so long as the Germans held their commanding positions on the Monte Cassino ridge. At the same time, Clark rejected Juin's route through the mountains: that way was too slow, too roundabout. Clark needed quick results. The means he chose to get those results were to have fateful consequences.

The problem was the Monte Cassino ridge. Seen from the Allied lines, the ridge was a promontory stretching 5 miles from the snow-capped peak of Monte Cairo in the north to the hill on which the monastery stood jutting out into the plain at the southern end. The side of the promontory facing the Rapido Valley and the Allied

125

positions was steep and rough and the Germans were well-entrenched upon it. But, if the Allies could somehow fight their way to the top of the ridge, they could either descend on the other side into the plain behind Cassino, or they could move along south of the ridge to capture the monastery and the heights on which it stood. Whichever they did, the effect would be to make the German positions in Cassino town untenable. And then at last the Allies could bring their overpowering armor up Route 6 and into the broad, level valley ahead. Then it would be a simple matter to drive up and take the Germans around the Anzio beachhead from the rear—and roll right on into Rome itself.

Clark ordered a two-pronged attack by the French and by the American 34th Division. The French, he told Juin, would abandon their current objectives and instead attack at the north end of the Monte Cassino promontory, near Monte Cairo. The Americans, to the left of the French, would cross the Rapido Valley and attack up the slopes toward the southern end where the monastery stood.

Juin was distressed by his new orders. Not only would he have to give up his cherished route through the mountains, but what Clark wanted was precisely what Juin wanted to avoid: the kind of frontal assault on strong positions that would just waste his men's lives. But Juin had no choice, and on January 25 the French launched their attack in the direction ordered by Clark. Now Monte Cifalco, its observation post unconquered, would be at their rear. The new objective of the French was a series of peaks of which the most prominent were Monte Belvedere and Monte Abate. The peaks looked out over a road—the only one in the area—that climbed in ten frightening hairpins to the village of Terelle on the ridge.

The morning of January 25 was typically clammy and dismal. It was raining when two battalions of the 4th Tunisian Infantry set out. They had to ford the Secco River, which was up to their waists and bitter cold, and then start on a 2,500-foot climb: their leaders, hoping for surprise, once again had chosen to take the hardest but perhaps least-defended route. That morning one company crawled up a rocky, steep gully that became known, after their commander, as "le ravin Gandoet." Two French armored cars managed to get part of the way up the hairpin road. The French were beginning to pierce the German positions.

The struggle that took place in those mountains over the next ten

126

days was full of episodes of horror and heroism. The North Africans attacked German bunkers by a suicidal method. A few men would rush—as fast as they could in that country—to the sides of the bunker. Of those who got there, some would throw grenades in the front opening, others would do the same at the entrance in the rear of the bunker. The guns within would be silenced, the Germans who manned them either killed or forced to surrender. But many times none of the attackers made it through the German fire to the bunker. Often the men on both sides ran out of ammunition, and both French and German chroniclers report instances when their men were reduced to throwing rocks at the enemy. A particularly grotesque incident of those days would later become celebrated: a French second lieutenant named Bouakkaz had sworn he would be the first to set foot on a peak known as Point 862. He was killed in the assault, but three of his men fulfilled his vow by carrying his corpse up to the summit.

As always in the mountain winter, any successful attack made it still harder to supply the soldiers fighting in isolation in the frontlines. Those who led the packtrains were not always sure where their comrades were, and with each advance the route grew longer and usually more dangerous. The Tunisian infantry up on Monte Belvedere began to run short of water, food, and ammunition. One night a supply train of 80 mules set out for the Tunisians, but only 2 of the mules reached their destination; the rest were cut down by German machine-gun and mortar fire. The German soldiers were no better off than the French. Among the peaks where they were fighting was a bowl-shaped hollow in which there was a small spring. By the end of the battle that spring was ringed with the bodies of French and German soldiers who, desperate with thirst, had gambled their lives, and lost, for a drink of water.

After four days of intense combat—some key places changed hands half a dozen times—the French had driven into the German positions but they had not broken through them. They could go no farther; it was difficult even to hold the ground they had won. The Germans were entrenched all around them, and the observation post at Monte Cifalco was watching them from the rear. The French losses had been heavy: two-thirds of the Tunisians were dead or wounded. The survivors were exhausted. The French had no reserves from which to replace the fallen. On January 29, Juin wrote to Clark that the French had "accomplished the mission you entrusted to them"—the capture of the Belvedere and Abate peaks—but that he could ask no more of them than they had done. Though the French fought on in that area, they were no longer a threat to the Monte Cassino ridge.

35

By late January the monks were living in their refuge. The shells that were hitting the monastery with increasing frequency had convinced them—even the reluctant abbot—that it was too dangerous to remain in their cells, which were on the exposed side of the Monte Cassino complex, the side facing southeast toward the Liri Valley and the Allied guns.

The monks moved their few personal possessions across the cloisters and into the place they had earlier chosen and prepared. Their place of refuge was two narrow corridors on the lowest floor of the *collegio,* the wing where the abbey's school was located. This was on the side that faced northwest, back toward the ridge behind the abbey, and so was best protected from the Allies' artillery. The monks had divided the corridors, which had housed the school's small natural history museum, into half a dozen small rooms, among them a room for the abbot; another for the rest of the monks; a makeshift kitchen; and, of course, a chapel in which the monks could conduct those daily rituals, from matins to compline, that gave meaning to their lives.

The huge monastery was almost empty now. The buildings that once had housed hundreds of monks and students were occupied by just seventeen people huddled in what seemed to be the safest corner: the monks and those few civilians who the Germans had decided were too sick to move when they had forcibly expelled the refugees in early January. But outside a swelling crowd was pressing against the walls of the empty buildings. Most of them were from Cassino town or from hamlets or farms in the plain. Driven from their homes by combat or shellfire, they had come to Monte Cassino in search of sanctuary, but the Germans, with the tacit backing of the monks, refused to allow them to enter the monastery itself. So during the days the civilians foraged for food, and at night they clustered as close to the monastery as they could. Some three hundred jammed into San Giuseppe, a small building immediately adjacent to the abbey on the side away from the guns. Another hundred or so sought refuge in the *conigliera*, the rabbit warren. This was an arched passageway, about 60 feet long, that cut through the foundation of the monastery below the north corner, the corner that faced the ridge. The passageway had been built for some long-forgotten purpose and was only called the *conigliera* because a few years earlier the monks had kept rabbits in cages there. The *conigliera* was almost directly below the monks' refuge, but there was no entrance from it to the monastery. The passageway provided protection from the Allied artillery fire and from the winter rain and snow, and that was enough to bring a crowd of civilians there every night.

Within the abbey walls the monks went about their daily routines as best they could. Though they had no fuel for heating, they had water and ample food and wine for themselves—the supply had been laid in for the normal number of monks—though this was not enough, in their opinion, to share with the refugees. In a letter to the monks in Rome, the abbot observed that since their employees had been taken away by the Germans "we must take care of everything ourselves. Dom Eusebio makes the pasta, builds caskets, digs graves, cooks, etc., dom Nicola makes ricottas, cheeses and sausages, dom Martino sweeps, dom Agostino performs the services, buries the dead, attends to the church. The lay brothers take care of the few cows, pigs, sheep and chickens left to us." There was plenty of work for the monks who served the dying and the dead: all the Italian civilians around Monte Cassino were suffering from hunger and exposure, and some were killed or wounded by the guns of the combating armies.

In accordance with Benedictine custom, each monk who was a priest celebrated a private daily mass. Martino Matronola, the tall, close-cropped monk who was the abbot's secretary and German interpreter, always went to Saint Benedict's crypt for his mass. The low-vaulted crypt lay beneath the basilica, and so was protected by tons of stone. But even there, as he said his mass amid the mosaic representations of the saint's career, Matronola could hear the pounding of the guns. If the crypt was safe, the way to it was not. To get there Matronola had to cross two cloisters and climb the monumental stairs that led to the basilica. One morning, when the monk was about to leave the refuge, he saw a great flash of light and stopped: the shell struck immediately outside the entrance to the *collegio.*

It was Matronola's habit, after his solitary mass, to make a tour of inspection of the monastery. He walked through the archive, empty since the Germans had evacuated the Monte Cassino treasures, and then down the long, deserted corridors where the monks had lived. From the cell that had been his home, Matronola could look down at the plain below where the armies were clashing. Once he saw a bomb hit the site of the little church of Saint Scholastica, which marked the legendary place where Benedict and his sister had met for the last time. From what he observed, the monk could guess at the progress of the war: when he saw that the Allies were still shelling the area east of the Rapido, he concluded accurately that their attempt to cross the river had failed.

Sometimes German soldiers or Italian civilians would give the monks reports and rumors of the war, but nonetheless their isolation grew greater every day. The noose of war had been drawn more tightly around the little group of men inside the abbey. Fewer travelers were able to cross the lines these days, so there were fewer opportunities to send or get news from their fellow monks in Rome.

Old Abbot Diamare's mood was gloomy. In the early days, when Dr. Becker came to see him, when the Germans evacuated the treasures, there was reason to hope. But now all the abbot's efforts on behalf of his monastery had come to nothing . He had sent Leccisotti to Rome to ask the Pope to intercede with the Allies, though in all those months the abbot had never directed a personal appeal to those he knew in the Roman hierarchy, notably Monsignor Tardini, the undersecretary of state, who had worked with Diamare in the prewar Catholic Action movement. In his isolation Diamare had no way of knowing what the Vatican had or had not done for Monte Cassino, but he could read the Allies' reply in the shells that were falling on his monastery. The abbot had asked the Germans to respect the 300-meter limit they themselves had set, but instead they had abolished the limit and moved their men and guns in closer to the walls. Every day the monks could look out and see armed Germans within what had been the neutral zone. And, on January 27, the German gendarmes who guarded the gate told the monks they were being withdrawn and would not be replaced. It seemed the Germans were abandoning the monks to whatever fate awaited them. No one cared what happened to Monte Cassino.

One morning the abbot was in bed with a pain in his leg, and the other monks had gathered around him in his little room in the refuge. He told them about a dream he had had long ago, during a journey he took in his first years as abbot. In his sleep one night on that journey Diamare heard a voice sobbing and crying out: "Monte Cassino! Monte Cassino! Monte Cassino!" That sobbing voice was an omen, the abbot told his monks: it prophesied that their monastery would be destroyed for the fourth time.

Two days later, on January 27, Diamare wrote his last letter to the monks in Rome—the German gendarmes had offered to send it. This was the abbot's final effort. He did not again attempt to address any plea to the Germans or to the Vatican. Thereafter the old abbot seemed passively to be waiting for his dream of many years ago to become reality.

On February 4, a company of American infantrymen captured
the place known, from its elevation in meters, as Point 445. Point 445
was close to the top of the Monte Cassino ridge. About two hundred
yards above, up a bare slope, was San Onofrio, a hamlet of half a
dozen stone houses now in ruins. Up there were the Germans.

To the south of Point 445, about four hundred yards away across
a deep ravine, stood Monastery Hill. The ravine that separated the
Americans from the abbey was a tangle of steep slopes, rocks, and
thorny brush. In the middle of the ravine, bisecting it, was a knoll
on which were the remains of the small building known to the monks
as Il Fortino.

The Americans' capture of Point 445 was the furthest advance of
the 34th Division in its attack on the Monte Cassino promontory.
While the French were fighting to their north, the Americans aimed
their offensive close to the southern end of the promontory, where
the abbey was. They had succeeded with great difficulty in crossing
the swampy floor of the Rapido Valley, and now a week of bitter
combat on the steep rocky slopes of the promontory had brought that
one company to Point 445.

The next morning, February 5, two patrols of that company were
sent out with the unlikely objective of capturing the monastery itself.
The third platoon was to go around the east, or downhill, side of the
knoll topped by the ruins of Il Fortino. The second platoon was to
go around the uphill end of the knoll and work its way up the ravine
to the monastery. What happened that day to the second platoon was
later reconstructed by six of its members.

Fifteen men led by a sergeant set out just after dawn. Through the
early morning mist the soldiers saw a huge gray blur ahead of them:
the monastery. The snow that had fallen during the night had already melted, leaving the ground muddy. Once the patrol had gotten
around the knoll of Il Fortino, they spread out and moved cautiously
down a gully toward a small stream that ran between banks higher
than a man's head. The sergeant was the first to reach the bank. He
surprised three Germans getting water from the stream. The sergeant

covered the Germans with his rifle and they surrendered. The Americans decided the Germans were an outpost designed to give early warning of any attack such as theirs. The sergeant chose a squad leader and three men to take the prisoners back to the company command post on Point 445.

The rest of the platoon, a dozen men now, crossed the small stream and started up the slope on the other side. It was slow going. The hillside was extremely steep, almost a cliff, and it was covered with heavy brush that still had many of its leaves. Further up the slope the men came upon a black-topped road. This was the main road to the monastery, coming up the hill on the other side and looping around the monastery just before it reached its gate. The Americans were now looking up at the abbey's eastern face.

Across the black-topped road was a stone wall, and in it was a break that appeared to the Americans to have been made by shellfire. Through that break, in the steep hillside immediately below the foundations of the monastery, was what the Americans took to be the entrance of a dugout. It was, in fact, a natural cave that the Germans back in December had enlarged with explosives and outfitted for their quarters. It was one of two caves—the other housed ammunition—about which Abbot Diamare had repeatedly complained to the Germans, to no avail, because they were located far inside the 300-meter perimeter of the supposed neutral zone.

The soldiers ran across the open road one at a time. No one shot at them. The sergeant then signaled to his men to surround the entrance of the cave. A soldier found and cut a telephone line leading out of the cave. When a single German came out, the Americans captured him. The sergeant, in his fragmentary German, told the prisoner to call the others out. The German refused. The sergeant pulled the pin from a grenade and threatened to throw it inside the cave. The German then called to those inside. One by one seventeen Germans, one of them a captain, filed out and surrendered. Three Italian civilians came out with them; these were local men the Germans had conscripted for labor. When some of the Americans ventured inside to see if anyone else was there, they found a two-room cave. The first room was empty. In the second room, separated from the first by a door and a curtain, were bunks and tables, food, and the telephone.

The scene at the mouth of the cave had been witnessed by a monk looking down from a monastery window. According to the monks' diary, Fra Zaccaria told his fellow monks that in the early morning he had seen a patrol of what he perceived to be "about thirty Italian soldiers" take prisoner the same number of Germans. He saw two or three soldiers approach the mouth of the cave, weapons in hand, while others waited in the road. One of the soldiers said, in Italian: "*Su via, presto* [come on quickly]." The Germans came out with their hands on their heads. Fra Zaccaria saw the patrol with its prisoners go down the hill and disappear from his sight.

The members of the patrol calculated that, from what they could see, they were the only Americans on Monastery Hill. They heard gunfire further up the hill, but it was not aimed at them. Fearing that the prisoners, who now outnumbered them, might seize an opportunity to overpower his men, the sergeant decided to take his patrol and its prisoners back to Point 445. From the cave, the Americans could see a foot or mule path leading downhill a short distance to the east of where they had climbed the hill. The sergeant decided to follow that path back.

He divided the prisoners into four groups. He then put two of his men in front of the procession, two between each group of prisoners, one man out on each flank, and two more at the rear. Because of the prisoners, the Americans could not dash across the road, so everyone walked across together without incident. They went along the road to the beginning of the path. Once they started down the path, they found that it had been cleared of brush—undoubtedly by the Germans, to improve visibility—for ten or twenty feet on each side.

The rising sun by now had burned off all the early morning mist. When the Americans were halfway down the path, the Germans spotted them. Snipers on both sides of the path and above them on the hill opened fire. Everyone, prisoners as well as Americans, hit the ground. The sergeant then detailed some of his men to fire back at the snipers while the rest watched the prisoners. When they had beaten down the snipers, the group got up and moved down the path until the Germans started firing at them again.

The patrol with its prisoners went on down the path that way: hitting the dirt when shot at, returning fire till the Germans were silent, getting up and moving a short distance before the Germans started shooting and they had to hit the ground again. An American corporal was hit in the leg the second or third time the Germans opened fire. A couple of the Americans moved quickly behind the German sniper and captured him. The sergeant ordered three Germans and an Italian to carry the wounded corporal. The eleven uninjured men in the patrol now had nineteen prisoners plus the three Italian civilians.

While the group was working its way down the hill, the four men who had taken their first three prisoners back to Point 445 were coming back to join the patrol. On the way they surprised a German machine-gun crew putting its gun in position to catch the patrol when it left the brush and entered the bed of the stream. The Americans opened fire and put the machine-gun crew out of action. They then took up positions to fire at the snipers and thus help cover the patrol's return.

The American patrol was still far from even the dubious safety of Point 445 when providence intervened in the form of a smoke screen. Smoke was a weapon commonly used by the Americans to blind enemy gunners. This smoke screen had been laid down on Cassino town, in the plain, and now it was drifting up the ravine. The Americans could see well enough to keep control of their prisoners, but the smoke shielded them from the eyes of the Germans up on the hill. With this protection, the patrol was able to move quickly back across the ravine and deliver its prisoners to the command post on Point 445. Its only casualties were the corporal who was shot in the leg and another man who was nicked in the ear by a bullet.

Once back at their command post, the Americans learned that the other platoon, which had taken a different route toward the monastery, had been driven back by German fire almost immediately after it started out. The second platoon had not of course carried out its impossible mission of capturing the abbey. The Germans evidently did not realize they were trying—the diary of the 14th Panzer Korps reported "no major actions" for that day. The following day the monks noted that the Germans were once more in control of the Il Fortino knoll in the ravine below the monastery. Except for another patrol that briefly approached that same wall a few days later, the foray by the second platoon was the closest the Americans ever came to the monastery during the long battle on the Monte Cassino ridge.

37

The approaching tide of battle terrified the hundreds of Italian civilians who were clustering outside the walls of Monte Cassino. Now that the Allied soldiers were on the ridge itself, within a few hundred yards of the monastery, the civilians were caught in the cross fire between the two combatants. Wherever they went, whatever they did, they were likely to be shot at by one side or the other, if not both. There was no place to hide—no place but one.

On the morning of February 5, not long after the American patrol had captured the Germans in the cave, about ten women pounded on the gate of the monastery and demanded to be let in. The German gendarmes who had guarded the gate for three months were gone: now that the battle on the ridge was nearing its climax, the Germans had no men and no time to spare for Monte Cassino. The monks refused to let the women in. But the desperate women were not to be denied. They threatened to set fire to the gate. At that, the abbot ordered the gate opened to admit the women.

The trickle of women that the abbot thought he was letting in quickly became a flood as other civilians pressed in behind the women. Without the Germans, the monks were powerless to stop them. Soon about eight hundred frightened civilians—men, women, and children—had poured into the monastery. Now the buildings that had been deserted were suddenly crowded far beyond their capacity.

The flood of shabby, desperate people poured into the cloisters, up the monumental stairs, through the adjoining rooms. The monks, seeking to protect the privacy of their refuge, posted one of their employees and his family at the entrance with orders to keep everyone out. He succeeded. Though the civilians had forced their way into the abbey, they evidently were still in awe of the monks. Despite their overwhelming numbers, and although the monks had food while they were starving, the refugees made no effort to break into the refuge or to seize the monks' food supplies. Four women from Cassino town reported, in an account taken by American interrogators later that month:

We slept on the floor. Most people had brought some food of their own along; those who had none bought maize at 15 lire a kilo, wheat at 25 lire and meat, whenever a beast was killed by shellfire, at 50 lire a kilo. It was sold by a civilian who, it was said, obtained the food from the monks. There were large quantities of wine and other food in the Abbey, but they were never distributed. We got some only when some shells knocked down the walls of the storeroom.

All the civilians were fleeing the war, but the men, especially the young men, were also trying to escape the periodic German labor roundups. At San Giuseppe, the building next to the monastery that housed many refugees, a German soldier informed the men he was conscripting that the Americans would have sent them to work in Russia. On one occasion, the Germans even went into the *conigliera,* the passageway through the foundation of the monastery, to requisition labor. Once the monk Matronola, looking out a monastery window, saw forced laborers carrying ammunition from a cave just below the monastery to the German strongpoint at Monte Venere, the knob on the hill overlooking Cassino town, where there was a mortar as well as an observation post.

The civilians milled around in the cloisters despite the monks' warnings that this was the place of maximum danger from the artillery. That first afternoon, the monk Matronola saw a man killed while getting water at the cistern in the first cloister. Later that day another young man was killed by a shell in the same cloister, and two women died of exposure. Many of the refugees were sick with what appeared to be an infectious disease, and two of the monks were also down with fevers. So, when a German doctor came that evening— the only German to enter the monastery in those days—and asked the monks for a place to put wounded men, they offered him the women's guest quarters at Sant' Agata, a building near the abbey on the side away from the frontlines, and asked him to visit the sick monks in the morning.

Till that great influx of refugees the monks had been able at least to bury the civilians who died in and around Monte Cassino. Now that was beyond their capacity. A few days later, young Fulvio de Angelis, who with his family was living in the *conigliera,* entered the abbey and found it "a tragic spectacle." He saw corpses lying on the

137

ground. In his diary, he wrote: "Monte Cassino, by now half destroyed. The people are on the verge of madness. A sunless day. Leaden."

38

For a while, in the early days of February, it had seemed that the battle would pass by Monte Cassino. This was when the monks could look out back and see the Americans fighting along the ridge toward the monastery. On February 4, Matronola saw German and American patrols shooting at each other in and around the half dozen houses of San Onofrio, 300 meters from the abbey, and the following day the monks saw the American patrol that crossed the deep ravine, past the ruins of Il Fortino, and came right up to the abbey walls. "I believe before long Monte Cassino will be on the other side," Matronola wrote in the monks' diary.

Not that the monks of Monte Cassino were hoping for an Allied victory: there is no such suggestion in their accounts of the war. What they hoped for, indeed fervently prayed for, was that the front would move away—in any direction—in time to save what was left of their home. But it was not to be. The American assault had spent itself, and the next day, February 6, Matronola was surprised to observe that the Germans were back at Il Fortino. Monte Cassino was still in the frontline.

The great monastery was being battered by both belligerents. The Allied artillery was shelling the ridge on which the abbey stood from positions several miles away in the hills south of the Liri Valley. After the 300-meter zone was abolished in early January, the Germans moved in close to the building itself. On two sides of the monastery, just below the foundations, were caves that the Germans used as bunkers or as storage places for ammunition. In the side away from the ridge, starting on February 4, Matronola noticed two "armored cars"—tanks or self-propelled artillery—which at night fired across the abbey at the Allies. On the side facing the ravine, where the Americans had come so close on February 5, and immediately below the abbey, there were a machine-gun and an observation post which, Matronola later said, signaled the location of Allied positions to the German gunners. Since the German positions that the Allied gunners were shooting at now were around, below, and behind the monastery, it was inevitable that some of their shells would hit the building itself.

In early February, with the American advance along the ridge, the monastery also came within the sights of the German artillery. When the German gunners, located in the valley below, fired at the Americans on the ridge, the monastery was in their line of fire. From the first days of February on, Monte Cassino was hit daily by shells from both sides. On February 10, Matronola, who was still striding around the monastery on his daily inspection tour, estimated that Monte Cassino had been hit by "several hundred" shells. The next day he wrote: "We are impotently watching the gradual destruction of the monastery, with our hearts full of bitterness." The monks often could tell from the trajectory of a shell which side had fired it. The shell that plunged through a window of the basilica and ruined the painting by Luca Giordano had come from the Allies. The Germans fired the shell that wrecked the famous bronze doors.

The monks, now spending most of their time in their refuge deep in the subterranean part of the *collegio* wing, were doubly prisoners. The shells raining down on the monastery made it ever more dangerous to venture out in the open space of the cloisters, and there was continuing tension between the dozen monks and the hundreds of hungry refugees who effectively controlled most of the monastery. Occasionally the monks had to go out to fetch water, but only the tall, strong-willed Matronola still crossed the dangerous cloisters daily to say mass in the crypt. February 10 was the feast day of Saint Scholastica, and Matronola noted sadly that his was the only mass said that day at the tomb of Benedict's sister. In the darkness on the stairs leading down to the crypt Matronola saw a couple stretched out: the man was dead and the young woman was dying; the monk stopped to pronounce absolution. In the shelter it was dark and cold both day and night; the racket of the artillery went on without end. The monks were idle, two were sick, all melancholy, and most apathetic. As if to preserve their sanity, they clung to the one constant of their lives: the Rule of Benedict. With its series of fixed daily rituals, in a world gone mad it remained as unchanging as the North Star.

By now the isolation of the monks was total. No messages came from Rome anymore, or from anywhere else, and no one offered to carry messages out. Other than the refugees who went out to forage for food, no one left or entered Monte Cassino except the one German military doctor. He came at Matronola's request and treated the two sick monks, both suffering from high fevers, and he removed a shell splinter from the leg of one of the employees' wives. He also treated some of the many sick and dying refugees.

Through the German doctor Matronola made one last attempt to reach the belligerents and save the monastery from the pounding that was destroying it. Matronola, who, with the old abbot sunk in depression, was the effective leader of the monks, asked the doctor if it would be possible to put out a sign or in some other way tell the belligerents that their shooting was misdirected. The doctor replied that the Anglo-Americans—he said nothing about the German artillery—must be able to see from their observation posts that they were hitting the monastery and that no return fire was coming from there.

39

Harold Bond hurried into the old stone building known as Iannucelli's house. He was out of breath after his frightened dash across the 300 hundred yards of open space in full sight of the monastery from which, he assumed, the Germans were watching. The house, he was relieved to see, was in a gully and shielded from the view of the Germans up the hill. The house was a bit warmer than the bitter cold outside. It was full of American soldiers, about forty of them, milling around and talking. The ancient odors of a peasant household mingled with the smell of wet wool given off by the Americans.

Bond was looking for Lieutenant "Stuart." (In his account of his wartime experience, *Return to Cassino,* Bond uses fictitious names except for the generals.) He found Stuart in a corner with another officer. Bond reported that the men of his mortar platoon were digging in—or trying to—at a small rocky field about a thousand yards down the mountain. Stuart told him an attack was planned for that night. On a map Stuart showed Bond a hill, to the right of the monastery. He said, "You haven't got much time"—it was late in the afternoon—"but zero in your mortars before dark so that you can fire on this hill when we need it." He told Bond to string a phone line from the command post in Iannucelli's house back to his platoon.

Harold Bond was a second lieutenant, twenty-three years old, and newly in command of a mortar platoon. His platoon belonged to the 141st Infantry Regiment of the 36th Division, one of the two regiments that had been so badly battered at the Rapido. The platoon had only eighteen men, two-thirds its normal strength. Bond had been sent up to the front after the Rapido. He and his men were just getting to know each other when they were ordered up to join the Americans fighting on the mountainside. They had made the arduous climb earlier that day. Bond remembered the six dead Germans he saw by the trail. The sodden, gray-faced corpses were barefoot but otherwise fully dressed; a veteran told Bond an Italian peasant had probably stolen the shoes from the corpses. It was Bond's first experience of combat.

The way back down was slow going because this time Bond had to string his phone line. He could not run across the open space. Again he passed the two pairs of dead Americans that had startled him just before he reached the farmhouse. At the rocky field he found the members of his platoon building sangars, small stone enclosures, to give them some protection against both the Germans and the elements.

141

The mortars that Bond's men were now setting up were a crucial weapon for the Americans fighting in the mountains. Because the mortar travels in a high, short trajectory, the Americans could lob shells on the German positions concealed on the far side of the ridges above them, positions that the big guns with their flatter trajectories, in the plain below, could not hit.

The mortar is normally fired from a protected position according to instructions telephoned by an observer placed where he can see the target. Bond took two men and went back up the hill in search of an observation post from which he could direct the mortars' fire. Behind them the three men strung the phone wire. They followed the trail for about five hundred yards, then they branched off to the left, in the direction of the southern end of the Monte Cassino promontory. They came out on a ridge. The three Americans could see the great bulk of the monastery across a deep ravine about four hundred yards away. They were at Point 445, the place from which a few days earlier the American patrol had ventured to the abbey wall and captured the Germans in their cave.

To the right Bond could see their target. Monte Calvario, Point 593, is the summit of a spine that runs along the top of the Monte Cassino promontory; because of its twisting shape, the spine was known to the Americans as Snakeshead Ridge. Bond decided to direct the fire from where they were. He telephoned the mortar crew to get ready. Then a flock of German shells came screaming down near them. The Americans hit the ground, and when they got up they found that the phone was dead, the line severed by a shell. Bond and another man went down in search of the break. They managed to splice it, but because their fingers were numb with cold it was slow, tedious work. It was almost dark by the time they got back to their observation post.

Bond ordered the mortar crew by phone to fire. The mortars, he knew, were aimed in the general direction of the monastery. He heard the characteristic hollow pop of the mortar. He saw the shell explode—on the roof of the monastery itself. He could have immediately shifted fire to the target he was supposed to hit. Instead Bond ordered three more shots aimed so that they would explode immediately in front of the abbey wall.

Bond thought he was the first American to hit the monastery, though he also knew a small mortar shell could do no serious damage to those massive stone buildings. In later years Bond would be less than proud of what he had done, but at the time his feelings were different. He had been seeing the abbey from the plain below ever since he had arrived in the area; once, by moonlight, it floated "mysterious and beautiful," up in the night sky. He had seen its hundreds of windows looking down like so many eyes watching every movement below. He had heard the veterans, the survivors of the Rapido, talk about the abbey. Almost all of them were convinced the Germans were watching them from the great building that stood up there seemingly untouched amid the devastated country all around. Certainly the Germans were watching from *somewhere*— that much the Americans knew from the deadly accuracy of the German artillery. Because the abbey so dominated the landscape, so filled the soldiers' vision, it was logical to believe the enemy had his eyes there. The soldiers hated the abbey. The abbey was killing them.

After the three shots fired in front of the abbey wall—Bond's idea was simply to scare the Germans away from the windows—the phone line was cut once more by a German shell. With darkness now falling, it was too late to fix the line, so Bond took his two men back down to rejoin the rest of the platoon. When he told the men their mortars had hit the abbey they were delighted. They told him that Lieutenant Stuart had phoned down from Iannucelli's house—before that line also went dead—to say that the night's attack had been called off.

The next morning Bond went up to the command post at Iannucelli's house. He saw that the two pairs of dead Americans were still lying by the trail. Stuart asked him, "Was that you yesterday firing at the abbey with your mortars?" Bond said the abbey had been the best target to zero in on. Stuart laughed and said: "Division called up last night to find out who was firing at the abbey. Someone at army headquarters was hot about it. The army commander says that you can fight around the abbey but you can't hit it." Bond sensed from the other man's sarcastic tone that he did not need to justify what he had done.

Twice in the next few days Bond was questioned by other officers about the abbey: had he seen any evidence of Germans there? Both officers said they had been directed to ask. As Bond recalled it, the question was neutrally phrased: it did not seem to push him toward either a yes or no answer. "I replied," Bond later recalled, "that I had not actually seen anyone in the abbey but was pretty sure the Germans were using the grounds for observation."

Soon Bond and his platoon were in almost as bad shape as the other Americans they had found on the mountainside. The first night they hardly slept: it rained and then turned cold, and in their stone shelters the men could not escape the elements. They tried to fasten down the canvas over their trench with stones, but the freezing water kept seeping in anyway, and soon they and their clothes and blankets were all soaked through. They were terrified as well as cold. That night the Germans shelled the American positions for a full two hours, and, because they had dug in by the junction of two trails, Bond's platoon was in a target area. The ground under the Americans shook with gigantic explosions, and when a shell exploded close by, it flung a shower of earth over them. They did not dare leave their shelter to relieve themselves. Bond found in the morning that his feet were numb; neither walking around nor rubbing them seemed to help. It was the beginning of trenchfoot. Fortunately he had packed an extra pair of wool socks, and these saved his feet.

The Americans all around were in desperate condition, and some of them, Bond saw, had been driven past the limit of endurance. He sent his orderly out to deliver a message, and the young man simply vanished; Bond was certain he had fled down the mountain. He was told that a wounded man being taken down the hill, to safety and warmth, had shot himself in the foot: just what soldiers were said to have done in the First World War. On the trail between the field where his platoon was dug in and Iannucelli's house Bond saw a shocking sight: a young lieutenant was standing by the trail stopping everyone who passed. He had drawn his pistol. The battalion commander had told the lieutenant to prevent any but the seriously wounded from going down the hill. Bond watched the lieutenant force two sullen soldiers at gunpoint back up to the front. Harold Bond had never thought he would see an American officer draw a pistol on American soldiers.

Bond and many others wondered whether the commanders down in the plain—warm and safe—had any idea of the state of the men up on the mountain. Certainly Bond had never seen or heard of a senior officer up there. The generals might know, as a statistical fact, that it took a mule train an average of fourteen hours to make the

ABOVE: The monastery, seemingly unscathed, as seen from the valley floor in the early days of February 1944. The ruins of the castle at Rocca Janula, below the monastery, are enveloped in the smoke of combat. BELOW: American gunners near the Rapido River. Monte Cassino and Monte Cairo are in the background.

ABOVE, LEFT: Lieutenant-General Bernard Freyberg, commander of the New Zealand Division on the Liri Valley front. ABOVE, RIGHT: Major-General Francis Tuker, commander of the 4th Indian Division. BELOW: Correspondent Martha Gellhorn talking with Gurkha soldiers of the Indian Division.

round trip to the lines. But did they know how many of the mule trains either were shot down by the Germans or dropped their loads short of their destination in order to get off the mountain before daybreak? And did they know what the failure of the supplies to arrive did to the morale as well as the physical condition of the lonely men waiting on the mountain? It seemed inconceivable that the commanders could order these men to attack—as they had done again and again. It was one thing to defend a position, as the Germans were doing—that did not take much more than waiting and pulling the trigger—but to attack in that forbidding terrain was an altogether different challenge. It meant scrambling, heavy-laden, and fast if you wanted to live, across and around rocks and gullies and through brush, always up, up in the teeth of the well-entrenched enemy. Bond thought most of the men around him were no longer capable of that effort.

Four days after he had climbed the hill, Bond learned that his battalion was being moved to a position farther north on the mountainside, more than twice as far from the monastery. Not many men were left to move. From its normal complement of about 800, Bond's battalion, the second, was down to 94 men and 12 officers.

The Americans were to be replaced by newcomers to the Cassino front, troops from New Zealand. One morning Bond watched officers from the New Zealand Division come up the hill to look over the positions their troops would occupy. They struck the Americans as experienced, self-confident men who knew their business. The newcomers seemed to be in a good mood; some of the officers even sported walking sticks. They looked clean and rested and strong, compared to the filthy, weary Americans. But the Americans did not envy the men who would be taking their place on the mountain.

40

The men from New Zealand began arriving in the Liri Valley in the first days of February. In mid-January, the Allied commander in Italy, General Alexander, had taken them out of combat on the Adriatic front. In the valley of Alife, just north of Naples, the New Zealanders had enjoyed two weeks of peace. The men had caught up on their sleep; the mechanics had caught up on the maintenance of vehicles and weapons; the training exercises had not been too rigorous. Now they were going back to the war.

From the rest area the New Zealanders had set out along Route 6, the highway along which the Fifth Army had fought earlier in the winter. As they went by, someone pointed out "Million-Dollar Hill," so named by the Americans for the cost of the artillery fire they spent in taking it. This was where, according to Ernie Pyle, two artillery men figured out that it was costing about $25,000 in shellfire to kill a single German; one of them wondered if it would not simplify things all around to offer the Germans that amount to surrender. The newcomers were impressed by the endless stream of trucks traveling in both directions along the highway, a stream to which they added the 4,500 vehicles of their division. Going up the road the trucks were carrying clean soldiers like themselves; the men in the trucks coming back were filthy and hollow-eyed. The New Zealanders, these tall, raw-boned men who had come from halfway around the world, now contributed their distinctive accent to the polyglot medley of shouts and curses along the road. One of their officers described his introduction to the multinational world of the Fifth Army:

Running up Highway Six we were nearly put in the ditch by American Negro drivers. An Indian military policeman warned us to waste no time at the San Vittore corner, beyond which we overtook an Algerian battalion with French officers. We passed through an English field regiment's area, several hundred American infantry working on the road, and reached Corps headquarters immediately behind two Brazilian generals. In the first room I was astounded and mystified to hear that the Japanese had taken the castle.

The "Japanese" were the American Nisei of the 100th Infantry Battalion, and the "castle" was the ruin on top of Rocca Janula, the hill between Cassino town and the Monte Cassino ridge.

In the Liri Valley itself the New Zealanders saw the evidence of combat all around them. They saw rusty, burned-out wrecks of tanks; tangles of phone cables; signs warning: ROAD UNDER SHELL-FIRE; small clumps of shallow graves at roadside. Both German and Allied artillery had raked over the landscape time and again, leaving scorched, splintered trees and craters that soon filled with stagnant water. "It looks like Passchendaele," said an officer old enough to remember that battle in the earlier war.

Alexander had brought the New Zealand Division over because the Fifth Army was running short of troops. The French attack on the Monte Cassino promontory had been stalled because they had no reserves, and neither did the Americans fighting alongside the French. Even if the Fifth Army should succeed in breaking through at the Liri, as Mark Clark kept saying it would, Clark could not exploit the breakthrough because he had no fresh troops to send up the valley to Anzio and Rome.

The pressure on Alexander and Clark kept on growing. Their superiors in London and Washington, peering down at the tiny spot on the map, saw that the Americans on the ridge were only a mile and a half from the other side and wondered why they could not break through. The American Joint Chiefs of Staff, on February 4, observed that "in spite of a considerable weakening of German strength on main [Cassino] front there has been no heavily mounted aggressive action. . . ." Churchill passed that observation along in the form of a question to Henry Maitland Wilson, the 300-pound British general known as "Jumbo," who on January 8 had succeeded Eisenhower as commander of Allied forces in the Mediterranean and, as such, was Alexander's superior. Wilson, who was headquartered in Algiers, answered, with much optimism but little accuracy, that "we have almost secured the whole of the Cassino feature [the Monte Cassino promontory] and are hopeful of getting the Monte Cairo massif."

Churchill was particularly worried because of the threat to the

Anzio beachhead. Anzio had been Churchill's idea. Now it seemed about to turn out as disastrously as an earlier Churchill inspiration, the Allied landing at Gallipoli in 1915. If only to save Anzio, the Fifth Army had to keep pounding at the Germans in the Liri: ". . . we have a great need to keep continually engaging them and even a battle of attrition is better than standing by and watching the Russians fight." No doubt Churchill would have had trouble finding men up on the Monte Cassino ridge who agreed with him.

The generals in command in Italy did not know much more than Churchill and the Joint Chiefs about what it was like up there on the ridge. The generals could gaze across the valley to the ridge, only 3 miles away, from their observation posts on Monte Trocchio. They could pore over aerial photographs of the ridge taken by their aircraft. But neither looking across the valley nor aerial photos conveyed the realities of the ridge. You could not see from either perspective how difficult it was to move around in that terrain. You could not see that the approaches were so narrow that the number of men who could advance together was never enough to overwhelm the German positions. You could not tell how rapidly the conditions of life were sapping the fighting strength of the Americans up there. You could not tell that the Allies' great superiority in firepower was of little use because the artillery, firing from miles away in the valley at German positions often only a hundred yards from the Americans, was almost as likely to hit their own men as the enemy; but usually the artillery hit no one at all. You could not tell, finally, that the "mile and a half" that separated the Americans from the other side of the ridge might as well as have been the distance to the moon. So the generals, like the Joint Chiefs, kept thinking one more push would do it. The troops Alexander was bringing over were to provide that push.

The New Zealanders now arriving in the Liri were a distinctive body of men with a dramatic leader. Lieutenant-General Bernard Freyberg was a great barrel-chested man, over 6 feet tall, of enormous physical prowess, and with an astonishing combat record in two wars. Trained as a dentist, Freyberg discovered his true calling in 1914, when he was 25. He met Churchill just as the war was starting, and the following year he shipped out to Gallipoli, where he distinguished himself by swimming ashore to the beachhead. Back on the Western front in 1916, Freyberg was wounded four times and won the Victoria Cross, Britain's highest and rarest honor. In the 1920s, he tried twice to swim the English Channel but failed both times. By 1939, Freyberg was 50 and ready for another war. New Zealand's government put him in command of the division it raised and sent to the Middle East in 1940. The division had been in action all around the Mediterranean ever since: in Egypt, in Crete, again in North Africa, now in Italy.

The gregarious, outgoing Freyberg was popular with his men. These New Zealanders were used to the lonely life of isolated farms and sheep stations, and many of them knew each other from before the war. At times the division seemed less like a military organization than a family business run by a lot of cousins. They called themselves "the great amateur division." Such men had no patience with the spit and polish and protocol of the professional military. Once, in North Africa, General Montgomery had asked, "Don't your fellows salute anymore?" Freyberg had answered: "They're all right. If you just wave to them they'll wave back." These men liked a commander who joked with them and who looked after their needs: in Cairo, Freyberg arranged for his division, men and officers alike, what was widely believed to be the biggest beer bar in the world. The British press lionized Freyberg, in part because it provided an opportunity to underline the contribution the members of the Commonwealth were making to the mother country in her hour of need.

Those who had to work most closely with Freyberg saw a different side to the man. Even those who admired him said also that Freyberg was impulsive in his decisions, that he lived in a world of boyish fantasy, and that he was naive about issues larger than those involved in leading men into battle. He was a sloppy administrator whose subordinates often had to call each other to try to figure out what he wanted. General Freyberg—this thought was expressed with varying degrees of delicacy—did not have a brain equal to his powerful physique.

This man of great bravery and limited intellect had been placed in a position of great political subtlety. The New Zealand Division, like all the Commonwealth forces, had been sent where it was by its home government and could be withdrawn at any time. Australia, in fact, already had withdrawn its troops from the Middle East after war had started in the Pacific; after all, Japan was far closer to Australia—and New Zealand—than was Germany. There had been great pressure at home on the New Zealand government to withdraw its soldiers. The reason for which the troops had first been sent—the threat to the Middle East—had now disappeared. Keeping the troops over there, plus another division in the South Pacific, was straining the resources of the little nation. Of its 2 million people almost 10 percent—163,000 men and 5,000 women—were in uniform. The casualties the 2nd Division had suffered were particularly troubling. It had lost 18,500 of a total of 43,500 men. As a proportion of the nation's manpower, this was equivalent to the loss to the United States of almost 1 million men. Less than a year earlier, on May 20 and 21 of 1943, the New Zealand Parliament had debated the question of bringing its men home; three cabinet ministers had sons serving in that one division. Churchill had sent a characteristically theatrical plea. Freyberg also had said he thought the division should stay, and his voice was apparently the deciding factor in the Parliament's decision to leave the division in the European theater for the time being.

A few days after he had ordered the New Zealanders over to the the Liri, Alexander decided that Mark Clark was going to need still more troops. So Alexander stripped the Adriatic front of another division, just as his German counterpart, Field Marshal Kesselring, was stripping his side of that same front of troops destined for the same purpose: the battle on the Monte Cassino ridge. Alexander took the new division, the 4th Indian, and combined it with the New Zealand Division in what he called the New Zealand Corps. This he put under the command of Freyberg.

The 4th Indian Division added still another exotic flavor to the incredible variety of Clark's Fifth Army. The division was part of the army of India and was an elite professional organization. Two-thirds of its units were Indian and Gurkha, one-third British; the senior officers were British. Its members were all volunteers, many were career men, some were following their father's careers. For members of the British units qualifications were higher, and so was the pay, than in the regular army. The Indian Division was experienced in mountain warfare; years ago they had fought on India's northwest frontier, recently in East and North Africa. Its three battalions of Gurkhas from Nepal were the only men on either side who could match the North Africans man for man as mountain warriors.

Major-General Francis Tuker, commander of the Indian Division and now Freyberg's subordinate, was about as different from Freyberg as it was possible to be. Tuker was aloof, almost shy, an intellectual who had devoted himself to the study of war. He was also a sharp-tongued man, an individualist, a professional who did not suffer gladly the fools and amateurs he detected all around him. His judgment of Freyberg, as expressed in a postwar letter, was: "personally brave, without any tactical talent, had no brains and no imagination." Tuker contemplated the chain of command and he did not like what he saw above him, from "an obstinate dunce" (Freyberg), through "a flashy ignoramus" (Clark), to "an indolent fifth wheel" (Alexander).*

Since the division had arrived in December, Tuker had devoted much thought to the problems of war in the Italian mountains. He had concluded that fortified places on the tops of mountains could not be taken by ground forces without the help of massive air bombardment. It was entirely typical of Tuker that, when he was transferred to the Liri, he sent a young officer to Naples to search bookstores for whatever written information he could find about Monte Cassino. He came back with a grab-bag collection that included four copies of an illustrated publication of the Italian Fine Arts Society, an automobile guide for 1920, and a book dated 1879 that purported to give details of the abbey's construction. After studying this miscellany, Tuker fired off to Freyberg a memorandum that said in part:

> After considerable trouble and investigating many bookshops in NAPLES, I have at last found a book, dated 1879, which gives certain details of the construction of the MONTE CASSINO Monastery. The Monastery was converted into a fortress in the 19th Century. The Main Gate has massive timber branches in a low archway consisting of large stone blocks 9 to 10 metres long. This Gate is the only means of entrance to the Monastery.

*So Tuker wrote after the war. But at the time, when he fell ill and had to give up his command, Tuker wrote to Freyberg: "I am ever so thankful my division is being looked after by yourself. With you there, I know that no single life will be squandered and that those that are spent will be well spent." When, long after, his letter was quoted, Tuker tried to explain it away: "I wrote that note precisely because I was pretty certain the division wouldn't be safe. This was a last desperate attempt to induce Freyberg to take my advice and not attack the Cassino features as he and Mark Clark planned, but to outflank them."

. . . The walls are of solid masonry and at least 10 ft. thick at the base. Since the place was constructed as fortress as late as the 19th Century, it stands to reason that the walls will be suitably pierced for loopholes and will be battlemounted. . . . [It] is therefore a modern fortress and must be dealt with by modern means. It can only be dealt with by applying "blockbuster" bombs from the air, hoping thereby to render the garrison incapable of resistance. The 1,000-lb. bomb would be next to useless to effect this.

Tuker observed that field engineers could not "cope" with the monastery. This seemed to be his reply to the engineer who had suggested they use the method "adopted at the Kashmir Gate, Delhi, in the Mutiny." On September 14, 1857, two engineers and some men blew open the gate with bags of powder, ending the siege of Delhi. Tuker concluded in typical style:

I would point out that it has only been by investigation on the part of this Div., with no help whatsoever from "I" [intelligence] sources outside, that we have got any idea as to what this fortress comprises although the fortress has been a thorn in our side for many weeks.

Tuker's first preference was not to attack Monastery Hill at all. Like Alphonse Juin, and perhaps because he too commanded men who were at home in the mountains, Tuker advocated a wide swing to the right that would bypass and cut off the German defenses at Cassino and on the hill above. Freyberg's first plan, put out on February 4, reflected Tuker's thinking. The Indian Division, and some of the New Zealanders, would join the French in an attack in the area where the French already had a foothold in the mountain. The plan differed from what had been done before only in that it provided for trying to put more soldiers up on the mountain, without any certainty that more soldiers could be maintained by supply lines that were long, exposed, and already overstrained.

Within a couple of days Freyberg had abandoned this plan and gone back to the old frontal assault on Monastery Hill. He never said why he changed his mind. Certainly Freyberg was feeling pressure from above for quick results. Probably also Freyberg, who like the other generals had never been on the ridge, shared with them the mirage of the 1½-mile gap that separated the Americans from their objective. Put some fresh troops up there, and one good push should do it. Accordingly, Freyberg ordered part of the Indian Division to go up the mountain, replace the Americans, and take Monastery Hill. The New Zealanders meanwhile would attack Cassino town along the highway.

Tuker was not around to argue his case against the frontal attack. In early February, about the time Freyberg was putting out the first plan, Tuker was stricken with a recurring rheumatoid arthritis while visiting Juin at his headquarters at Venafro in the Abruzzi. Tuker was taken in his trailer to the military hospital near the palace in Caserta. His place as commander of the Indian Division was taken by Brigadier H. W. Dimoline, an artillery officer and a much less forceful personality.

The soldiers of the Indian Division began climbing up the murderous hillsides where so many French and American soldiers had struggled and died. When they got to the part of the ridge where the Americans of the 34th Division had been in combat for two weeks, the newcomers were appalled by what they found. Corpses lay all around and the living were not much better off than the dead. The Americans had fought up to and beyond the limits of human endurance. Fifty men still defending their positions were found to be too cramped and too weak from exposure even to walk. The men of the Indian Division had to lift them bodily from their stone shelters and carry them out on stretchers. Not all of them made it. Some of the stretcher bearers, and the exhausted men they were carrying, were killed by German shellfire on the long, difficult journey down the mountainside. The Indian Division also discovered—in contradiction to what they had been told by the American commanders—that the Americans up there did not hold the crucial Hill 593. These discoveries seemed to confirm the disapproving judgment of Major-General Howard Kippenberger, Freyberg's successor as commander of the New Zealand Division, after a discussion with the American commanders, that "it was plain that none of them had been forward or was at all in touch with his men."

Now that the Indian Division had been given the task of taking the monastery, its new commander, Brigadier Dimoline, adopted his predecessor's thinking. Tuker later recalled: "I always told Freyberg quite clearly that nothing would induce me to attack this feature

[Monte Cassino] directly unless the garrison was reduced to helpless lunacy by sheer unending pounding for days and nights by air and artillery, that all the bombers of Italy, the Mediterranean, and Great Britain would be needed for the job, and the Infantry attack must follow in at night on the heels of the bombardment."

On the evening of February 11, at 10:45, Dimoline asked that the Abbey of Monte Cassino be bombed. The operating instructions of the Indian Division record: "Requests have been made for all buildings and suspected enemy strongpoints on and in vicinity of the objectives [Monastery Hill] including the monastery to be subjected to intense bombing from now onwards." Freyberg said he would transmit the request with his own approval.

41

General Freyberg waited almost 24 hours, till the evening of February 12, before he transmitted the request for the bombing of the Abbey of Monte Cassino.

During that day General Tuker fired off another memorandum to Freyberg from his van at the hospital in Caserta. Tuker said he had spoken with Brigadier Dimoline, acting commander of the Indian Division during Tuker's illness. Tuker reiterated his case for the bombing of Monastery Hill, the objective his division was supposed to capture:

> It is apparent that the enemy are in concrete and steel emplacements on the Monastery Hill. From a wide experience of attacks in mountain areas I know that infantry cannot "jump" strong defenses of this sort in the mountains. These defenses have to

be "softened" up either by being cut off on all sides and starved out or else by continuous and heavy bombardment over a period of days. Even with the latter preparation, success will only be achieved if a thorough and prolonged bombardment is undertaken with really heavy bombs a good deal larger than "Kitty Bomber" missiles.

Tuker also repeated his opinion that if such bombing were not possible the alternative was to "turn the Monastery Hill and to isolate it. This course I regard to be possible. . . ." In fact, it had been Tuker's preferred course from the beginning.

Freyberg himself could not order the bombing. Only his superior, Mark Clark, could do that. The tactical air forces—the medium and light bombers used in close support of ground forces—were under the control of the commander of the Fifth Army. The strategic air force—the heavy bombers used to bomb targets far in the enemy's rear—were controlled not by Clark but by Lieutenant-General Ira C. Eaker, commander of the Mediterranean Allied Air Forces. These aircraft were not normally used in support of ground troops.

At 7:00 P.M., Saturday, February 12, Freyberg telephoned Clark at his command post at Presenzano, a town in the mountains south of the Liri Valley. Clark had moved the trailer in which he lived up there from the grounds of the palace in Caserta in late January. Freyberg reached Major-General Albert Gruenther, the Fifth Army chief of staff, who told him that Clark was up at the Anzio beachhead.* Freyberg told Gruenther: "I desire that I be given air support tomorrow in order to soften the enemy position in the Cassino area. I want three missions of twelve planes each, the planes to be Kitty Bombers, carrying 1000-pound bombs." Gruenther said Clark had directed that the main effort the next day be concentrated at Anzio, and he was therefore not sure Freyberg could be given what he wanted. Freyberg repeated his request and said he thought it was a minimum requirement. Gruenther said he would look into it at once.

Gruenther checked the list of targets for air attack, if planes were available, that Freyberg's headquarters had routinely submitted to Clark earlier that day. He then called Freyberg and told him he could

*Gruenther wrote a detailed account that same evening of the critical telephone conversations in which he had taken part. He was the only participant to do so. Our account is based on Gruenther's memorandum.

155

get a 36-plane squadron of A-36 fighter-bombers carrying 500-pound bombs. This amounted to half the weight in bombs that Freyberg had requested, which in turn was far less than the enormous tonnage Tuker had advocated. Gruenther asked Freyberg which of his targets he wanted the planes to attack. Freyberg said, "I want the convent attacked." Gruenther said he assumed this meant the monastery and that it was not on Freyberg's list of targets. Freyberg said: "I am quite sure it was on my list of targets, but in any case I want it bombed. The other targets are unimportant, but this one is vital. The division commander who is making the attack feels that it is an essential target and I thoroughly agree with him." Gruenther said that he would have to consult Clark because of restrictions on bombing the monastery.

Gruenther could not reach Clark by phone. That morning Clark had gone off in his Piper Cub, flying just above the water under a Spitfire escort, up to the place that was most on his mind in those days—the endangered beachhead at Anzio. Clark later recalled that a messenger found him at the beachhead with a radio message from Gruenther saying Freyberg wanted to talk to him about bombing the abbey and advising Clark to "get back if possible because this is a hot one." Soon after that Clark flew back to his command post in the mountains.

For Mark Clark, the arrival of Freyberg on the scene had only added to the stress of trying to command his heterogenous army in a situation that seemed always to get more difficult. From the beginning, Clark had found it disturbing to be in charge of an army in which American troops were in the minority. Of the five corps under his command, two were American and one each British, French, and now the corps from New Zealand and India. Clark had British generals under him, and British over him: Alexander, and, since Eisenhower had left, the British general Maitland Wilson over Alexander. If he had been winning, it would have been tolerable, but he had been defeated at the Rapido, the 34th Division had failed to break through on the Monte Cassino ridge, and the Anzio landing, far from solving his problems, was only offering another chance for disaster. "I never had more headaches than in that period," Clark later recalled.

Now, with the arrival of Freyberg and his troops, Clark would be commanding soldiers from two parts of the old empire, India and

New Zealand, in the battle of Cassino and would be responsible to two British superiors. He was feeling encircled. "I was the only American in that show," he recalled. Freyberg himself was a formidable personality. Clark knew that this man who was technically his subordinate was ten years older and far more experienced in battle. Clark also knew about Freyberg's favored position in that Commonwealth to which Clark's own commander, Alexander, also belonged. He remembered Alexander saying to him when he brought the New Zealand Division over and put it under Clark's command: "Freyberg is a big man in New Zealand, a big man in the Commonwealth. We treat him with kid gloves and you must do the same."

Clark was also aware of the reason behind Alexander's "kid glove" policy: the special political status of the New Zealand Division, and Freyberg's power to pull his troops out of combat on his own authority. Freyberg was only under his and Alexander's orders as long as he wanted to be. Freyberg was known to have broken off an engagement at Orsogna on the Adriatic front because he thought his division was suffering too many casualties. He told Clark that when his casualties reached a thousand he would abandon the attack unless it was about to achieve success. Since his division had already endured many more than that number of casualties, Freyberg must have been referring to the New Zealanders' coming attack at Cassino, where the Americans already had lost many more than a thousand men.

These two strong-willed, egotistical men—the flashy young upstart and the veteran full of past glories—were soon at odds despite their efforts to get along. As Clark later recalled, he made a point of flying over frequently for lunch with Freyberg at the latter's headquarters; when he got back in his Piper Cub after lunch, he would find a bottle of New Zealand brandy on the seat. But brandy or no brandy, on February 4 after a meeting of New Zealand and American officers, Clark wrote in his diary: "Freyberg is a sort of a bull in a china closet. He feels he is going to win the war, and with his 15,000 vehicles is going to clutter up the entire Liri Valley area. He immediately clashed with [Major-General Geoffrey] Keyes when he indicated where he was moving artillery, his New Zealanders, his Indians, and other impedimenta. I turned it over to my staff, telling Freyberg that he could move into no area until he had coordinated with all other Fifth Army activities." Clark thought Keyes was "a bit belligerent about the whole affair, having been through a difficult period of attack in which he got very little sleep." So he wrote Keyes: "These are Dominion troops who are jealous of their prerogatives. They have always been given special consideration by the British and I intend to make their relations with the Fifth Army happy and successful. You must help me all you can."

That night Clark informed his diary that he was "about ready to agree with Napoleon's conclusion that it is better to fight allies than to be one of them."

Freyberg's Saturday night call about the Abbey of Monte Cassino did not come as a complete surprise to Clark. They had talked about the problem of the abbey on a couple of occasions, and on February 9, according to Clark, Freyberg had said it should be knocked down by artillery or aerial bombardment, if necessary. Clark had said it was not necessary, and that ended the matter for the moment. According to Freyberg, in one of their conversations, "I suggested to drop a token bomb, to show what lay in store for the defenders, and to get them to clear the refugees out. Mark Clark poured ridicule on this, and said that nothing would do but to bring in the heavy Fortresses with delayed-action 1,000-pound bombs."

Clark's own position on the abbey was taken in the light of a directive from his friend Eisenhower, then the Allied commander in the Mediterreanean and now the Supreme Allied Commander in Europe. In a December 29 message to "all commanders," Eisenhower had said:

> Today we are fighting in a country which has contributed a great deal to our cultural inheritance, a country rich in monuments which by their creation helped and now in their old age illustrate the growth of the civilization which is ours. We are bound to respect those monuments so far as war allows.
>
> If we have to choose between destroying a famous building and sacrificing our own men, then our men's lives count infinitely more and the buildings must go. But the choice is not always so clear-cut as that. In many cases the monuments can be spared without any detriment to operational needs. Nothing can stand against the argument of military necessity. That is an accepted principle. But the phrase "military necessity" is sometimes used where it would be more truthful to speak of military convenience or even of personal convenience. I do not want it to cloak slackness or indifference.

It is a responsibility of higher commanders to determine through A.M.G. [Allied Military Government] officers the locations of historical monuments whether they be immediately ahead of our front lines or in areas occupied by us. This information passed to lower echelons through normal channels places the responsibility on all commanders of complying with the spirit of this letter.

Clark had also received the several messages in October and November asking that Monte Cassino be preserved if possible. Clark had said repeatedly that he would not destroy churches and other religious monuments unless they were being used for military purposes; he had no wish to be seen as a barbarian conqueror. Clark knew that his political superiors, beginning with President Roosevelt, who faced an election campaign in less than a year, were much more sensitive than the British to Catholic and Vatican opinion. (The point was made explicit on February 17 by Acting Secretary of State Edward Stettinius in replying to a British suggestion: "We cannot agree to permit British channels only to be used for the communication of Vatican observations and protests concerning extraterritorial Vatican property or other religious property in Italy, particularly in view of the relatively much greater interest in the United States in problems affecting the Catholic Church.") On January 29, Clark instructed his subordinates to avoid attacking Vatican or church property if possible. This order was generally interpreted to cover Monte Cassino, as its intent certainly did, although technically the monastery had been the property of the Italian state since the nineteenth century.

Before Freyberg's entry on the scene, the only generals who could have requested the bombing were Americans: General Keyes, the commander of II Corps, and the divisional commanders under him, Walker of the 36th and Major-General Charles Ryder of the 34th. None of them had made such a request. None of these generals believed that "military necessity"—the magic phrase—justified the destruction of Monte Cassino. All of them, by February 12, were on record as opposing the idea. Walker in particular disliked bombing civilians. Of the bombing of a village named Altavilla, he had written in September: "The bombardment of this village, full of helpless civilian families, was brutal and to no purpose."

159

Despite the unanimity among the American generals in the Liri Valley, the immune status of Monte Cassino and other religious sites was coming under increasing criticism. An important indication could be seen in the response to the bombing of Castel Gandolfo, the Pope's summer residence in the Alban Hills between Rome and Anzio. Alexander's November 5 message to the Fifth Army had listed Castel Gandolfo and Monte Cassino as the two sites about which special care was to be exercised. On February 1, Allied bombs hit a convent just outside the gate of Castel Gandolfo, killing seventeen nuns. The bombing was approved by all the Allied military commanders in Italy and by the Joint Chiefs of Staff in London on the grounds that the area bombed contained not German fortifications or forces but "essential road communications."*

The Vatican protested the bombing of Castel Gandolfo, but about Monte Cassino it had said nothing to Allied diplomats for more than a month. Its last communication had been on January 8, when the Vatican had passed on part—the weakest, least meaningful part—of the German ambassador's statement denying that the Germans were using the abbey. On February 11, the day before Freyberg made his telephone call, D'Arcy Osborne, the British minister to the Vatican, had suggested the possible consequences of their silence. As he reported to the Foreign Office:

> I have thought it well to remind the Vatican, both verbally and in writing, that if the abbey *or* its territory were used by the Germans for military purposes, the Allied military authorities would be obliged to take necessary counter measures; also that I have never received any reply to my suggestion [of November 1943] that the Vatican should ascertain from the Germans whether their assurance that the Abbey would not be occupied by German troops covered occupation or utilization of the Abbey or its territory for any military purpose.

Monte Cassino's representative in Rome, the monk Tommaso Leccisotti, was still haunting the corridors of the Vatican in the hope of finding out what, if anything, could be done to save his monastery.

---

*The neutral territory of Castel Gandolfo was also where Lieutenant Paul Freyberg, the general's son, found a safe refuge later that month after he escaped from the Germans who had taken him prisoner at Anzio.

160

On February 11, the Benedictine heard there was talk of sending a neutral observer to Monte Cassino. The observer would see for himself whether the Germans were using the abbey, and if they were not, he would so inform the Allies. Apparently this was no one's formal proposal, just an idea discussed among Vatican officials. It was also the suggestion that Leccisotti thought he had discerned in the Vatican's account of a statement made in December by Baron Weizsaecker, the German ambassador. At that time the prospect had alarmed Leccisotti, and he had not made it known to the abbot of Monte Cassino. Now, according to what Leccisotti heard at the Vatican, it was Weizsaecker who was offended at the thought of a neutral observer at Monte Cassino. "You don't believe my word!" was said to have been his reaction.

The press in both the United States and England had begun pointing to Monte Cassino as the obstacle that was blocking the advance of the Allies in Italy and costing the lives of Allied soldiers. On January 29, the *New York Times* published a dispatch from C. L. Sulzberger under this headline: CLARK ORDER PROHIBITS 5TH ARMY FROM ATTACKING CHURCH PROPERTY. . . . COURTESY TO VATICAN HANDICAPS ADVANCE AS ENEMY IS SAID TO USE RELIGIOUS SITES FOR ARTILLERY OBSERVATION. Sulzberger listed three sites as "obstacles": Monte Cassino, Castel Gandolfo, and the three bridges across the Tiber in Rome near the Vatican (used by German trucks). Of Monte Cassino, he wrote: "There seems little doubt that [the Germans] are employing it as an artillery observation post, for which its position, dominating the valley, is wonderful. . . . The Fifth Army's abstention from shelling Monte Cassino Abbey . . . hampered our advance greatly." Of Clark's order concerning the sanctity of religious property, Sulzberger observed that "many lives may be lost."

The same newspaper's foreign affairs writer, Anne O'Hare McCormick, titled her February 9 column on the editorial page: THE SYMBOLIC BATTLE FOR MONTE CASSINO. She philosophized:

> What makes this war different from all the wars of history is that nobody on the earth can find a refuge from it. You can't run away anywhere. The battle on the slopes of Monte Casino proves it. . . . Monte Cassino, spared through all the warring centuries, has not been spared in this conflict. . . . The Ameri-

cans have strict orders not to shell the monastery, which is Vatican territory, but the Germans are established on the hill and apparently pay no more attention to the signs warning that it is neutral territory than to the Red Cross signs marking the hospital tents they bombed yesterday at Anzio.

Similarly, the *Times* of London on February 10 published a dispatch dated two days earlier under the headline: MONASTERY USED AS OBSERVATION POST. The story said that the Americans' guns "are careful not to make it [Monte Cassino] a target. . . . The Germans trade on this discrimination and our men can see wireless aerials established on the roofs and telescopes at the windows." The next day the headline was: MONASTERY USED AS GUN-POST. And the story read: ". . . men of the Fifth Army, groping their way up the slopes, have seen German machine-guns along the abbey wall."

In England, and to some degree in the United States, there was a countercurrent of opposition to indiscriminate bombing, but it represented the opinion of only a small minority. In a pamphlet titled "Seeds of Chaos," Vera Brittain argued that bombing detracted from the real goal of the war because it was "steadily creating the psychological foundations for a third world war." The bishop of Chichester, George Bell, the best known of the small band of critics, rose in the House of Lords on February 9 to oppose the needless destruction of cultural monuments.

The English critics were usually concerned about either the wholesale killing of German civilians or, in Italy, the fate of Rome. On January 31, a letter from Archbishop Lang of Lambeth—"Rome is not like any other city"—touched off one of the *Times*'s classic exchanges of letters. Of the fifteen letters published in the next few days, one of them signed by A. A. Milne, a small majority held that the lives of Allied soldiers were more important than the monuments of Rome.* Mollie Panter-Downes, London correspondent of *The New Yorker,* summed up her view of the debate in a cable dated February 13 and published on the nineteenth:

---

*Milne wrote that the lives sacrificed to save Rome would be those of Allied soldiers and concluded: "It may be that they will be ready to make that extra sacrifice, but it is not one a sensitive man would care to demand from them." His letter appeared in the *Times* for February 8.

A verbal battle is going on between the school of thought that holds that Rome should be tenderly treated by Allied gunners and those who believe a military advantage in the hand is worth two Michaelangelo frescoes on the wall. Perhaps worried families weren't precisely in the mood last week for figuring out whether they would rather know that St. Peter's or their Bert was all right, but Archbishop Lang, former Archbishop of Canterbury, found time to lead the chorus of anxious concern over the fate of Rome—concern which, judging by the extreme solicitude the Allies were showing over the Monte Cassino monastery, hardly seemed necessary.

Correspondents covering the Cassino front were reporting the opinions of the soldiers, as they heard them, or more likely heard *about* them, concerning the immunity of the abbey. The generals were extremely sensitive to this reporting: it was on the basis of these news stories that they were being judged, surely by the folks back home, and to a large degree also by their political superiors. In early February the correspondents' reports were overwhelmingly hostile to Monte Cassino. A flurry of stories in the press reported that the Allied soldiers bitterly resented the abbey's immunity from attack. On February 11, for example, the Associated Press correspondent, Lynn Heinzerling, wired that:

> Allied artillerymen were still carefully avoiding the Abbey with artillery fire though officers say the old monastery was definitely being used as an observation post. Many soldiers are bitter that it is left unmolested while their comrades die below it.

That same day Clifton Webb, a *London Daily Herald* correspondent, was quoted as saying that it was his "definite opinion" that the abbey's days "were numbered." He added:

> Allied artillerymen have been scrupulously careful to avoid shelling the building, but information advanced by an Italian civilian on Wednesday makes it fairly certain that the Germans have already wrecked the abbey interior, dynamiting it to turn it into a fortress. . . . None of the American soldiers who have been fighting around it for weeks would regret its disappearance.

Some of the press reports from Cassino raised the religious question that had always lurked beneath the surface of debates about Monte Cassino and other religious shrines in Italy. On February 11 the *Des Moines* (Iowa) *Register* ran a dispatch from its correspondent, Gordon Gammack:

> The Catholics in the artillery battalion would be only too glad to do the firing. "We could do a job on the abbey in nothing flat," a Catholic officer said. "CATHOLIC BOYS ARE DYING BECAUSE WE ARE LEAVING IT ALONE."

Two days later the United Press reported that an American artillery battery commander, perhaps the same officer, had said a week earlier: "I don't give a damn about the monastery. I have Catholic gunners in this battery and they've asked me for permission to fire on the monastery, but I have not been able to give it to them. They don't like it."

The abbey's visual prominence, the way it dominated the entire landscape, had much to do with the soldiers' conviction that the enemy must be up there watching them. From every perspective in the valleys below, on the steep slopes of the hill, those windows glared down at them. Fred Majdalany, who served in the Lancashire Fusiliers, described how it felt to approach the ridge on which the abbey stood: "As the road became less crowded, you began to get the feeling the monastery was watching you. When you have been fighting a long time, you develop an instinct for enemy observation posts. . . . it is like being suddenly stripped of your clothes. We were being watched by eyes in the monastery every inch of the way up the rough little road through the olive groves."

The news stories from the Cassino front produced angry protests at home. The Chief of Staff received messages saying: "Dear General Marshall: All the stone monuments of Italy, be they 3,000 years old, are not worth the life of one of our boys. General Clark is unfair to his boys." Or: AM A CATHOLIC BUT DO NOT BELIEVE PRESERVATION BENEDICTINE ABBEY WORTH SINGLE AMERICAN LIFE. Or: "Why don't you give orders to blast that blazing monastery in Italy off the face of the earth? Everyone I know is blazing mad to think the lives of our soldiers are lost to save that building. Many say that F.D.R. is afraid of what his Catholic brethren will say and do." Or even: "As a loyal American with his only son in the armed forces I protest the War Department's policy of giving special consideration to the Roman Catholics in the war in Italy. My boy's life is worth more to me than Gen. Clark's feelings for the Italian-Fascist Pope and the slimy hypocrites who are Vatican serfs first before they are Americans. DO SOMETHING."

Such was the background against which Gruenther that Saturday night told Freyberg he would have to consult Clark before answering his request. While waiting for Clark to respond to the radio message he had sent to him at the Anzio beachhead, Gruenther called General Alexander's headquarters down at the great palace at Caserta. He reached his counterpart, Lieutenant-General John Harding, Alexander's chief of staff. He told Harding about Freyberg's request and added: "General Freyberg expressed to General Clark his considered opinion that the destruction of the monastery was a military necessity, and that it was unfair to assign to any military commander the mission of taking the hill and at the same time not grant permission to bomb the monastery. I am quite sure that General Clark still feels it is unnecessary to bomb the monastery. However, in view of the nature of the target, and the international and religious implications involved, I should like to get an expression of opinion from [Alexander] as to the advisability of authorizing the bombing." Alexander and Harding had visited Freyberg's headquarters that afternoon at 3:30, so they presumably knew the request was coming. Harding now promised to find out Alexander's opinion and report it to Gruenther.

Shortly after that conversation Gruenther finally spoke to Mark Clark. Clark told him to restate his views to Harding when the latter called, and went on to say that Freyberg's "extremely strong views" caused him some embarrassment and that he, Clark, would be put in a difficult position if the attack of the Indian Division on Monastery Hill should fail. By this time it was clear that what was taking place, as Clark said much later, was a "contest of wills" between himself and the New Zealander.

Now Gruenther, apparently in an effort to round up support for his commander's position, called General Keyes, the highest-ranking American field commander. It was about 9:15. Keyes said, as he had said before, that he did not think the bombing was a military necessity, that three senior officers with commands in the combat area

165

(Generals Ryder and Butler and Colonel Boatner) shared his opinion, and that he further thought that bombing the abbey would enhance its value to the Germans as a military obstacle. Gruenther then asked to speak to Lieutenant-Colonel Mercer Walter, the G-2 (intelligence) officer of II Corps.

Until the arrival of the New Zealand Corps, the only military sources of information were the American intelligence officers of the Fifth Army and its component parts, II Corps and the 34th and 36th Divisions. The records of the Fifth Army show only scattered reports suggesting that the Germans might be using the abbey itself. On February 4, a II Corps staff message reported that: "1st battalion 135th Infantry has direct observation above the monastery and can see people observing the battle from the hill."

On February 6, according to the Fifth Army History, Company L of the 168th Infantry reached a "narrow defile covered by enemy machine guns on the Abbey walls."

On February 8, a telephone message reported that: "Germans have been observed in the monastery using same as an observation post."

Also on February 8, 34th Division received a message that: "A battery 133rd Infantry reports seeing a [telescope] in the middle row of windows on the East face of Abbey of Monte Cassino. This window had no pane and was covered by a blanket. On the same date, this officer observed a scope in upper right hand window of East face of Abbey. Enemy have been observed moving around the base of the building on North side."

On February 9, 34th Division received this message: "Italian interrogated by CIC [counterintelligence] reports he left Monte Cassino area February 7 and had frequently been in abbey in past 30 days. He says approximately 80 enemy officers and soldiers and 30 machine guns are in the buildings." It is not clear from the report whether the Italian was referring to the abbey itself or to its several buildings outside the walls of the abbey.

On February 12 an artillery unit reported: "Our observers had noted a great deal of enemy activity in the vicinity of the famous monastery, and it became ever clearer that they were using the abbey as an observation post, and also had gun emplacements installed. One man seriously wounded by a sniper hiding in the monastery."

The 34th Division monthly intelligence report for January states:

"Enemy artillery was provided with exceptional observation on the high ground all along the line, and particularly by the use as an observation post of the Abbey de Monte Cassino, from which the entire valley to the east is clearly visible. Orders preventing our firing on this historical monument increased enormously the value of this point to the enemy."

Sometime on February 12 the New Zealand Corps put out a document called "Intelligence Summary No. 22." On March 9, in a report from the Algiers headquarters of General Wilson, the content of this document was summarized as follows: "A prisoner of war staff sergeant from the 3rd Battalion, 132nd Infantry Regiment, states its headquarters and operations battalion and battalion aid station were all together in the abbey." But the original document reads: ". . . are all together in the abbey on Hill 468 (G. 8321) marked with a Red Cross flag." Hill 468 was the location, not of the abbey (it was on Hill 516), but of the stone house at the Albaneta farm, some 2,000 yards from the abbey, and "G. 8321" is the geographical coordinate of Albaneta. The Albaneta house was indeed used by the Germans and was marked with a Red Cross flag. No Red Cross flag was ever reported seen at the abbey.

It is not known whether this report reached Freyberg before he made his call to Gruenther, and if it did, whether it was in such a form as to make him think it was about the abbey.

These scattered bits of evidence and guesswork could have been interpreted in either direction. On the face of it they do not add up to proof or even a strong suggestion that the Germans were in fact using the abbey itself. However, an intelligence officer determined to find that the Germans were in the abbey could have combined those few sightings with the overwhelming opinion of the soldiers in combat to make a case plausible enough at least to convince anyone who wanted to be convinced. The New Zealanders, after all, persuaded themselves on little or no evidence. That the Germans denied they were in the abbey only reinforced the belief that they were. In wartime you expect your enemy to lie, and if he is Nazi Germany you find it hard to believe that he will ever tell the truth. In this case, the American intelligence officers did not follow what seemed the easy line of reasoning. Perhaps they all sincerely believed the Germans were not in the abbey. On the other hand, intelligence is notorious for seeing what its superiors want to be seen. Perhaps, then, the intelligence officers were acting on what they sensed to be the un-spoken desires of Mark Clark and, above him, President Roosevelt: that it would be better all around if they did not have to destroy the Abbey of Monte Cassino.

In any event, the intelligence officer of the 34th Division summarized his knowledge as follows to Gruenther:

> Colonel Walter told me that from two civilian sources he had reason to believe that there were refugees in the building, one report stating that there were probably as many as 2,000. Colonel Walter stated that artillery OP's [observation posts] had submitted several reports concerning the use of the monastery as an OP, but that he had no reports of any actual fire coming from the building. He stated that the evidence pointed to the fact that there were enemy strongpoints very close to the walls of the building.

The intelligence officer of the Fifth Army itself, Colonel Edwin Howard, did not take part in the telephone exchanges of that evening, but he had discussed the issue of German use of the abbey with Clark on previous occasions. In an interview long after the war, Howard summarized what he had said at the time: "I had sufficient information to indicate that the abbey was not being used by the Germans for defensive purposes. I told them there was no reason whatsoever to bomb it. I also said once you bomb it to make it rubble, it will be a better defensive position for the Germans. They listened to me and said nothing."

Howard stressed the importance of aerial photographs in reaching his conclusions: "I had that place photographed almost every day. We studied the photos. We pinpointed every single [German] weapon and overprinted them on maps. I never saw any indication the abbey itself was being defended." He went on to say: "I can't say they didn't have an O.P. up there. . . . A photo wouldn't necessarily show one man. . . . There might have been Germans in there, but no defense installations. . . . To take a million-dollar plane and drop a million dollars worth of bombs on a place like that, you've got to have more reason than a few Germans standing around."

In a postwar interview, General Keyes said he thought at the time that the Germans would be "glad to entice us into bombing such a religious and cultural monument." This idea, that the Germans hoped for rewards in the form of propaganda if the Allies bombed Monte Cassino, was one that Keyes shared with D'Arcy Osborne, the British minister to the Vatican. Later in that month of February Osborne cabled the Foreign Office:

> I am informed, on what seems to be good authority, though I cannot guarantee it, that German agents are instructed from time to time to spread, in circles believed to have Allied sympathies and connections, information to the effect that certain churches, ecclesiastical property or cultural monuments are being used by the Germans for military purposes. Thereby it is hoped that Allied bombings of such edifices will provide propaganda material for asserting Allied vandalism, or at least incompetence. . . . Is it possible that the Germans used this trick in this [Monte Cassino] case?

According to one of his aides, General Keyes flew over Monte Cassino in a small plane to find out for himself if it was being used by the Germans. Colonel Robert Porter, deputy chief for plans and operations of II Corps, said in a postwar interview that Keyes made more than one flight and always reported that he had seen no evidence the Germans were in the abbey. About the rumors that reached him that one person or another had seen Germans in the abbey, Keyes said: "They've been looking so long they're seeing things." Porter said it was the general view of the American officers at II Corps that there was no one in Monte Cassino except the monks. The Americans did not as a rule pass along their information to the New Zealanders "because we weren't asked." Porter thought the New Zealanders and Freyberg had a "patronizing attitude" toward the less experienced Americans. Porter told his counterpart on Freyberg's staff that the Americans' information was that the abbey was not being used by the Germans, but, Porter later concluded, "it didn't matter because Freyberg did his own planning."

Mark Clark himself, in a postwar interview, recalled the information from Italian civilians as essential to his conviction that the Germans were not using Monte Cassino. Enough Italians crossed the lines at night and told the Allies' intelligence people what they knew that, said Clark, "I knew everyone who went in that abbey."

At 9:30, Gruenther spoke for the second time to Alexander's chief of staff down at the headquarters in Caserta. Harding reported his chief's position:

> General Alexander has decided that the monastery should be bombed if General Freyberg considers it a military necessity. He regrets that the building should be destroyed, but he has faith in General Freyberg's judgment. If there is any reasonable probability that the building is being used for military purposes General Alexander believes that its destruction is warranted.

Gruenther made yet another effort. He said that he had spoken with Clark since his earlier conversation with Harding and that Clark had said that if Freyberg were an American commander he, Clark, would give specific orders that the monastery not be bombed. But, Gruenther continued, the situation was delicate because of Freyberg's position in the Commonwealth forces, and Clark "hesitated" to forbid the bombing without first referring the matter to Alexander. Gruenther then repeated Clark's view that there was no military necessity for the bombing, that it would endanger the lives of many civilians, and that the ruins would be more useful to the Germans than the unbombed building.

Harding did not budge. He said: "General Alexander has made his position quite clear on this point. He regrets very much that the monastery should be destroyed, but he sees no other choice." But he added: "If General Clark desires to talk personally to General Alexander about the subject, I am sure that General Alexander will be pleased to discuss it with him."

Gruenther reported this exchange to Clark, and, at Clark's direction, called Freyberg once more. He repeated Clark's opposition but said he would "defer" to Freyberg's judgment if the latter had evidence that the monastery should be bombed. Freyberg said the commander of the Indian Division—which could have meant either Tuker or his acting substitute, Dimoline, but more probably the former—was indeed convinced the bombing was necessary. Freyberg also told Gruenther that "he did not believe that it would be sound to give an order to capture Monastery Hill"—the order Clark had in fact given him—"and at the same time deny the commander the right to remove an important obstacle to the success of this mission."

And then: "He stated that any higher commander who refused to authorize the bombing would have to be prepared to take the responsibility for a failure of the attack."

Prepared to take the responsibility for a failure: Freyberg's threat to his superiors could hardly have been more clearly stated. Clark and Alexander were both already in a good deal of hot water, without any trouble from Freyberg. Their campaign in Italy was going badly, especially compared to Allied successes on other fronts; the capture of Rome was long overdue. If, as seemed more than possible at the time, the Germans pushed their troops into the sea at Anzio, they would both be in a great deal more trouble, and Clark—as Alexander pointed out to him a few days later—would surely lose his command.

So neither man was in a strong position to resist this new threat from Freyberg. In the first instance, the threat had only been addressed to Clark, who had the authority to approve or deny Freyberg's request without consulting Alexander; had Clark done so, Alexander would have been politically in the clear whatever the outcome. But once Clark, in the person of Gruenther, had taken the issue to Alexander, then Alexander was as fully involved as Clark. In fact, as a member of the Commonwealth, Alexander was even more vulnerable than Clark; he was also far more politically aware than his younger American colleague. Neither man could help seeing the rock that loomed ahead of them in the imposing shape of Bernard Freyberg. The Indian Division would attack Monastery Hill, while the New Zealand Division attacked Cassino town, and the coordinated attacks would fail with heavy—more than a thousand—casualties. This was far from unlikely: it was, after all, just what had happened to the American 34th Division. Freyberg would then tell the government of New Zealand—and the rest of the world—that Clark and Alexander had caused his attack to fail by denying him the bombing of the abbey. The government of New Zealand would pull its division out of Italy in the middle of the campaign, giving as its reason casualties that were not only heavy but also needless. This would be a political disaster of major proportions for the Allies, and above all for the British who had lobbied so hard to keep the New Zealanders in the Mediterranean. Churchill would be purple with rage. The press, which had been reporting the American soldiers' anger over the abbey's immunity, would not be slow to fix the blame.

Clark and Alexander would walk the plank. At the supreme moment of their professional lives, the moment to which the long years of peace had only been a prelude, the careers of both men would be ruined.

All this because they refused to bomb a single stone building. A *Catholic* building, at that. Against the recommendation of the great war hero. While their own men were dying because of that building. . . .

It was hardly a contest: Freyberg won the test of wills. More accurately, perhaps, it was Tuker who won. It was Tuker who had argued so persistently for the bombing, not Freyberg. Freyberg seemed mainly committed not to the bombing as such but to having his way, the way that had been selected by Tuker. Freyberg may well have been just as reluctant to overrule the sharp-tongued, independent Tuker as Clark and Alexander were to overrule him. It was, after all, Tuker's Indian Division, not Freyberg's New Zealanders, who had to make the assault on Monastery Hill. Yet Tuker did not want to attack the hill at all—he wanted to bypass it.

The rest was aftermath, though Clark did hold on to one last slim hope. Gruenther told Freyberg that the air mission was on, and that Freyberg should arrange to move back any troops so close to Monte Cassino that they would be in danger of being hit by bombs. Freyberg was to determine when the area was safe for the bombing. Gruenther then arranged for the bombing to take place the following morning, the thirteenth, at some time after 10:00 A.M. Next he called Harding to say that Clark would talk to Alexander before 10:00 A.M., so that the mission could be canceled should Alexander change his mind.

Early the next morning Alexander appeared at Clark's command post in the mountains. Face to face they went over the ground that they had debated the previous evening through their subordinates. Alexander told Clark, "I would like you to comply with [Freyberg's] request." As Clark remembered their conversation years later, Alexander never argued the military merits of the bombing but stressed the nature of Freyberg's threat: "Remember, Wayne, he is a very important cog in the Commonwealth effort. I would be most reluctant to take responsibility for his failing and for his telling his people 'I lost 5,000 New Zealanders because they wouldn't let me use air as I wanted.' " Finally Clark asked Alexander to take the responsibility: "I said, 'You give me a direct order and we'll do it,' and he did."

The debate over the fate of Monte Cassino was over. Freyberg had won, or Tuker had won through Freyberg. What was perhaps most notable in that long evening and morning of telephone calls and conversations back and forth was that no one had changed his position in the slightest in response to the information and arguments advanced by any of the others.*

As it happened, the bombing did not take place that morning or that day. Freyberg had called Gruenther at midnight to request a delay because the troops near Monte Cassino could not be moved back in time.

42

General von Senger was skeptical about his soldiers' chances up on the Monte Cassino ridge. The Americans attacking across the northern end of the promontory had captured Monte Castellone and had pushed the Germans back almost to the edge. Only a thin line of German positions remained on the ridge between the Americans and the lifeline of the Via Casilina in the valley. So far Senger's troops were holding, but his army was being used up at the rate of about three hundred men a day, as they were killed, wounded, captured, or incapacitated from exposure up on the bitter mountain. Senger

---

*It is not entirely certain how high the issue was taken for final decision. Many believe that Alexander checked with his superior, General Wilson, the Allied commander in the entire Mediterranean, but neither man ever said so, and there is no written record of any exchange between them at the time. What does seem certain is that the decision was not referred still higher up than Wilson, to the political or military leaders in England or the United States.

calculated that he was outnumbered in men by two to one and in artillery by five to one.

When Marshal Kesselring made one of his frequent trips to the headquarters at Castelmassimo, Senger suggested that he abandon the battle on the ridge and withdraw his troops all the way up to a line behind the enemy beachhead at Nettuno-Anzio. But Kesselring, ever the optimist, knew how Hitler felt about giving up territory for any reason. He told Senger to hold his position at Cassino and on the Monte Cassino promontory. After his chief had gone—he left at 4:00 A.M. to avoid Allied aircraft—Senger told an aide that Kesselring was too naive for his liking. Not that it mattered much anyway, for, as Senger often said to his aide, "The rotten thing is to keep on fighting and fighting and to know all along that we have lost this war."

Whatever his innermost thoughts, Senger maintained a cheerful manner before his soldiers and his fellow officers. He was now living with four other officers in a fifteen-room Italian home that belonged to the Campanari family. Anna Campanari remembered that the Germans installed electricity for the first time—the Campanaris used oil lamps—and a direct telephone line to the front at Cassino. The Campanaris were living in a smaller house a few miles away. Though the Germans had taken over their home, the Campanaris were on good terms with Senger himself, who stopped by often to visit them.

The four officers who shared the house at Castelmassimo were carefully chosen by Senger. He picked men who were personally congenial and politically reliable. He wanted to be able to speak his mind without worrying that one of the men around him was going to repeat his words to the Gestapo. The tension between the Nazis and the men of the officer class was growing. On January 28, Hitler had issued an order to Kesselring in which he'd said, along with the usual exhortations, "The fight must be hard and merciless, not only against the enemy, but against all officers and units who fail in this decisive hour." None of the men Senger chose would report their chief for defeatist talk. At least two of the four had some links to the group planning the attempt to kill Hitler that was to culminate on July 20. The father of one of Senger's aides, Joachim Oster, was a leader in the plot, but none of the aides was an active participant. Like Senger himself, they stood aside and went about their assigned duties.

Senger knew Burghard von Cramm from before the war, when von

174

Cramm was a reserve officer in the cavalry regiment that Senger commanded. In January 1944, Cramm, a captain, was stationed in Berlin after two and a half years in Russia. When an order came down that younger officers—Cramm was 37—must go to the front, Senger arranged to put Cramm on his staff. The robust, ruddy-faced, smiling Cramm was the officer who spent the most time with Senger. Years later Cramm would recall the days with Senger at Castelmassimo.

The five men—Senger and his four aides—usually gathered for dinner around seven o'clock. They would openly discuss the course of war in the privacy of Castelmassimo, though, Cramm recalled, one subject was taboo—the plot against Hitler. After dinner, which was cooked by an invalid German soldier, they moved into the living room. The four younger men usually played cards, but Senger never joined them. After an hour or so he would get up, bow slightly, and murmur, "I wish you all a good night, gentlemen." Then he would go to his room and read for an hour or two. Unless, of course, they were showing *Der Weisse Traum* (The White Dream). This was a movie that they had gotten on loan and were able to keep when the loan records were destroyed in a bombing. Even after they had shown it a dozen times, Senger still loved to see it. On the evening of his birthday, Cramm said to him around ten o'clock: "Herr General, a small surprise for you. Come with me into the next room." There the projector had been set up, and Senger saw *Der Weisse Traum* one more time.

Cramm accompanied the general on his frequent tours of inspection. "Tomorrow we are going to drive out to take a look at [such-and-such] regiment," Senger would say in the evening, and at eight in the morning they set out in the open Volkswagen jeep, the driver in front, Cramm sitting next to Senger in the back with a pistol in his lap. The jeep would take them as far up into the mountains as it could go. Senger would set off on foot with his characteristic loping gait—more like a sailor than a soldier—and Cramm, though fifteen years younger, found it hard to keep up. Then riding back in the jeep from the frontlines Senger would talk about what they had seen. "That man is crazy, and what he says is nonsense, but still he is a good officer," he might say of the commander they had visited up on the ridge.

Often Senger wanted to relax and be entertained. Cramm's role was to distract Senger from his essentially tragic thoughts about the war with jokes and stories about boyhood pranks. Senger enjoyed spending time with the Italians, and often he would stop the jeep to talk with a group of peasants. It was, Cramm reflected, a strange war in a strange place: up there on the ridge men were fighting and dying in bitter cold, and a few miles away Italian peasants by the roadside were selling oranges. Senger and Cramm would fill the jeep with oranges for their colleagues at headquarters. Sometimes Senger would make a detour and stop to visit the Benedictine nuns at Veroli, 6 miles from Castelmassimo. He would ask about their needs and arrange for food to be sent to them. Cramm recalled that Senger more than once interceded at the request of a priest to try to save civilians taken hostage by the SS. These efforts were to win Senger a kind of immunity later on, when partisans began ambushing German officers: his jeep was never attacked.

This morning in early February Senger told his aide he had heard Major-General Ernst-Guenther Baade's 90th Division was being attacked by American tanks. "Come on, let's drive over and see if there's anything we can do to help," Senger said. Baade and Senger knew each other from prewar army days. They came from the same background of petty landowning aristocracy, shared intellectual interests, and both men and their wives were passionate horse lovers. In fact, Baade and his wife were international-class jumpers. Baade was notably eccentric in appearance and behavior. He liked to wear a Scottish kilt over his uniform, and instead of a pistol he sported a huge bone-handled dagger. Just before the war, when he was serving under Senger, Baade said, "I assume that in my service records, I must have been given the worst confidential report of any army officer." But Senger thought Baade had done an exceptionally good job of training his unit. That memory made him arrange to get Baade in his sector and then to put him in command of the critical front up on the Monte Cassino ridge.

Senger knew that the many anecdotes about Baade's eccentric behavior made him popular with the troops. The time Baade got an English prisoner to guide him through a minefield, and then rewarded the man with his freedom. His habit when returning from the frontlines of radioing to the enemy: "Stop firing. On my way back. Baade." In January Senger got a distressed call from an officer at headquarters who had heard that Baade had dined on Christmas with the English. Senger knew even Baade would not do that, though he did send New Year's greetings to English commanders he had fought earlier in North Africa. Some of Baade's messages had a serious purpose. When his division captured a number of Americans, Baade ordered their names to be radioed to their units the next night. "That's a great favor for mothers and wives and fiancées," he said.

Senger and Cramm went to Baade's bunker, a kind of concrete cylinder dug into a hillside on the road north of Cassino. Baade's bunkers were as distinctive as he was. It was his custom, like a marooned mariner, to leave in each bunker a letter in a bottle in which he informed posterity of the date of whatever battle had occurred, his name, that of his adjutant, and the name of his dog. Senger had been surprised on his first visit to the bunker to find that Baade had only two aides with him. When he asked Baade what help he had, Baade called a young soldier out of a corner of the bunker and said, "This is Count Arnim, my adjutant for the front positions." Arnim was the eighteen-year-old son of friends of Baade that he had taken under his protection. "Stuetzen over there answers the telephone, and that's all I need." Senger made no issue of the fact that Arnim at eighteen was far too young for the responsibility Baade said he was giving him.

In the bunker Baade kept a monk's cowl and a red dress. If he were ever threatened with capture Baade intended to escape disguised as a monk. The red dress was for young Arnim. "He looks like a girl anyway," Baade said. Baade had a morbid fear of capture. For many other career officers being captured by the Anglo-Saxons offered a graceful way out of the losing war in which they were trapped. Not for Baade. Though he was an Anglophile, the thought of captivity horrified him, and so he kept his disguise always close at hand.

This particular morning Baade was not at the bunker. He was up front, Senger was told, so Senger and Cramm got back in the jeep and went on toward the front. Baade was not at regimental headquarters either, but still farther forward. The jeep had to remain where they were, so Senger and Cramm got out and walked on. Senger was not surprised: Baade was known as a commander who liked to get up close to the fighting. Usually Senger disapproved of generals who spent too much time at the front; they lost control of their larger operations, he thought, and many of them were just showing off to impress Hitler. But Baade's style was well-suited to

177

the peculiar conditions of combat in these mountains, where it was so difficult for the commander to keep informed about the state of his men who were fighting up on the ridge.

They found Baade in the basement of a shattered farmhouse. He was peering through a binocular telescope so intently that he did not notice their arrival. Senger tapped Baade on the shoulder. Baade jumped when he saw who it was, then saluted. "What's going on?" Senger asked. Baade said: "They're driving past us. See for yourself." He indicated the telescope. Senger looked through the telescope and saw, 1,500 yards away, about fifteen American tanks lumbering along like a herd of tame elephants. "What are you going to do?" Senger asked, and it was characteristic of him that he did not intervene in a decision that, according to German military doctrine, belonged to his subordinate. Baade grinned and said: "Nothing at all. They can only keep on going till their gas runs out, and then they'll have to stop. Or maybe they'll have turn back before that. As for me, there's nothing I can do, nothing at all!" Everybody laughed. Senger roared with laughter and he slapped his thigh time and again. There was nothing he could do either.

In his first days of command Baade had justified Senger's confidence in him. He rearranged the German positions up on the ridge so as to get the maximum defense from his limited resources in men, guns, and munitions, and the frequent presence up there of their flamboyant general raised the morale of soldiers suffering through the bitter mountain winter. Baade immediately saw the importance of Monte Calvario—Point 593—the summit of the winding ridge at the top of the Monte Cassino promontory. Point 593 changed hands several times in the early days of February, but each time they lost it the Germans kept on attacking, at Baade's insistence, until it was again in their hands. Baade thought the weakest point in the German defense was not around the monastery but at the other end of the promontory, where the Americans had taken Monte Castellone and were close to the Albaneta farm. Senger knew the area; a few days earlier he had climbed the hill to the Albaneta and had found the trail marked by the blood of wounded men. Baade won Senger's agreement to a counterattack with the objective of retaking Monte Castellone. It was not an easy effort to mount. The attack had no chance without a heavy artillery barrage, but by now the German forces were chronically short of ammunition. Baade's attack had to be

178

postponed from the ninth, when it was originally scheduled, while the gunners accumulated supplies.

Baade's counterattack, code named Operation Michael, started at 4:00 A.M. on February 12. It was accompanied by the heaviest artillery barrage the Germans had mounted during the Italian campaign. In the early morning dark two battalions moved forward across the bare slopes of Monte Castellone. It was bitterly cold. The Americans found that some of their weapons were frozen; one man was lighting matches to try to thaw out his machine gun. At first the attack by the Germans was successful—they captured the near slopes of Monte Castellone. The Americans were in disarray: the German artillery had severed their telephone lines, and no one knew just what was going on.

Later in the morning, after sunrise, the Germans were struck by a double disaster. Now the attackers up on the slopes were being cut down in droves by their own artillery. Because the forward observers could not properly operate the Italian radios they were using, and because the German guns were worn out and inaccurate, the Germans could not correct their fire and the artillery kept on shooting at their own men. And the Americans in front of them now were holding firm and methodically shooting down the attackers exposed on the bare slopes. An American officer noted after the battle how many of the German dead were shot between the eyes and concluded that the strain of combat on the ridge had quickly turned the Americans into veterans.

At noon Baade called off the attack. The Germans had lost almost all the ground they had briefly gained. They left at least one hundred fifty dead men, most of them killed by their own artillery, on the slopes of Monte Castellone. The Germans were learning the same lessons that the terrain had been teaching the Americans: up there the defense has an immense advantage, and artillery is as likely to hit your own men as the enemy. Not only had Operation Michael been a fiasco, it had also been unnecessary. The Americans had no plans to attack in the area of Monte Castellone.

The next day, February 13, the German regimental commander sent an English-speaking officer to ask the Americans for a truce in which the Germans could pick up their dead.

43

The air support officer of the American II Corps was Captain George Walton. His job was to set the bomb safety line, the line beyond which bombing was forbidden because of the proximity of American troops. As long as American soldiers were on the Monte Cassino ridge, Walton was primarily responsible for deciding what could be bombed in the vicinity of the monastery.

According to his postwar recollection, Walton had set the bomb line so that the abbey was included within the forbidden zone. As Walton told it, when Freyberg first brought up the idea of bombing Monte Cassino, General Keyes—to whom Walton was responsible—had said that his air support officer would not move the line, "unless I give him a direct and written order, which I am not about to do." Walton wrote:

> Terrific pressure was brought on me to change my position during this period. . . . I was told that the President of the United States and the Prime Minister of Great Britain wanted that abbey bombed and here an obscure captain like me was holding it up. But so long as Clark and Keyes were tacitly encouraging me to hold on, I refused to change the line. Finally, even they had to give in. II Corps elements in front of the abbey were relieved in a few days by New Zealand troops, and this permitted Freyberg to set his own bomb line.

None of the other actors in his recollections, written or oral, described the bomb safety line as figuring in the decision. But the records of II Corps show that at midnight on February 12, the day of the decision, Captain Walton reported that the "mission was scheduled for some time after noon February 13, that the BSL [bomb safety line] was garbled but that the trace appeared to be our front line."

At 8:10 A.M. on February 13, the 34th Division reported to II Corps: "Our air officer has coordinates of bomb line given by NZ Corps. That bomb line in one place is on our troops, will have to be changed. They also request bombing of the Abbey but don't think General Ryder [commander of the 34th Division] will approve as it's too close to our troops. Bomb line is also too close. He has talked to General Keyes about it." At 8:40, Ryder himself said to II Corps: "Make clear with air force that I will not accept that bombing. I am in command of this sector and will not permit any other bombing than what I put out myself."

At 10:50 A.M. II Corps got word that "Mission on Ab called off" —the postponement requested by Freyberg late the night before.

Sometime during that day Freyberg went to Fifth Army headquarters at the mountain town of Presenzano to discuss the timing of the bombing and of the Indian Division assault on Monastery Hill. The decision to bomb was definite—it had been confirmed that morning by Alexander—but the timing was not. The Indian preparation had been slower than planned: it was snowing heavily that day, to add to the obstacles of terrain and the Germans, and some of the Indian Division had been diverted to help the Americans repel the German counterattack on the previous day. In the early morning hours their attack had been put off for the second time.

That the bombing of Monte Cassino was imminent was announced that day to the world. In Algiers, headquarters of the Allied Mediterranean command, a spokesman told the press that it "might" be necessary to attack the abbey because the Germans not only were using it as an observation post but had turned it into a fortress.

The Germans, for their part, were making what propaganda they could out of the Allied air offensive over Europe. That same February 13, according to a German broadcast monitored by the Allies, a Nazi propaganda official said in a speech that "our enemies have unleashed an air war against cultural monuments which are the eternal heritage of all humanity. The U.S. and Britain no longer even try to hide their anticultural intentions, but quite openly propagate in their newspapers the destruction of all cultural monuments." But, the official said, efforts to smash Germany's cultural institutions were hopeless because bombed-out theaters resumed without delay in new quarters and concerts were held shortly after even the heaviest attack.

FROM THE MONKS' DIARY

FEBRUARY 13

At 3:45, *pie obit in Domino d. Eusebius Grossetti, monachus et sacerdos Montis Casini. R.I.P.* The acute abdominal pains from

181

which he was suffering yesterday evening continued in the night and morning. At 1:00 P.M. he suddenly got worse. The abbot was called. I got him ready to receive the Sacraments; he understood what I told him; he nodded that he wanted to receive the Sacraments. The abbot administered extreme unction and immediately after gave the blessing of San Mauro. The abbot imparted the apostolic absolution *in articulo mortis* and recited the prayer of the dying. We monks were around his bed: the only ones missing were three lay brothers who were outside; we could not go out to call them because of the artillery fire. He died quietly. Quite likely he contracted the illness that took him to his grave because of the aid he gave to the sick. At 4:15, Sunday vespers. The body of dom Eusebio was dressed in his monk's habit and rested in the second corridor of the refuge. ... Taking turns during the night, we stood vigil over his corpse.

That day an unusual visitor called on General Alexander at his headquarters down at the great ornate palace in Caserta. The visitor's voice was urgent and his hazel eyes burned under black brows and shaven skull. Lieutenant-General Wladyslaw Anders, 61, was a man of passionate resolve—he had to be to have made his way from a Soviet prison cell to Italy and the palace at Caserta.

Anders led the Polish Corps of 50,000 men who were the latest exotic addition to the polyglot Fifth Army. He and his men had emerged from a world of nightmare unimaginable to the Westerners around them. They came from an Eastern Europe that two monstrous tyrants between them had turned into a place of torment and slaughter such as the world had never known. In their homeland, Stalin had done his worst during the twenty months he ruled half the country, and the Nazis were now staging an unforgettable demonstration of the principles on which they based their rule of those they conquered.

All the Poles now in Italy had suffered under either Hitler or Stalin, and some under both. Anders himself had fought both his nation's enemies in the brief battles of 1939. A career officer, he had led Polish troops at Warsaw in losing combat against the German invaders. The Russians then attacked the Poles from the rear, and Anders was wounded and captured by these second invaders. Anders was taken to a windowless cell in the Lubyanka prison in

Moscow. He was held there for almost two years.

In August 1941, Anders was taken from his cell and brought before Lavrenti Beria, the chief of the Soviet secret police. After Hitler's June invasion of the Soviet Union, Stalin had agreed to the formation of a Polish army made up of men being held in his slave labor camps. Anders was to be its commander. This army of men, weak from hunger and mistreatment, gathered in tents on the steppes of Central Asia in the winter of 1941–42. After some time in Iran, the Polish Corps had arrived in Italy in December 1943.

The Poles were desperate to salvage something from the horror that had engulfed their homeland. Like the French in Italy, they were fighting to free their country from Nazi occupation. Unlike the French, however, the Poles could not count on the defeat of Germany to bring them freedom from foreign tyrants. The Poles had entertained the hope that perhaps after Rome fell the Allies would advance through Central Europe and get to Poland before the Russians. But Russian troops had already crossed the old Polish border, and at the Teheran conference in December Roosevelt and Churchill had effectively conceded postwar control of Poland to Stalin.

That day in the palace at Caserta Anders was discussing ways of getting reinforcements for his army. Anders told Alexander "that reinforcements would come over to us from the other side of the front, as all Poles who had been taken by force to serve in the German army would take the first opportunity to escape and join us." General Alexander agreed that all Polish prisoners of war should be transferred to separate camps.

A month later the Poles would enter the battle of Monte Cassino.

By the end of that day, February 13, some units of the Indian Division had installed themselves on top of the Monte Cassino ridge in the positions held by the Americans they were replacing. Lieutenant-Colonel J. B. A. Glennie, commander of the First Battalion of the Royal Sussex Regiment, had set up his headquarters in a small stone farmhouse on the ridge. From the farmhouse Glennie could look across a ravine at the monastery, 1,000 yards away but barely visible in the snowstorm. The Germans on the ridge were only 200 yards away.

The position of these newcomers to the corpse-littered ridge was precarious. The mule trains that brought them what supplies they got came over an exposed 7-mile route and were often cut down by German shellfire. The men were short of grenades and they were short of rations. In that bitter cold, they had, Glennie noted in his diary, "barely one blanket per man." While the Germans were ensconced in their caves, the men of the Indian Division had for protection only the shallow stone shelters scraped together by the Americans who preceded them. Such was the situation of the men who were supposed to conquer Monastery Hill.

44

"Let's go have a look," General Eaker suggested after a conference at the palace in Caserta. The generals had been discussing, not for the first time, whether the Germans were using Monte Cassino.

Eaker was an American, commander of the Mediterranean Allied air force, and as such the highest-ranking air officer in Italy and the Mediterranean. He had just been transferred from England, and he was unhappy about that. In England, Eaker had been the apostle of daylight "precision" bombing, the American alternative to the British night bombing that targeted entire cities and often missed them. Eaker had been moved out of England before he had time to prove his case in the skies over Germany.

In his new assignment, Eaker sent bombers from Foggia, the great air base in south Italy, to bomb targets in north Italy and Central Europe. Eaker had quickly found out that strategic bombing in Italy involved him in issues that did not apply when striking targets in Germany. On February 1, his British deputy, Air Vice Marshal John E. Slessor, had written him that he was "disturbed at reports of bombing Siena marshaling yards through overcast on Jan. 30. . . .

It would rightly cause serious bad impression if known at all widely." To bomb a target in the beautiful and historic town of Siena when the planes were blinded by clouds was not in keeping, Slessor thought, with the policy of avoiding damage to valuable sites if at all possible. "British Air Minister has previously been given impression we are trying our best in complicated business of avoiding such damage. Siena makes me a bit doubtful." As Slessor pointed out in a second message a week later, this was "most important from the point of view of repercussions in the House of Commons and Congress and in public opinion towards the air forces in Britain and America."

Eaker made his suggestion to "have a look" to another American, Lieutenant-General Jacob L. Devers. "Our recommendations will have more authority if we can say we looked down on that courtyard, if we see the radios in the abbey," Eaker said. Devers was deputy to General Wilson, the overall Allied commander in the Mediterranean. Devers had no part in the Monte Cassino decision, but he and Eaker had become close friends when they were both in England. The two generals went up in an L-5 Courier plane, the kind usually employed in running messages between headquarters. It seemed like a lot of brass to chance in a small plane, but in fact the risk was not great. The Germans on the ground did not usually fire at such planes for fear of giving away their locations, and the generals' flight was escorted by three fighter-bombers flying 1,000 feet above them.

As he recalled the event many years later, Eaker was certain before the plane took off about what he would find at Monte Cassino. Eaker had told Wilson and Devers that he was sure the Germans were using the monastery at least as an observation post. "Any soldier would know the Germans had to use it," he said.

The small plane flew over the Monte Cassino promontory at an altitude, Eaker recalled, of 1,200 to 1,500 feet. The weather had improved during the night, and the day—February 14—was clear and sunny. From his seat Eaker looked down into the cloisters of the horseshoe-shaped abbey and the robin's-egg blue of the cupola of the basilica. What he saw, as he later described it, was a radio mast that, he assumed, was used by soldiers manning an observation post to report what they saw; German uniforms hanging on a clothesline in the abbey courtyard; machine-gun emplacements 50 yards from the abbey walls. In this interview Eaker never said he saw anyone in a

German uniform, but of course "everyone went to cover" when the plane came over. On another occasion Eaker was quoted as saying: "We clearly identified German soldiers and their radio masts. I could have dropped my binoculars into machine-gun nests less than fifty feet from the walls." In response to a question, Eaker said he was certain the radio mast could not have been that of the meteorological station that had been operated at Monte Cassino until the previous fall.

The plane was over the Monte Cassino promontory for no more than ten minutes, Eaker recalled, and by noon of February 14 the generals were back on the ground. That afternoon they reported what they had seen at still another conference in the palace at Caserta.

45

For Lieutenant-Colonel Hal Reese, February 14 started at 5:30 A.M. in the village of Cervaro, in the hills across the Rapido Valley, where the 36th Division had its headquarters. The Germans had asked for a three-hour truce, from 8:00 to 11:00 A.M., to pick up the bodies of the soldiers they had lost in their costly attack two days earlier. Reese had been assigned to supervise the truce.

The moon was still up when Reese went out that morning to look for his jeep and driver. It was very cold. In the moonlight he could see the wrecked buildings of the village. As they drove across the Rapido Valley, they passed a group of filthy, exhausted American soldiers staggering slowly to the rear. Day was breaking, and to his left Reese saw the monastery gleaming white far up on its hill. He wondered when the Germans would start shelling the road they were traveling.

The jeep trail ended. They were at the foot of the Monte Cassino promontory, at its northern end, near the village of Caira, below the place where the Germans had been defeated. Reese told the driver to wait for him at a farmhouse now occupied by a medical aid station. He set out uphill on the mule path. It was 7:20. He had 40 minutes to reach the front, up on Monte Castellone, before the truce was due to start.

Reese followed the mule tracks—they looked like the marks of miniature horseshoes—in the thin soil that showed him the trail up the rocky mountainside. He passed soldiers trying to sleep in uncomfortable positions on ledges alongside the trail. Boxes of rations and ammunition littered the route, as did the gory, swollen bodies of dead mules. Three infantrymen manned a position in a stone shelter facing the enemy. Reese looked again and saw they were all dead. As he climbed he was stepping across the corpses of Germans and Americans alike. One dead German, lying on his back, had the bluest eyes Reese had ever seen.

Reese found the battalion commander looking across a valley, up on the ridge, where the battle had taken place. He was watching for a signal from the Germans. "There's one now, with a flag," he said. "See him? See him?" The Americans started down into the valley, the battalion commander carrying a small American flag. At a plateau they found two Germans with a Red Cross flag. A third German was watching from behind a bush.

Though his German was rusty from years of disuse, Reese found himself the interpreter for this strange and tense battlefield encounter. The Germans said an officer would be coming soon. Reese said that American Red Cross men would bring the German bodies down to this point; the battalion commander did not want the Germans climbing the hill to where they could observe the American positions.

The battalion commander went back up to his command post. Reese was alone with about twenty Germans, and more were peering out from the bushes. The Germans gathered around him and made conversation. One German said he was from Koblenz and remembered the American soldiers stationed there when he was a child, at the end of the First World War. Reese said he had been one of those Americans, and when the Germans were skeptical, he pulled out an old I.D. card with a picture of himself taken in Koblenz in January 1919.

ABOVE: General Clark, at right, with his chief of staff, Major-General Alfred M. Gruenther (left), and the Allied commander of the Mediterranean Theater, General H. Maitland Wilson. BELOW: Lieutenant-General John Harding, chief of staff to General Alexander, who relayed the crucial messages of February 12.

ABOVE: Major-General Ernst-Guenther Baade, commander of the German 90th Armored Infantry Division. BELOW: American and German soldiers on the Monte Cassino ridge during the brief truce of February 14. At right is Lieutenant-Colonel Hal Reese, with whose camera the picture was taken by a German soldier. The second of the three Germans at left is "Heinrich from Hamburg."

Soon they were all pulling out wallets and showing photos of parents and wives and children. Reese showed them his camera and suggested taking some pictures. The Germans agreed, and he snapped away. One of the Germans asked if he could get prints. Reese, stumped, finally suggested he could send prints through the International Red Cross if they gave him their home addresses. The Germans dug out scraps of paper and began to scribble.

Reese found himself chatting in his broken German to a red-haired, blue-eyed sergeant from Hamburg named Heinrich, who seemed to be the acting leader of the Germans. The American said he had heard that Heinrich's hometown had been destroyed by Allied bombers. "Propaganda," Heinrich said; his family had written that most of the city was still functioning normally. Reese found out Heinrich had been a railroad inspector. Reese, who had been in the railroad equipment business, told Heinrich he would give him a job after the war. Heinrich grinned confidently and said there would be plenty of work in Germany after the war.

The American officer watched the German stretcher-bearers at work. Most of them were very young and slight of build. They made a litter by cutting down two saplings and tying a blanket to them. Reese also tried to observe whatever might be useful to the battalion commander back up the hill. He noted two men with heavy packs going into a thick clump of trees about two hundred yards away, in the direction of Monte Cassino. But then Heinrich, smiling, moved in close and engaged him in conversation as if to end his observation.

Time was running out. It was 10:30. Reese had only 30 minutes to get back behind the American lines before the truce ended and the killing resumed. The artillery was firing on both sides of them, and there seemed to be a lot of activity over near Monte Cassino. Reese shook hands with the sergeant and said he would see them all in Berlin after the war. Then he started back out of the strange interlude he had experienced.

"Come back, Colonel," a German called to him. "Here is an officer who wishes to speak to you in English."

The officer, a heavy-set man with a pleasant face, said in perfect English: "Could you please have the truce extended an hour? We will not have all the bodies removed by eleven o'clock."

Reese said he had no such authority but would try to get a message to headquarters. The request was shouted back up the hillside from one American to the next, then telephoned to headquarters, where General Walker agreed to an extension of 30 minutes. The news was shouted back the same way.

Reese shook hands with the German officer and headed back for a second time. He and a sergeant who had joined him decided to sit for a while on a rock to let the Germans know that in their minds the truce was still on. Reese surveyed the scene. A small plane was flying lazily over their heads. In the distance he saw two Spitfires on patrol. An occasional bullet ricocheted past the two men. Above them the towering peak of Monte Cairo gleamed in the sun. With its snow-covered slope above the brown soil, Reese thought the mountain looked like "a huge ice cream cone of vanilla and chocolate with the vanilla melting and starting to run down."

Reese borrowed the sergeant's field glasses and began to study the countryside ahead of them. He heard the ping of a bullet, then another, closer. The sergeant said: "Colonel, I think they're trying to let us know that they don't like us using those glasses on them." Reese's watch said 11:25: the truce would end in five minutes. In the valley the group of Germans was dispersing, disappearing into the bushes. Farther away Reese saw two groups of stretcher-bearers carrying their dead burdens down a narrow trail.

"Let's scram," he said.

The sergeant agreed and added, "You know, some kraut's watch might be fast."

They crossed a slope that took them out of sight of the Germans. Once he was behind the American lines, Reese heard a commotion behind him: it was a German soldier, hands raised, flanked by two Americans. The German, who seemed terrified, spoke to Reese in French. Reese agreed to take the prisoner back and he went down the hill, skidding and slipping, the German in front of him. He found out the prisoner was from Alsace, had been drafted six months ago, and had a brother fighting with de Gaulle. Reese turned the prisoner over to a military policeman to be taken to a prisoner-of-war enclosure.

It occurred to Colonel Hal Reese that this day, February 14, was Saint Valentine's Day.

The truce brought repercussions among the German brass. The regimental commander who requested the truce had not sought the required permission from his superiors. When news of the truce reached Berlin, the army command demanded an explanation—

Hitler detested truces. General Baade covered for his subordinates. He explained that the truce had been requested by the Americans. This was transparently untrue; the Americans had possession of the field of battle, so they had no need of a truce to pick up their dead. But Baade's cover story was allowed to stand. Two days later, in fact, the German press chief, Otto Dietrich, stated in Berlin: "It wasn't the Germans who asked for a cease-fire, but just the reverse. The American troop commanders were forced to ask the Germans for a three-hour cease-fire in order to bury their thousands of soldiers who had bled to death before the German lines."

46

The men of the Fifth Army Combat Propaganda Team could turn out a leaflet on very short notice. Some leaflets conveyed news that, it was hoped, would sap enemy morale; a common leaflet was a safe-conduct pass intended to encourage enemy soldiers to desert. Once the message to be delivered across the enemy lines had been approved by the chief of staff, General Gruenther, the text was translated and the leaflet was put into production by the team's mobile unit. It was composed on a Linotype and printed on a Crowell press, both of which were carted around Fifth Army territory on a giant captured German tank-carrier. The mobile press could turn out four-by-six-inch leaflets at a rate of 8,000 per hour.

The leaflets would be delivered by the artillery. The men of the propaganda team removed the smoke canister from a smoke-producing shell. They stuffed each shell with about seven hundred and fifty leaflets, put the ejection charge back in, and screwed the base of the shell on. When the time fuse was set—depending on the range—the propaganda broadside was ready to go. A leaflet shell had a range of about twelve thousand yards. The ejection charge forced the leaflets out, and, according to the army manual:

> When the shell is observed to burst, there is a small puff of black smoke . . . and a cloud of leaflets about five times the size of the smoke puff. The leaflets appear as a thin white vapor which sometimes flashes in the sun. They settle slowly to the ground. With a light breeze, if the leaflets leave the shell at a height of 300 to 400 feet, the area covered by the leaflets is approximately 150 yards in diameter. . . . Once grounded, the leaflet may be read easily. The dangers incurred in moving in the slightest degree on the battlefield make it highly desirable to get the leaflets directly on the enemy position. The ideal case was that of a German soldier from the 44th Infantry Division who had a leaflet delivered into his foxhole announcing the landings near Rome.

At 1:00 P.M. on February 14, a battery of American 105-mm howitzers located in the Liri Valley fired 25 rounds of leaflet-stuffed shells into the skies over Monte Cassino. The message was printed in both Italian and English. Headlined ATTENZIONE!, it read:

> Italian Friends,
>
> ### BEWARE!
>
> We have until now been especially careful to avoid shelling the Monte Cassino monastery. The Germans have known how to benefit from this. But now the fighting has swept closer and closer to its sacred precincts. The time has come when we must train our guns on the monastery itself.
>
> We give you warning so that you may save yourselves. We warn you urgently: Leave the monastery. Leave it at once. Respect this warning. It is for your benefit.
>
> ### THE FIFTH ARMY

Fulvio de Angelis and two other youths watched the leaflets drift down. They came to ground not far from the entrance of the *conigliera,* the passageway under the monastery in which a hundred or more Italian civilians had taken refuge. The youths ventured out and recovered several leaflets.

They took the leaflets to the monks in the monastery. It was now about 2:00 P.M. The monk Matronola delivered the leaflet to the old abbot in their shelter. The civilians were crowding in behind the monks and asking desperately what they should do. Young Fulvio suggested that they hang a lot of white sheets over the east wall of the monastery—the wall that faced the deep ravine and the Allied positions—and then come out in an orderly group in the hope of a cease-fire that would permit them to escape. Others said the Germans would just shoot them down as they had other civilians on similar occasions. The abbot advised them to get in touch with German soldiers who could inform their commanders.

A university student from Cassino, Nino Morra, volunteered to try. He and two friends set out from the rear of the monastery on the road that led to the hamlet of San Onofrio, where the Germans were, and to the Albaneta farm. They were carrying a white flag. But the three young men were soon forced back into the monastery; one of them later said the Germans had pointed a machine gun at them and ordered them back. A second attempt met the same rebuff. Inside the monastery the civilians milled around, frightened and indecisive. The monks finally told them that each person must do what he thought best for himself. But no one knew what that was.

47

The units of the Indian Division up on the Monte Cassino ridge were still having trouble readying themselves to attack. Supplies were lacking, two needed battalions were still miles away, and, worst of all, the crucial Point 593—Monte Calvario—remained in German hands. The commanders on the ridge decided that they would have to take Point 593, the summit of the ridge that led to the abbey, before they could attack Monastery Hill.

At 11:00 A.M. on February 14, the attack on Monastery Hill was put off till the night of February 15–16. A few hours later the Indian Division sent word to General Freyberg that the attack could not be made before the night of February 16–17. Point 593 would be attacked, and presumably captured, before the attack on the monastery.

The Indian Division that day put out a planning note based on the assumption that "the monastery and the enemy defenses around it would be bombed heavily" late on February 16. The troops would have withdrawn behind a line 1,000 yards from the monastery before the bombing. Attached to the planning note was a document called a "pro forma" in which the Indian Division planners specified what they expected in the way of bombing.

The first priority target was the abbey, which was to be hit with the "heaviest possible weight of demolition bombs, as late on the afternoon of February 16 as considered advisable," with the object of "reduction of the Monastery to ruins." Under "remarks" it was noted that "Reports up to February 14 indicate Germans are living in the building including the cellar."

Secondly, the planners asked that "15 percent of air attack available other than demolition bombs" be aimed at "enemy mortar and machine-gun posts beside abbey wall" and that this bombing "continue until dusk." Finally, they asked that "incendiary and smoke bombs" be dropped on the abbey and nearby woods "to prevent the enemy from reorganizing his defenses." This bombing was to be started when "smoke would no longer affect carrying out of other tasks and maintained until dusk."

Late that afternoon Brigadier Dimoline, who had replaced the hospitalized Tuker as commander of the Indian Division, spoke to Freyberg by telephone. He informed his superior of the new schedule, and Freyberg does not appear to have made any objection.

Each of the monks had packed a small suitcase with his meager belongings. In the abbot's small room the monks recited, as they always did, the matins and the lauds.* The old abbot, weeping, charged Matronola with asking the forgiveness of the absent members of his community. The monks ate their dinner in silence. Each was alone with his thoughts about the supreme moment that was approaching.

Around sunset young Fulvio de Angelis was back in the *conigliera.* As far as he knew, nothing had happened. Everyone—the monks and civilians in the monastery, his family and the others huddled in the passageway—was waiting passively for the blow to fall. Fulvio stood at the entrance of the passageway and "shouted to the four winds in German that someone should come to the abbey and tell us to evacuate."

From the window of the monks' refuge, above the *conigliera,* Matronola heard the young man screaming. Matronola called down and told the distraught youth that the student Morra had finally succeeded in speaking to two German soldiers by one of the abbey's outlying buildings. The Germans said that their officer would come to their post at ten o'clock but that the Italians could not see him until five o'clock the following morning. They had said the monk who spoke German—Matronola—should come accompanied by only one other person. If more came, the Germans said, they would shoot.

Mark Clark had two visitors the day of the 14th who discussed Monte Cassino. One was the French general Alphonse Juin, who stopped by Clark's command post in the mountains to say he was opposed to the bombing. Clark's other visitor stayed for dinner. He was Colonel Patrick J. Ryan, Catholic chaplain of the Fifth Army. The priest also knew the bombing was scheduled for the next day. Over dinner, Ryan wrote later, Clark said he had argued against the bombing: "He wanted me to know, so I could refer the matter to Cardinal Spellman [the politically powerful archbishop of New York]."

That evening General Freyberg called Dimoline, the commander of the Indian Division, and gave him some dismaying news. The bombing of Monte Cassino, which Dimoline had expected late on the 16th, about 48 hours away, would take place the following morning,

---

*It was customary in teaching monasteries to recite the morning hours the evening before in order to free the monks for their school duties.

in about 12 hours. Could Dimoline move up his attack accordingly?

Freyberg was acting in response to information he had gotten earlier during a visit to Fifth Army headquarters. He was told that the forecast was for clear weather around Monte Cassino on the morning of the 15th, but that clouds would move in around noon. Freyberg was also told that all or almost all Allied airpower would be preempted for Anzio starting on the 16th, when a German counterattack was expected. The combination of the forecast and the requirements of Anzio left only the following morning when both bombers and the clear skies they needed would be available.

On the telephone Dimoline went over his reasons for postponing the attack and explained why moving it up at the last minute would drastically reduce its chances of success. His arguments made no impression on Freyberg. In the opinion of General Kippenberger, the commander of the New Zealand Division, Freyberg was not paying much attention to what Dimoline had to say. "Poor Dimoline was having a dreadful time getting his division into position," Kippenberger wrote later. "He got me to make an appointment for us both with General Freyberg, as he thought his task was impossible and his difficulties not fully realized. The General refused to see us together: he told me he was not going to have any soviet of divisional commanders." The self-confident, acid-tongued Tuker might have forced his point of view on Freyberg, but Dimoline, new in his job, was in no position to stand up to the massive man with the massive reputation.

Freyberg told Dimoline that "the bombing had been put on at their [the Indian Division's] request, that if we cancelled the programme now we would never get the air again and that this delay from day to day was making us look ridiculous." He told Dimoline to tell him within half an hour whether he could withdraw his troops to the 1,000-yard safety line and advance the attack on the Monastery Hill. Dimoline said he could not do either.

At this point, then, the logic of the bombing had come unstuck. Its premise had always been that the infantry would attack immediately after the last bombs fell, before the dazed Germans could reorganize themselves to take advantage of the ruins. Since the Indian Division's plan was to attack at night—to attack by daytime was considered sheer suicide—the bombing had to be in the late afternoon. But now the monastery was to be bombed in the morning,

195

followed by no infantry attack at all. That night the Indian Division was scheduled to attack, not the bombed monastery, but Point 593, which was not scheduled for any bombing. The monastery was not due to be attacked till the next night or the night after that.

Only one man both knew that the plan had lost its logic and had the power to do something about it. That man was General Freyberg. But Freyberg made no effort to postpone the bombing till a time when the Indian Division was ready to do its part. Freyberg's failure to act determined the course of the events that began the following morning.

At 10:46 that night, the apostolic delegate in Washington, D.C., sent a cable to the Vatican in which he reported that the American press was advocating the bombing of Monte Cassino "because it has become (so it is said) not just an observation post, but an enemy fortress." The delegate asked for more information so he could make a "new approach" to the United States government.

48

Matronola awoke very early on the fifteenth. He said mass in the monks' refuge, and then he prepared to leave the monastery for his promised five o'clock meeting with the German officer. At a few minutes before five, he asked the old abbot to give him his blessing. Before he could leave, Matronola was told that the officer was in the monastery with an armed soldier. Matronola escorted the officer— a lieutenant named Deiber, who was in command of the two tanks stationed near the monastery—to the refuge to meet the abbot.

Matronola, the only monk who spoke German, then translated the leaflet dropped the previous afternoon for the lieutenant. Speaking for the abbot, who sat by in silence, Matronola asked the lieutenant to allow the monks, and only the monks, to cross the lines to the Allied side. He reminded the lieutenant that the German command had said the monks could await the coming of the Allies, and he assured him that among the monks there were no spies who would reveal German positions to the enemy. He asked that the civilian refugees in the abbey be allowed to go to the rear of the German lines.

The German lieutenant dismissed the leaflet as nothing more than propaganda designed to frighten the monks. (Similarly, refugees later said a German guard told them the leaflets were *"scheiss"* and advised them to stay.) The lieutenant said the Germans could permit no one to cross the lines, and that if the refugees ventured outside, they could expect that a good third of them probably would be killed by gunfire on the road. But, Lieutenant Deiber said, his commanding officer had arranged that the mule path that led down the mountainside into the Liri Valley, away from the fighting, would be open for the monks and civilians from midnight that coming night until five the following morning. He warned them to stick to the mule path itself; if they tried to go down the main road that wound through the German defenses to Cassino town the Germans would have to fire on them.

Matronola pleaded that midnight might be too late, but the German officer had nothing more to say. On his way up the stairs from the refuge the lieutenant asked Matronola if he could visit the basilica. It was still dark inside, and the officer lit his flashlight for a brief look around before leaving the monastery.

Refugees gave an account different from Matronola's of what happened in those early morning hours. Two groups of refugees told their stories to Allied reporters a few days later. They said that on the evening of the fourteenth, after the leaflets, they had been told the Germans would let them leave the next morning before six o'clock. But when dawn came the Germans forbade them to leave, locked the gate, and stationed guards with two machine guns outside to prevent anyone from escaping.

Matronola reported to the other monks what the German officer had told him. He suggested they tell the civilians once more that each should do what he thought best. Tension between the refugees and the monks was running particularly high since they had seen the leaflet. Some of the refugees had been virtually without food for more

197

than two weeks. They knew the monks would have liked to be rid of them, but they had no place to go. Now, according to what Matronola heard, some of them were saying the monks had arranged for the leaflet as a way of driving the refugees out of Monte Cassino.

At about 8:30 that morning the monks gathered in the small room in their refuge, below the northwest wing of the monastery, that they had arranged as a temporary chapel. There, before the altar with the Madonna they had brought from Saint Benedict's tomb, they recited the psalms and prayers of the divine office. They moved to the room occupied by the abbot to continue their devotions. On their knees they were reciting the Marian antiphon, *Ave, Regina Caelorum*. They had come to the phrase *"Et pro nobis Christum exora"* when above them they heard a sudden tremendous explosion.

49

The Second Bomb Group flew from a field just outside Foggia, the great air center in southern Italy where the Allies' strategic air forces were now located. The fliers were camped out in an olive grove, and they had improvised a club, PX, and theater inside some man-made caves.

After the usual breakfast of powdered eggs, the fliers gathered in their group headquarters. It was 5:45, late for a briefing, but the mission of the fifteenth would be unusually short. The group operations officer, standing by an enlarged photo of the target, told them its location, how they would travel, and what enemy opposition they should expect to meet. He told the fliers to be particularly careful in their aim because American troops were very close to the target. An intelligence officer then told them why this target was being attacked:

The target is a huge ancient monastery which the Germans have chosen as a key defense point and have loaded with heavy guns. It is located about one mile West of Cassino on a hill and stands out as a perfect target for heavy bombers. Those crew members who have served through the African campaign will remember how we did not bomb mosques because of the religious and humanitarian training all of us have received from our parents and our schools. Because of that and because the Krauts and the Eyties know this they lived in these mosques. They knew we would not bomb these places. The Germans are still capitalizing on this belief in our avoiding churches and hospitals. In the past few days this monastery has accounted for the lives of upwards of 2,000 American boys who felt the same as we do about church property and who paid for it because the Germans do not understand anything human when total war is concerned. This Monastery *MUST* be destroyed and everyone in it as there is no one in it but Germans.

Two fliers who attended other briefings recalled, years later, that they were told anyone who had religious scruples could refuse to fly the mission against Monte Cassino. At the briefing for the Second Bomb Group, however, the group mission leader, Bradford E. Evans, a 25-year-old major, heard no such offer. Nor did Evans later remember feeling any special emotion when the target was announced; Evans had flown on two missions against Rome itself, and neither he nor his fellow fliers had reacted then to the nature of their target. He thought any qualms the fliers might have had about deliberately bombing a monastery had been allayed by what the intelligence officer had told them. Their primary concern that day was about the risk of hitting their fellow Americans on the ground around Monte Cassino.

Evans was due to lead a flight of 37 B-17s, the four-engined bombers known as Flying Fortresses. These were the big strategic bombers usually sent against targets far from the field of combat. Most B-17s that day carried twelve 500-pound demolition bombs. Evans's group was only the first of four. All told, 144 B-17s were scheduled to drop their bombs on Monte Cassino. Nor was that all —they were to be followed later in the day by 86 medium bombers.

This was by far the largest concentration of bombers that the Allied air forces had ever sent against a target as small as a single building. It was also many times more than the 36 fighter-bombers General Freyberg had requested in his telephone call three days earlier. Who caused this enormous escalation, and why, has never been explained. In theory, the diversion of the B-17 strategic bombers from their usual missions would require an order from the overall Mediterranean commander, General Wilson, to the air commander, General Eaker. In an interview years later, Eaker said that Wilson did in fact order him to use the strategic bombers against Monte Cassino. But there is no record that Wilson even participated in the decision to bomb the abbey, much less in the details of its execution, and Eaker's British deputy did not think Wilson "felt all that strongly" about the whole Monte Cassino business.

It is tempting to believe that the American advocates of daylight precision bombing saw in Monte Cassino an opportunity to show the world—and their British rivals—the accuracy of their bombers. But Eaker himself said, though only much later, that he would have preferred to use lighter bombers and to rely on smoke bombs to blind the German observers in the monastery. Mark Clark had said to Alexander after the decision was made: "If you say to do it, we will, but not in a small manner. We'll give it everything we've got." But Clark did not have the authority to order the use of the strategic bombers and, in fact, there is no evidence that he participated in the execution of the bombing after the decision had been made.

Bomber 666, piloted by Bradford Evans, took off at 6:55 A.M. The next hour and a half was occupied by what was called the "rendez-vous"—the complex process of getting all the bombers aligned in the skies over Foggia in the formation they would keep to the target. As they circled into position, Evans took note of the landscape below. It was his forty-seventh mission, so the sights by now were familiar. Not much detail could be seen from 20,000 feet, but Vesuvius was clearly visible, and so were the Bay of Naples and the isle of Capri. Evans flew up the peninsula above the snowcapped Abruzzi, searching for the "initial point," a highway intersection just north of a distinctive bend in the Volturno River. From the initial point the bombers were supposed to proceed without altering their course or speed or altitude till they reached the target. Evans saw that they were too low, so he led his group in a huge 360-degree circle that brought them up to 21,000 feet.

The B-17s flew straight up above Route 6, above San Pietro and

200

Million-Dollar Hill, covering in minutes the route that had taken the Fifth Army so many bloody months on the ground. As bomber 666 approached the Liri Valley at an airspeed of 155 miles per hour, Bradford Evans noted the great white peak of Monte Cairo at the northern end of the Monte Cassino promontory. Clouds hovered to the north and to the south, but over the promontory the sky was clear and the sun was shining. The monastery was clearly visible, resplendently white, all alone on its mountaintop. It was a good day for bombing.

Now bomber 666 was essentially under the control of its bombardier, First Lieutenant James W. Harbin. Harbin and Evans had been chosen to lead the mission because of their record for accuracy on previous bombings. Harbin's job was particularly important because the 36 planes following his would drop their bombs according to his judgment: if he missed, so would they. Evans kept his eyes glued to a dial on his panel called the Pilot Directional Indicator, on which the bombardier signaled the course he wanted. The pilot meanwhile kept the speed and altitude constant.

Evans felt bomber 666 lift slightly in the air. He knew what that meant: the plane had lost the weight of its bombs. The bombs had been dropped. He moved out of the cockpit to watch them plummet toward their target. It was 9:28 A.M.

50

They had begun gathering early in the morning from all over the territory held by the Allies. Practically everyone in the Fifth Army, it seemed, had heard something was going to happen that day at Monte Cassino. Dozens of reporters were on hand. "This was,"

John Lardner wrote in *Newsweek*, "the most widely advertised single bombing in history."

A holiday atmosphere prevailed among the soldiers. For almost all the men of the Fifth Army, this Tuesday was a very rare day off from the war. Soldiers all over the Liri Valley and in the hills to the south scrambled for positions from which they could watch what was to come. Some stood on stone walls, others climbed trees for a better view. Observers—soldiers, generals, reporters—were scattered over the slopes of Monte Trocchio, the hill that faced Monte Cassino 3 miles away across the valley. A group of doctors and nurses had driven up in jeeps from the hospital in Naples. They settled themselves on Monte Trocchio with a picnic of K rations and prepared to enjoy the show.

Harold Bond, the American lieutenant whose mortar had hit the abbey a few days earlier, was with his platoon on the side of the Monte Cassino promontory. Their new position was about two thousand yards farther from Monte Cassino than they had been before, when they looked across a ravine at the abbey, but the building was still in plain sight. Bond remembered that the morning was unusually quiet: neither German nor Allied guns were firing much. After the incessant racket of the war, the silence was eerie. Everyone was waiting. Even up there the Americans had heard about the coming bombing.

The morning sun lit up the eastern face of the huge white monastery on the hilltop. The wind was blowing from the east. The trees around the abbey were scorched black and splintered from gunfire.

The great silvery B-17s appeared from the south, over the right shoulders of those watching from Monte Trocchio. "They flew in perfect formation with that arrogant dignity which distinguishes bomber aircraft as they set out upon a sortie," the English correspondent Christopher Buckley wrote. The motors of each bomber drew four white traces across the hard blue sky.

The first bombs as they fell looked to Harold Bond like a string of black stones. The monastery vanished in a sudden cloud of smoke —black smoke from the explosions, white from the flying debris— and the smoke was laced with jets of flame. Not until about fifteen seconds later did the watchers hear the explosions. The first bombs —those dropped by Bradford Evans's bomber 666—seemed to strike on and around the gate of the monastery.

The wind blew the smoke off to the west and the monastery

reappeared just before another salvo of bombs dropped, and the hilltop once more was shrouded from view. Each time the monastery emerged from the smoke the watchers could see the damage inflicted by the last set of bombs. The steeple and the robin's-egg-blue cupola of the basilica disappeared in the second salvo. Blue flames flared above the cloisters. The walls still stood, but now they were pocked and streaked with dark wounds.

All over the hills and in the valley soldiers cheered the bombers. "Touchdown!" one man shouted when the bombs hit squarely on target. A 21-year-old signalman from New Zealand, watching from the valley floor, recalled, "We acted pretty much like a group of chaps cheering on our favorite football team." An American anti-aircraft gunner shouted up to the skies: "Boy, oh boy, why didn't you do that weeks ago?" The members of Bond's platoon, watching from their foxholes on the hillside, all rejoiced as the bombs hit. One of them commented that the monastery "would be rebuilt with the pennies of American schoolchildren."

Some of the observers noted that not all the B-17s were scoring touchdowns. One of these was the commander of the strategic bombers, General Eaker. Eaker later said that he and his friend, General Devers, were lying on a rooftop on the far side of the Liri Valley. "Are those bombs going to land over there?" Devers asked at one point. "I'm afraid not," Eaker had to answer. The bombs landed behind them among their vehicles, 3 miles from the target. For Eaker, at least, the day was by no means a perfect demonstration of high-level precision bombing.

Nor was it for Mark Clark. The Fifth Army commander had stayed in his command post at Presenzano rather than go forward to watch the bombing he had tried to prevent. Presenzano was 17 miles away from Monte Cassino, but it lay beneath the flight path of the B-17s, and sixteen bombs exploded only yards away from the trailer in which Clark was doing paperwork.

The blasts rattled the doors and windows of the Italian mansion at Castelmassimo that General von Senger was using as his head-quarters. The men inside heard a mighty series of explosions. "What the devil was that?" one officer shouted. The general knew what it was. According to his aide, Senger kept saying over and over: "The idiots! They've done it after all. All our efforts were in vain."

February 15, 1944. ABOVE, LEFT: An American Flying Fortress bomber over the Abbey of Monte Cassino. ABOVE, RIGHT: The first bombs plummet toward the abbey (directly below). OPPOSITE, TOP: The Abbey engulfed by the smoke of bombs exploding on and around it. OPPOSITE, BOTTOM: Abbot Diamare's statement, in the German text written by Matronola, attesting that there were no German soldiers in the abbey. The statement is also signed by the German lieutenant Deiber.

Ich bescheinige auf Wunsch, dass sich im Kloster von Montecassino kein deutscher Soldat befand oder jetzt befindet.

15. 2. 1944

+ Gregorio Diamare

Vescovo-Abate di Montecassino

Senger and his aide, Captain von Cramm, drove down the Liri Valley in the open Volkswagen jeep to the bunker that General Baade used as his headquarters. From there they could see, about five miles away, the hill on which stood the abbey of Monte Cassino. They watched the great building disappear in smoke each time the bombs struck.

The units of the Indian Division up on Monte Cassino ridge were far closer to the monastery than any other Allied soldiers. They looked along the curving ridge at the abbey from positions that were as little as 300 yards away. But they were also, it seemed, just about the only soldiers in the Fifth Army that did not know that Monte Cassino was going to be bombed that morning.

The diarist of a Punjabi unit wrote that about 9:30 they heard a sound and "We went to the door of the command post, a derelict farmhouse, and gazed up into the cold blue sky. There we saw the white trails of many high-level bombers. Our first thought was that they were the enemy. Then someone said 'Flying Fortresses.' There followed the whistle, swish and blast of the blockbusters as the first flights struck at the monastery. Almost before the ground ceased to shake the telephones were ringing." The highest-ranking Allied officer on the ridge, Brigadier O. de T. Lovett, wrote: "At that moment I was called on the blower and was told that the bombers would be over in 15 minutes. I started to blow up myself, but even as I spoke the roar drowned my voice as the first shower of eggs came down."

The B-17s dropped twelve bombs among the Indian Division troops crouched behind their makeshift stone shelters waiting to attack Monastery Hill. The bombs caused 24 casualties, none of them fatal. Most of the injuries were only bruises caused by flying pieces of rock. After the first wave of bombers had passed, a company of Sikh soldiers withdrew to safer ground, and the Germans radioed that "Indian troops with turbans are retiring."

The commander of the Indian Division had requested the bombing, but it was not working out at all the way he had wanted or expected. Colonel Glennie, the officer in charge of the coming attack on Monastery Hill, told his diary what he thought about the way the bombing was conducted: "They told the monks and they told the enemy, but they didn't tell us."

204

When they heard the first bomb strike home, the monks had gathered on their knees around their abbot. The old abbot, standing stoop-shouldered, gave them each absolution. The monks thought the end was at hand. They said a prayer for their passage from life to death and life everlasting.

The thick wall of the buildings around them shuddered with one huge explosion after another, explosions far greater than any the monks had experienced from the artillery fire that had been hitting the monastery almost daily for the last two weeks. The sound was so loud they stuffed wadding in their ears. Dust and smoke blew into the refuge through the narrow windows. Outside they could see the flash of bombs exploding next to the abbey walls. A deaf-mute who worked for the monastery burst white-faced and distraught into the refuge. He knelt by the monks and, with signs, conveyed to them that he had been in the basilica when the bombs started falling. Now their basilica was gone. The deaf-mute showed the monks the medal he wore on his chest and let them know it had saved his life.

Fulvio de Angelis, one of the youths who had gone out to pick up the leaflets, was with his family in the *conigliera* when the bombs began to fall. Because this passageway was under both the monastery walls and its foundation, it was relatively well-protected. After what seemed to Fulvio to be the third series of explosions—it would have been about 9:45—he and his family and some friends decided to flee the *conigliera*. Outside, they found dozens and dozens of other civilians rushing around in a daze without any destination. Fulvio's group fled through the abbey's gardens toward the mule path that led down the mountain. Now what Fulvio thought were phosphorus bombs—from their smell and the flames they caused—began to fall around them among the abbey's half-destroyed trees. Fulvio hurried on toward the mule path, but soon he came into the line of fire of a German machine gun. Trapped between the machine gun and the fire bombs falling around him, the youth gave up his attempt to escape and turned back toward the monastery. He struggled back through two more waves of bombing to where he had started out: the old rabbit warren under the foundations.

Starting at 9:30, the German 90th Division began radioing reports of the bombing to the headquarters of Senger's 14th Panzer Korps. The headquarters summarized these first reports in a telegram addressed at 12:15 to the Tenth Army, the next higher level of the German military organization:

> The 90th Panzer Grenadier Division reports that the Abbey Monte Cassino was bombed on 15 February at 9:30 by 31, at 9:40 by 34, and at 10:00 by 18 four-motor bombers. Damage still to be determined. In the monastery there are numerous civilian refugees. Notice of the attack was given by dropping leaflets with the justification that German machine guns were in the Abbey. Commander Cassino, Colonel Schulz, reports in this regard that the troops had not installed arms in the monastery. The divisional order, that in case of extreme danger the severely wounded were to be brought into the monastery, has not been used up to now.

The news reached Kesselring's headquarters within an hour of the bombing. At 10:30, his chief of staff, Major-General Siegfried Westphal, asked by telephone, "Has it done us any harm from a military point of view?" He was told by his counterpart at the Tenth Army, "No, because we were not occupying it."

After the four groups of B-17s had bombed the abbey—and the various other places they hit—reports began to come in to Fifth Army headquarters that "Germans" had been seen fleeing from the building. Lieutenant Herbert Marks of the Counterintelligence Corps, who was observing through a telescope from Monte Trocchio at a range of 4,000 yards, reported, "At 10:30 I saw 50–75 Germans run out of the entrance of the abbey into the courtyard." At 11:10 a message to the Fifth Army said: "Approximately 200 Germans seen evacuating monastery on road at southwest side after first wave. Taken under artillery fire."

An intercepted radio message seemed momentarily to provide evidence that the Germans were indeed in Monte Cassino. David Hunt, then an aide to General Alexander, told the story after the war. Shortly after the bombing began, he was handed a translation of the intercepted message that read: "Is battalion h.q. still in the monastery?" Hunt asked for the original text. It read: *"Ist Abt noch im Kloester?"* and the answer was *"Ja."* Abt was a common German military abbreviation for "battalion headquarters." But *Abt* also means "abbot," and Hunt realized it was being used in this sense when he saw that the message continued: *"Sind Moenche darinnen?"* (Are the monks in there?), to which the answer was *"Ja, ja."*

In Rome that morning, Tommaso Leccisotti hurried over to the Vatican from the monastery 5 miles away where he was staying. He was hoping to see Cardinal Maglione, the papal secretary of state. But Maglione was getting dressed to see the Pope, the monk was told, so instead he sought out the undersecretary, Monsignor Montini. Montini was not available either. He was in a long meeting with the abbot primate of the Benedictine order, Baron von Stotzingen, and they were discussing the possibility of sending a neutral observer to Monte Cassino. Apparently the German ambassador, Weizsaecker, was also at the meeting, and told the abbot primate that there were no German troops or military installations in the abbey or its "immediate surroundings." Leccisotti had to leave the Vatican without having seen either of the diplomats.

At about 11:15 the monks became aware of a lull in the bombing. They waited, fearful, but the silence continued. They realized all the members of their little community were unharmed. Matronola paced around the two corridors that made up the refuge and found that though the windows were shattered all the walls were intact.

The abbot said he wanted to go up and see what had happened to his monastery. Matronola escorted the old man up the stairs and out into the first cloister. They saw that the lower part of the abbey, the buildings surrounding the first two cloisters, was still standing. But, looking up the monumental stairs, they saw that the roof of the basilica was gone. The façade stood, but the entire vault behind it had collapsed, just as the deaf-mute had tried to tell them.

Civilians were milling around the cloisters. Many were injured, and the monks were told more had been buried under falling rock. A larger number had fled the monastery between bombs. Refugees later said that the Germans manning the machine guns trained on the gates to keep them inside had fled when the first bombs fell. The civilians had then succeeded in forcing the gate open so they could escape. Now three tenant farmers and their families pleaded to be allowed into the monks' refuge. Matronola told them the refuge was no longer safe, but the farmers would not listen and they and their families crowded into the small rooms of the refuge.

The abbot, having witnessed the destruction outside, said he wanted to go back to the refuge. Matronola went down the stairs with him; the younger monk stayed at the abbot's side all the time now. He helped the old man clean away the debris in his tiny room to make way for the sacred communion wine and wafers that the monk Agostino Saccomanno had gone to get from the sacristy. While the two monks were thus engaged, they heard a new explosion and the walls around them began to shake.

Medium bombers flew from bases on the island of Sardinia off the western coast of Italy. The 319th Bomb Group was stationed near the southern tip of the island, at Decimomannu, a onetime Luftwaffe base that was still littered with the wreckage of German planes and abandoned equipment of all kinds. The plane this group flew, the B-26 Marauder, was a two-engine bomber that carried four 1,000-pound bombs.

Twenty-two B-26s took off from Decimomannu at 10:57 A.M. The flight commander, Major Frank B. Chappell, later recalled that he had been especially careful at the briefing to explain to the flight crews why the monastery had to be destroyed. Twenty of the 22 planes reached Monte Cassino. One had returned early because of mechanical trouble, the other because of "pilot sickness." The sky was overcast, but the clouds cleared just as the planes approached their target. The B-26s dropped their bombs at 1:32 P.M. from between 10,500 and 12,000 feet. They encountered no anti-aircraft fire and none of the planes was damaged. Staff Sergeant Kenneth E. Chard, on board the lead bomber, recorded in his diary: "Target cabbaged real good."

At 1:50 P.M., after the last wave of bombers had left, an American observation post reported, "Can see white flags from East side of abbey." The message transmitting this news to the Fifth Army added, "II Corps not taking any action. May be laundry." It was on this side of the abbey that young Fulvio de Angelis had suggested the day before that they hang white sheets in the hope of getting a cease-fire that would allow the civilians to escape before the bombing. The abbot was quoted as saying three days later: "We laid out white cloths in order to say to them 'do nothing to us.'"

At 2:30, from his observation post on Monte Trocchio, Lieutenant Marks saw about two hundred civilians leave the abbey. He later said they "all went the same way the soldiers did [the 'Germans' he saw at 10:30], across the courtyard and down below the wall."

Matronola and the abbot huddled in a corner of the room to escape the fragments of stone and metal that were flying in through the slit of the window. After a particularly severe explosion, the building heaved and Matronola saw that the door of the room was blocked by fallen stone. He told the abbot as calmly as he could that they were now cut off. Through the walls they could hear the women and children of the tenant farmers screaming. They heard the voice of Agostino Saccomanno, who had just gotten back to the refuge from the sacristy when the bombs began to fall.

This bombing ended in about a quarter of an hour. Matronola called out from the isolated room asking for news of the others. Saccomanno called back that the others were safe and that the entrance to the refuge was usable although partly obstructed. Matronola now began to search for a way out of the room; if he could not find or make one, the room would be his tomb and the abbot's. He discovered that the stone of the walls did not extend all the way to the ceiling; the upper part of the separation was made up of a metal screen. Matronola succeeded in breaking the screen from his side. Because he was unusually tall and strong, he was able to lift the old abbot up through the hole where the screen had been and monks brought him down on the other side.

The monks now all fled their refuge with the suitcases they had packed the night before. When they emerged from the underground rooms they found a scene of devastation far greater than that created by the earlier bombing. They could hardly recognize their monastery. The cloisters and their colonnades were all smashed. Where the monumental stairs had led up to the basilica they saw only a jumble of fallen rocks. The upper floors of the surrounding buildings were in ruins. There was a crater filled with reddish liquid where the cistern had been. The statue of Saint Benedict still stood in the cloister, but it had been decapitated.

More of the refugees had been killed and wounded, the monks were told, and more of them had fled. But there were still hundreds of men, women, and children hiding here and there among the ruins and in underground passages that were intact.

The monks and a few civilians clustered around and asked the abbot what he intended to do. Diamare said he would stay with Matronola, the monk who was now his right arm, but, he repeated once again, the others—monks as well as refugees—should do as they thought best: he was no longer able to lead them. Five of the monks—half of those who had chosen in October to stay with their abbot—now said they could no longer bear to remain in the wreckage of their home. They had decided to try to escape as best they could. The other four monks said they would stay.

The monks saw that the *torretta,* the tower that had been built over the oldest part of the monastery, the cell where Saint Benedict lived and died, was still standing, though damaged, and that its entrance was passable. It was here, in an underground room, that the officer Schlegel had advised them to take shelter from bombing. The monks had chosen their other shelter because it was on the far side of the complex of buildings from the source of the Allies' artillery fire. Now the monks decided to change their place of refuge to the *torretta.*

Matronola told a monk to try to get their little store of supplies and bedding from the refuge they were abandoning. The monk was able to make two trips to the half-wrecked underground rooms before the wall collapsed and made entry impossible.

Now Matronola went to inspect the *torretta.* On the stairs, in its rooms, he found hundreds of civilians. Some were sleeping or nursing wounds; others sat in a daze; no one knew what to do. He heard someone screaming outside, and following the sound, he found a woman who had lost both her feet. He and some other men carried her into the *torretta.* The monks settled themselves in the chapel of the Pieta. They found a chair for the abbot; he sat silent by the altar. A monk who was running a high fever lay on a mattress. One of the monks who had left, Fra Pietro, had changed his mind and returned to be with his abbot. The deaf-mute was with them. They had some bread and cheese they had rescued from their other refuge, but, with the cistern destroyed, they had no water.

By 5:30 that afternoon all the fliers had safely landed their bombers at their bases at Foggia and Sardinia. They had encountered little anti-aircraft fire over Monte Cassino, and none of their aircraft was seriously damaged. The last two to return were two medium bombers whose pilots stopped in Naples for gas. For the B-17 fliers, the mission had lasted three hours and fifteen minutes. Bradford Evans remembered enjoying Red Cross coffee and doughnuts after the flight; another pilot recalled his "two ounces of whiskey." The fliers were questioned by intelligence officers at a "debriefing" right after they landed. The officers would put together the fliers' accounts with aerial photographs to determine what the bombing had accomplished. Evans recalled that his commanding officer, a "tough old codger," had told him, "Well, Evans, I guess you plastered the place."

In the four hours between 9:28 A.M. and 1:33 P.M., 239 heavy and medium bombers in eight attacks had dropped 453½ tons of bombs (66½ tons of which were incendiaries) on the Abbey of Monte Cassino. In this attack, as in so many during the course of the war, air officers made exaggerated claims about the amount of death and destruction accomplished by their bombs. The War Diary of Army Air Support Control reported that:

A heavy effort by strategic and tactical air forces was directed against [Monte Cassino]. In some cases our forward troops were only 600 yards from the aiming point but few casualties were reported and in view of the vast quantity of bombs dropped results were astoundingly accurate. Four groups of Fortresses and four groups of Mediums attacked the one target and were able to provide a remarkable spectacle for the many ground observers who were able to see that precision bombing is a fact and not merely an expression. This medieval fortress has been gutted and now lies in ruins. It is difficult to see how any of the occupants of the building could have survived the weighty attack.

In fact, of course, none of the monks was killed or even injured by the bombs. No one would ever know how many of the one to two thousand refugees in Monte Cassino were killed. The most careful estimate, by a local historian, is that about 230 civilians died in the abbey and that half of those lost their lives in the bombing. After the war 148 skulls believed to be those of civilians were found in the ruins, but the bones of others may never have been found, and, on the other hand, some of the dead may not have died on February 15. Other estimates have run up to several hundred. But all the estimates by those who were at Monte Cassino during or after the bombing agree that the majority of the refugees survived that day. In any event, the *only* people killed were among the civilians. There was never any evidence, then or later, that the bombs dropped that day killed a single German.

Those who witnessed the bombing of the abbey would look back on the day with varying emotions. The 21-year-old New Zealander who had cheered because, like most soldiers, he thought the bombs were hitting Germans later wrote: "Had we known that civilians were taking refuge within the precincts of the abbey I'm sure our reaction to the bombing would have been quite different, sorrow and compassion rather than elation."

For an English writer, Geoffrey Cox, the event was memorable as theater: "Only rarely in a whole war do you get the truly spectacular. You had it in the great air bombardment of Monte Cassino, for there the hills and the monastery and the ruined castle provided a truly theatrical backdrop."

One American, an artist charged with saving the work of other artists, found in the day's destruction a source of savage gratification. Sidney Biehler Waugh was, at 39, a noted sculptor. He was an army captain assigned—much against his will, he said—to the Monuments, Fine Arts and Archives staff. Waugh detested his work. He wrote his brother that it was run by "sentimentalists in uniform . . . who would gladly have held up the whole progress of the war to have saved some little remnant of their particular hobby, or who are really here to make up lecture notes for the first five years after their return to Princeton." Waugh claimed that the ban on bombing Monte Cassino was lifted "partly through my efforts." In his diary for February 9 he had written: "I honestly believe it is all the fault of that damned Abbey— of the sentimental criminals who cling to the idea of the holy church of Rome." After he had witnessed the destruction of Monte Cassino, Waugh wrote in his diary: "I can't remember anything I have seen or done that made me as happy as the sight of the abbey being blown off the top of the hill. . . . I loved to see the symbolic breakdown of the church and monument tradition."

Martha Gellhorn, one of the most talented writers to cover the war in Italy, looked back in rue: "I remember the actual bombing of Monte Cassino. I watched it, sitting on a stone wall or the stone side of a bridge, and saw the planes come in and drop their loads and saw the monastery turning into a muddle of dust and heard the big bangs and was absolutely delighted and cheered like all the other fools."

After dark, at about 8:00 P.M., the German lieutenant returned to the monastery. He had a message for the monks. What they understood him to say, as interpreted by Matronola, was as follows:

Upon the request of the Pope, Hitler himself was asking the Americans for a truce to evacuate the monks and civilians from Monte Cassino. The abbot and the monks, the wounded civilians and the children, all these would be transported to safety by the Germans, but first they would have to make their way on foot down the mountainside. The rest of the civilians would have to find their own way to safety. Kesselring would ask for the truce that same evening. They would have to wait till the next day or perhaps the day after that for the answer.

Lieutenant Deiber said he hoped the Americans would grant the truce; otherwise, the blame would fall on them. Matronola concluded from this that the Germans wanted to get the monks and civilians out so they could occupy the ruins for military purposes.

Deiber then asked the abbot if he would declare in writing that there were no German soldiers in the monastery at the time of the bombing. The old abbot readily agreed and wrote out a brief statement in Italian, which Matronola then wrote out in German. The abbot signed both copies "Gregorio Diamare, Bishop Abbot of Monte Cassino" on the altar of the chapel. The German officer countersigned both copies "Deiber, Lieutenant."

Matronola then sought out the civilians clustered around in the *torretta*. He told them about the truce and said it was the only hope for all of them. But the civilians said they did not believe him.

Matronola lay down on his mattress but could not go to sleep. Should they leave or should they stay? The decision was more up to him than anyone else. Even if the Americans granted the truce, how could the 79-year-old abbot make the journey on foot down the mule path, a distance of 4 miles of often difficult going? But if the monks stayed, how could they survive with all these sick and wounded people around them? Would they not just die slowly in the ruins of Monte Cassino?

At 9:45 in the evening, the British minister to the Vatican, Sir D'Arcy Osborne, cabled the Foreign Office in London what the Vatican had told him:

> On February 14th the German Ambassador to the Holy See transmitted to the Abbot Primate of the Benedictines the following statement: "German military authorities assert that the news of German defense works at Abbey of Monte Cassino are false. It is absolutely untrue that there are artillery, mortars or machine guns there. There are no large [*grossere*] troop concentrations there (in the neighborhood of the Monastery). Everything possible has been done to prevent Monte Cassino from becoming a traffic point [*durchgangplazt*]."

A similar statement reached the State Department in Washington the following afternoon.

President Franklin D. Roosevelt called a press conference at 4:06 P.M. In Italy the time was 10:06 P.M., more than twelve hours after the first bombs had fallen. By then the bombing had been reported on the radio and in the afternoon newspapers. Roosevelt said: "I was reading in the afternoon paper about the shelling of Cassino Abbey by our Fortresses. It is very well explained in the story that the reason it was shelled was because it was being used by the Germans to shell us. It was a German strongpoint—had artillery and everything up there in the abbey." He gave the reporters copies of Eisenhower's directive on the preservation of monuments in Italy, which had not previously been made public.

Sometime around one o'clock in the morning the monks and civilians in the monastery heard an enormous explosion in the *torretta*. Apparently it was a bomb with a delayed-action fuse. The blast filled the chapel in which the monks had taken refuge with dust and smoke, but none of them was injured. About an hour later four women clambered out of the monastery through a hole in the wall. They made their way in the dark along the ridge heading north from the abbey. They were trying to reach the home of the mother of one of the women. At around three o'clock they came across some Indian soldiers—they had succeeded in passing by the German positions.

214

The soldiers advised them to keep on going because their area was under shellfire. The four women kept on along the ridge until they encountered an American soldier who, after hearing their story, sent them to the 36th Division headquarters at Cervaro across the Rapido Valley.

During the night the Indian Division at last made its attack. What they attacked, of course, was not the hill on which the bombed monastery had stood, but Hill 593—Monte Calvario—the summit of the ridge that led to the monastery. Hill 593 had not been bombed except for the few bombs that had fallen there by mistake, and those fell among the Indians, not the Germans.

At noon that day, while the bombing was going on farther up the ridge, the commanders of the Indian Division had met in a farmhouse and decided they could not hope to take Monastery Hill—the objective they had been assigned—unless they first took 593. They so instructed Colonel Glennie, the commander of the Royal Sussex Battalion.

The attack Glennie had to plan was extremely difficult. Soldiers could not move around up there in daylight and survive, so the Royal Sussex had been able to learn very little about the terrain they had to cross. They did know the ground was hard and littered with loose stones, which would make it almost impossible to move silently in the dark. And Glennie knew there was no place he could safely concentrate any large number of men, and, had he been able to, there was no route along which they could advance together.

Glennie sent out only a single company of 66—63 soldiers and 3 officers. They had crept ahead for about fifty yards when the Germans opened up on them with deadly machine-gun fire. Groping around in the dark, the men of the Royal Sussex found that their way ahead was blocked by a deep gully that had not appeared on any of their maps. They were short of grenades, the fatal consequence of a 7-mile supply line along which the mules were constantly being killed by enemy fire. Dawn was approaching. It would be suicide to be caught out there in daylight. The attack was doomed.

The remaining men of the Royal Sussex withdrew. More than half of the members of that company—32 men and 2 of the 3 officers—had been killed or wounded.

51

With the first light almost all the remaining civilians fled the ruins. Young Fulvio de Angelis and his family took the mule path down the mountainside; others, like the four women who left in the dark, tried to make their way through the German positions up on the ridge. By early morning on February 16, there were only about forty people left in Monte Cassino: the six monks, the three tenant farmer families, and some orphaned or abandoned children and badly wounded people.

The monks were waiting for the truce that the lieutenant told them the Germans were requesting from the Allies. They tried in the wreckage to continue their usual rituals. In an upper hallway of the *torretta* where they had spent the night, they gathered to recite the divine office for the entire day. The monks were standing; a bitterly cold wind was blowing through the battered tower. The sound of explosions nearby drove them down the stairs and they finished their reciting at a landing under a fresco of Moses on the Mount with Aaron.

Abbot Diamare told Matronola to leave the ruins without him, as if he had guessed that the younger monk was wondering how the abbot could make the journey down the mountainside. Matronola refused, citing the part of Benedict's Rule that requires the monk to care for his abbot.

That afternoon the Allied bombers came back to Monte Cassino, but they dropped only a small fraction of the previous day's huge amount. Forty-eight fighter-bombers dropped 24 tons of bombs. This amounted to two-thirds of what General Freyberg had first requested. Apparently the monks did not notice that the bombs were anything different from the artillery fire that had been hitting the monastery all day.

The monks waited with decreasing hope for the German officer to return. In the evening they decided they were waiting in vain and that, as Matronola wrote, "we could hope for nothing from human beings."

At 11:20 that night the Indian Division attacked once again, and once more their objective was Point 593. Colonel Glennie noted in his diary that his Royal Sussex Battalion was not ready for what it had been ordered to do. They still lacked ammunition, information about the terrain, aerial photographs. But, Glennie recorded, they went ahead. "We had the superiority complex common to the rest of Fourth Indian Division," he wrote, "and we were not given to bellyaching." Again the Royal Sussex started out crawling through the terrible terrain that led along the ridge toward Monte Cassino. Again the Germans drove them back. This time the Royal Sussex had attacked in greater force, and twice as many men were killed and wounded. Some of them were struck down by the Allied artillery.

52

The monks debated what they should do. They were standing in an upper floor of the *torretta*. The early morning sunlight came through the gaping holes in the roof of the old tower. Matronola had led the abbot up there to show him how the rubble was weighing down on the ceiling of the little chapel in which the monks were staying.

Soon, Matronola said, the ceiling would collapse on their refuge. There was no place in the ruins for the monks to hide from the endless shelling and bombing. There was no hope the Germans would produce the truce they had promised. To stay in the ruins meant sure death. They had taken a vow to remain in this place all their lives, but, Matronola argued, since the house of Benedict had been destroyed they had no choice but to take the remaining civilians and leave. And the time was now, in the early morning lull in the artillery fire.

In the last moments before departure Matronola had to make life and death decisions about three small children abandoned by their father after their mother was killed in the bombing. The four-year-old girl was "in extremis"; she had only minutes to live, and to try to take her would only add to the agony of her end. Her brother screamed when Matronola tried to pick him up. Both his legs were gone; there was no hope for him either. The third child's legs were paralyzed, but Matronola thought he had a chance, so he asked another monk to carry him.

At 7:30 A.M. the procession began. The old abbot walked slowly at its head. He was carrying a big wooden crucifix, and under its weight his posture was more than usually slumped. Matronola—taller, more erect—walked at his side and helped the abbot over the barriers of rocks and shell holes. Behind them hobbled about forty monks and civilians, picking their way through the debris as they passed, at last, through the monastery gate. Men were using ladders as stretchers to carry the sick wife of a tenant farmer and the woman who had lost her feet. Matronola had told the civilians to spread out, in case they were fired on, but they clustered behind the abbot. As they walked, the monks recited the rosary and the civilians gave the responses.

> *Hail, Mary, full of grace; the Lord is with thee; blessed are thou among women, and blessed is the fruit of thy womb, Jesus. . . . Holy Mary, Mother of God, pray for us sinners, now and at the hour of our death. Amen.*

From the gate the abbot led them down the slope, gentle at first, on the south side of the monastery. They passed the ruined station of the funicular that had connected the monastery with Cassino town until a German pilot flew into it in October. On their left was the German strongpoint at the knob on the hill called Monte Venere, known to the Allies as Hangman's Hill. They started down the mule path of Saint Scholastica.

> *Glory be to the Father, and to the Son, and to the Holy Spirit. . . . As it was in the beginning, is now, and ever shall be, world without end. Amen.*

218

ABOVE: The monastery after the bombing, as seen from the air. BELOW: The front page of the *New York Times* on February 16 called the bombing "the worst aerial and artillery onslaught ever directed against a single building."

The interior of Monte Cassino after the bombing. Note the ruined choir stalls of the basilica (opposite, top) and (opposite, bottom) the decapitated statue of Saint Benedict.

ABOVE: The monastery seen from the ridge after the bombing. The monks took refuge in the lower floors of the *collegio* (to the right of the near corner of the building). Beneath the lower windows of the *collegio* can be seen the arched, partially closed entrance of the *conigliera,* where many civilians took refuge. BELOW: Another view of the abbey from the ridge. At left, caught by the sun, is the road from Cassino. Just above the road is the cave where the Germans were captured by the American patrol.

The mule path was a trail about six feet wide, stony and sometimes steep, that was cut into the side of the mountain. It led down to the Liri Valley about four miles north of Cassino. The path was well behind the German positions, and the small group must have been clearly visible to Allied observers across the valley. The sun had burned off the early haze, the few trees were bare and scorched, and the monks' black gowns—the civilians wore rags of all colors—stood out against the snow-streaked winter hillside. A small observation plane circled over them. But the few shells that went by did not seem aimed at them. Matronola wondered if the Allied observers had realized they were unarmed and innocent.

They passed an inscription carved on a rock under a wooden cross. The inscription read, in apparent reference to the early Benedictine missionaries sent to England:

> *Padre Nostro que sei nei cieli*
> *Affratella a noi l'Inghilterra*
> *Nell' Unita della fede*
> *(Our Father who art in heaven*
> *Join England to us in brotherhood*
> *in the Unity of the faith)*

Matronola heard a monk shouting at him from the trail up behind them. He said the men carrying the woman who had lost her feet were refusing to go on. Matronola called back that he could not leave the abbot. Could the men carry her just a little farther?

They were at the point where the trail reached the foot of the mountain when shells began to fall around them and all the monks and civilians scattered. When they finally were gathered again, Matronola saw that the men carrying the woman who had lost her feet were there—but she was not. They had abandoned her up on the trail. No one went back for her.

One of the monks was also missing: Carlomanno Pellagalli, a 79-year-old lay brother. Fra Carlo had worked in the olive groves and lands of Monte Cassino, and in his spare time he liked to go to an abandoned chapel in one of the monastery's outlying buildings. The monks never saw Fra Carlo again. Months later they learned that their old brother monk had gone back to the monastery. German paratroopers saw his black-clad figure wandering around the ruins. Some of them thought he was a ghost. Fra Carlo died about six weeks later, on April 3, in obedience—so noted the monk who chronicled his end—to his vow to spend the rest of his days in Monte Cassino.

About ten o'clock the monks reached the seasonal stream known as the "dry torrent." This place is holy to Benedictines. According to the chronicle, Benedict and his sister, Scholastica, met here for the last time. Scholastica asked her brother to stay the night in prayer with her. Benedict refused; he had to be back in his monastery by nightfall. Scholastica then wept so much that the flood of her tears —the dry torrent—prevented Benedict from leaving till the following morning. For centuries, a small, very simple church—it looked like a farmhouse—had stood on that spot. In 1939 it was razed, and its reconstruction had been interrupted by the war.

The monks saw a Red Cross sign on a small building near the site of Scholastica's church. It was a German first-aid shelter. The soldiers advised the group to keep on going because the shellfire there was heavy. But they gave the exhausted old abbot some coffee and let him and Matronola rest in the shelter. A soldier then appeared and said that Kesselring himself had ordered a search for the abbot and any others who had survived the bombing. The soldier told Matronola an ambulance would come that afternoon and take the monks and their wounded. While he and the abbot waited in the shelter, Matronola recited the divine office for the octave day (the eighth day after the feast day) of Saint Scholastica.

The ambulance arrived about 4:30, carrying an officer who had a letter for the abbot from General Baade. The boy whose legs were paralyzed was lifted into the ambulance. Three women refugees got in, followed by the abbot and Matronola. The officer gave them all oranges. They started out for the bunker that was Baade's headquarters. Matronola peeked through the curtains that covered the windows of the ambulance. He looked back at Monte Cassino. He saw planes flying over the mountaintop, black smoke rising from the ruins, and he heard great explosions. It was his last sight of the monastery.

Erwin Randolph Silsbee was one of the American fliers who bombed the ruins that day. Silsbee was leading a flight of eight fighter-bombers. When his plane was over the abbey, Silsbee could see nothing, he later recalled, but "a general outline of the walls and almost total destruction." But Silsbee and the other fliers had been told at their briefing that the appearance of the ruins was deceiving. In fact, they were told, below the ruins, and virtually undamaged, were underground passages filled with German soldiers and military installations. As he took his plane into its dive to drop its 1,000-pound bomb, Silsbee thought he saw flashes of gunfire in the rubble.

In all, 59 fighter-bombers dropped 23 tons of bombs on the ruins that day. It is unlikely that anyone in the abbey was alive when the bombs fell. The monks and civilians had left that morning and the Germans had not yet occupied the ruins. But Fra Carlo, the old monk who went back, may have been in the ruins by then, and the two children Matronola thought were dying may have still been alive.

53

Gregorio Diamare awoke on February 18 from his first good night's rest since the monks had moved into their cramped refuge three weeks earlier. Late the day before, the abbot and his secretary, Martino Matronola, had been brought to General von Senger's headquarters at Castelmassimo. "A sad encounter," the general had said, but he entertained the monks with his usual fluent courtesy. At dinner he told them not a single German had been killed in the bombing. The abbot, weak and apathetic, said little and took only tea and a piece of zwieback.

That morning Senger asked Abbot Diamare to be interviewed on the radio. The abbot said he thought the statement he had signed in the ruins was sufficient. General von Senger insisted. According to

Matronola, he told the monks that "in England they are beginning to blame me for the bombing." Senger himself wrote that he had been ordered by the army high command to interview the abbot and had done so reluctantly because it seemed "a breach of hospitality."

The interview took place in the general's living room. Diamare sat hunched over, horn-rimmed glasses down on his nose. His black robe contrasted with the flowered print of the slipcovers. Next to him sat a dark-haired young man in uniform—Lieutenant Owsnicke, a correspondent and interpreter. The lieutenant's left hand was in a sling; with the right hand he held out the microphone. In the armchair across from the couch sat the elegant General von Senger, his long legs crossed. After an introduction by the correspondent, the general asked questions to which the abbot made answers that he and Matronola had prepared in writing. The correspondent translated the abbot's statements into German. Newsreel cameramen and photographers recorded the scene. This film would be added to a film of the ruins that had already been sent to Berlin.

The two surviving reports of what Abbot Diamare said in that radio interview differ in three important respects. One account is by Matronola, the other is a German "condensed" and "approximate" account that appeared in the records of the 14th Panzer Korps.

Their most important difference concerns the 300-meter neutral zone. The German narrative quotes Diamare as saying to Senger: "You ordered that within a specified perimeter around the abbey there be neither weapons, nor observation posts nor billeting of troops. You have tirelessly taken care that these orders were most strictly enforced." Matronola's text does not mention the "perimeter" but rather the "enclosure"—that is, the area enclosed within the walls of the monastery. The German version is, of course, inconsistent with the monks' own testimony that the 300-meter zone was ended on January 5, and that even earlier the abbot was repeatedly protesting German violations of the supposed limits.

The German text quotes General von Senger as saying that "no leaflets were dropped over our German positions" so he did not know of the warning till after the bombing. To this the abbot is quoted as answering, "I have the feeling that the leaflets were intentionally dropped so late in order to give us no possibility to notify the German commanders, or, on the other hand, to bring the 800 guests of the monastery out of the danger zone." None of this exchange appears in Matronola's diary, nor did the abbot express such an opinion about the leaflets on any other occasion. In Matronola's text—but not the German—Diamare stresses how many of Monte Cassino valuables were not evacuated by the Germans but left and destroyed by the bombing.

It remains unclear whether the abbot's testimony was altered by the correspondent when he translated it into German for the broadcast, or only in the later written report of the interview.

After the interview the squat old abbot shuffled out of the headquarters, flanked by Senger and Matronola, both men towering above him. He and Matronola got into the touring car Senger had provided them. As the car pulled away, General von Senger saw them off, smiling, with a graceful bow and a salute. The car set out for Rome and, as the general had instructed its driver, the monastery of San Anselmo, where the two monks could be back with the monks who had left in October. There would at least be some comfort after the loss of their home in being united with the other members of their monastic community.

At a checkpoint on the outskirts of Rome a German officer told their driver to follow him. He led them, not to San Anselmo, but to a large office building in the center of the city. Another officer escorted the abbot and Matronola to a small room and told them to wait there for the "German ambassador." But Matronola thought the place looked like a broadcasting studio, and, in fact, they were in the offices of EIAR, the Italian national radio, in the Vittoria section. While they were waiting, the Germans telephoned San Anselmo and reported that the monks who fled the ruins with them had safely arrived in Rome. Relieved, the abbot, though exhausted, agreed when the Germans insisted on another radio interview, this one for the Italian audience.

Now, instead of San Anselmo, the two monks were taken to the office of the German ambassador. Weizsaecker asked Abbot Diamare to sign still another statement, this one in German, that had already been prepared for him. According to Senger, Weizsaecker had been ordered to get the statement by his chief, Foreign Minister Joachim von Ribbentrop, who was jealous because Goebbels had gotten the earlier radio interview with the abbot. But this time Diamare refused and held his ground despite the German's urging. The two monks made their way through a crowd of reporters and photographers. The abbot, silent, with his cloth-covered head bowed low, got back in the car with Matronola and proceeded at last to join their fellows at San Anselmo.

The news of Monte Cassino was all over Rome. The Germans and Italian Fascists had put up posters showing photographs of the ruined monastery and reproductions of the abbot's handwritten statement given to Lieutenant Deiber on the evening of the bombing. "This is certainly a trump card in the German propaganda game," the American nun in Rome who wrote under the name "Jane Scrivener" noted in her diary.

It certainly was a trump card. Nazi propagandists were in full cry. They had seized joyfully on the destruction of Monte Cassino as evidence for their current line. Now that the war had turned against them, the Nazis were portraying themselves as the defenders of European culture against the barbarians of East and West. Otto Dietrich, the Reich press chief, wrote in his diary the day after the bombing: "The willful destruction of the historical buildings of the Cassino monastery . . . is just as much a cultural scandal as the bombing of Pompeii, and it is to be comdemned as sharply as possible." The German News Agency added that the Germans had "again proven their sense of cultural responsibility at the expense of their military interests." In Rome, Kesselring said he had "ordered that German soldiers must keep out of the monastery and its vicinity. Strict adherence to this order was ensured by the competent commanders." But now, Kesselring went on, the inclusion of the ruins "into the German defensive installations is an entirely natural step from a military point of view." The Foreign Office in Berlin told all its diplomats abroad, "Please use all means at your command to exploit the destruction of the Monte Cassino monastery."

On February 17, the German News Agency let loose all its verbal firepower:

> In this senseless lust of destruction is mirrored the whole fury of the British–U.S. command, which first announced the capture of Rome by Christmas with great verbosity, and then discovered that the road to Rome is just as far as that to Tipperary. . . . The British press states . . . "The monastery of Monte Cassino has already been destroyed several times, why should

ABOVE: On February 18, Abbot Diamare, with Matronola at his side, reads a statement for a German radio interview in the living room of General von Senger's headquarters. BELOW: Abbot Diamare leaves the headquarters of General von Senger (right), accompanied by Matronola (left), on his way to Rome after the bombing.

A Benedictine goes home.

it not be destroyed again?" These British or Jewish scribblers are not far off. The monastery has been destroyed several times, but then it was by barbarians. . . . Today these barbarians are called British and Americans, whose wish is to exterminate these phenomena of a superior European civilization. Everything that has made our old continent beautiful, great and strong is to be systematically destroyed. . . . Thus it has been decided by Jews and pro-Bolsheviks in Moscow, London and Washington. . . . One cannot help asking how Roosevelt will explain the destruction of such sacred religious places to his Catholic electors.

The destruction of Monte Cassino made headlines all over the world. It was the lead story in virtually every newspaper in the United States and Britain and in most of the press of the neutral nations as well.

In the middle of a popular war that they were winning the American and British leaders could expect general support for the bombing, and they were not disappointed. Press accounts of the bombing took the presumed German presence in the abbey as established fact and the German identity of the two or three hundred people seen fleeing ("like rats," said the Associated Press) during the bombing as a certainty. Sulzberger in the *New York Times* wrote, under a six-column headline reading U.S. BLASTS NAZIS IN MONTE CASSINO ABBEY, that the monastery:

> . . . crumbled slowly into ruins beneath vast clouds of dust as the German soldiers who had violated all civilized codes by employing the sanctuary for military purposes met their day of wrath. . . . More than two hundred persons, many of whom were positively identified as German soldiers, fled in panic over the hillside from the disintegrating mass.

Public opinion was overwhelmingly favorable. In the United States, Roman Catholic prelates hurried into print with statements of support. The statement by Archbishop Michael J. Curley of Baltimore and Washington was typical: "The Germans evidently took advantage of the American attitude toward such a monument, and, according to all information, they took possession of that sacred place in order to carry out their nefarious warfare. Every Catholic throughout the world, I am sure, will understand the bombing by our boys." In Britain, two Benedictine abbots endorsed the bombing, and one, Bruno Fehrenbacher of Buckfast Abbey, said: "Much as I regret the destruction of our mother house at Monte Cassino, I realize that the Allies did everything they could to preserve it."

Still, those who listened carefully could hear a disquieting undertone. It was the first time the Allies had deliberately targeted a religious monument. Those previously destroyed had been hit while striking at a normal military objective. There was something strange about dropping such an enormous tonnage of bombs on a single building—and a monastery at that. Strange, too, that the bombing had not as yet produced any results on the ground. Support for the bombing was based entirely on the belief that the Germans were putting the monastery to military use. No doubt the Germans were lying, but what about the abbot's statement that there had been no Germans in the monastery? Suppose the Allied military commanders could not come up with convincing evidence? The Allies would be guilty then of a blunder, if not a crime.

The question was asked in the British Foreign Office soon after the bombing. Officials there had been reading D'Arcy Osborne's cables from the Vatican. On February 17, a Foreign Office official named A. B. Dew wrote to Colonel L. J. Carver of the War Cabinet:

> We should like to be able to supply Osborne with a short statement for him to pass on to the Vatican describing as precisely as possible the military use which the Germans have in fact been making of the abbey. Could you possibly furnish us with such a statement? If there has not been any report from Allied Force Headquarters, perhaps you could ask for one.

Thus was set in motion an inquiry that would stretch well past the end of the war.

In the worldwide clamor after the bombing one voice was conspicuously absent. The Vatican had nothing to say for three full days. Not till February 18 did *Osservatore Romano,* the official newspaper of the Vatican, mention Monte Cassino, and when it did, in an article headed THE TRAGIC HOUR OF MONTE CASSINO, what it had to say was notably bland:

It is known that the Holy See did not fail to make timely and persistent efforts to preserve the wonderful monastery from any possibility of attack. . . . It will only be in the more or less remote future that it will be possible for judgment to be passed on the causes of so great a misfortune.

The Pope himself was silent, but his secretary of state, Cardinal Maglione, was neither bland nor silent in a meeting with the American minister. According to the notes made by the minister, Harold Tittmann, Cardinal Maglione said there were no Germans in the monastery or "the immediate vicinity" and that the bombing was "a colossal blunder . . . a piece of a gross stupidity." When Tittmann said the Allied military must have had some overriding reason for their action, Maglione got very annoyed and said: "I know what I am talking about and I have access to sources that are undoubtedly not open to you." Tittmann had to admit his only source of news was the radio: the State Department had sent him nothing about Monte Cassino. In a separate report Tittmann took pains to state there was "of course no truth whatsoever" to an account published in the *Giornale d'Italia* that he had told Maglione Monte Cassino could be rebuilt with American money, to which the cardinal was supposed to have answered "disdainfully" that even if "rebuilt in gold and precious stones it would no longer be the monastery."

One of Maglione's assistants, Monsignor Tardini, was thinking about the possible link between the destruction of Monte Cassino and the prospect that Rome might suffer a similar fate. In notes he wrote on February 19, Tardini said the bombing proved that the Allied commanders in Italy were possessed of a "mania for destruction." He recalled the principle that had been attributed to General Alexander: where there is a single German, we will bomb. That principle had been applied in the Allied bombing of the Pope's summer residence at Castel Gandolfo, on the property and even under the eyes of the Pope. Would the same principle be applied by Alexander to Rome? Tardini thought Castel Gandolfo and Monte Cassino were a "sad prelude." Public opinion ruled in democratic countries, Tardini knew, but he could hope for little in nations where even Benedictine abbots endorsed the destruction of their mother house. If there was to be any hope of stopping the tide of destruction before it reached Rome, the only way—"in my humble opinion,"

Tardini wrote—was if the Vatican could fix the responsibility for the destruction of Monte Cassino.

That there was a connection between the fate suffered by his abbey and the danger to Rome was a thought that had also occurred to Abbot Diamare. Diamare believed, and perhaps it was the only meaning he could find in the destruction of his beloved monastery, that Monte Cassino had been sacrificed to save Rome. In the first days after he arrived at the monastery of San Anselmo, the old abbot said to a fellow Benedictine about the bombing, "The Lord willed it, and it was a good thing for the salvation of Rome."

54

General Freyberg was embarrassed, and with excellent reason. At the request of General Tuker, he had thrown his political and personal weight around and had forced the Americans to bomb Monte Cassino on the assumption the Indian Division would capture the ruins right after *and because of* the bombing. Here it was two days later and the Indian Division had not even attacked Monastery Hill, much less captured it. All they had done up there in those two days was to fail in two attempts to take the obscure place known as Point 593. For all the difference it had made, the bombing might as well not have happened. Was it for this that Freyberg had laid his prestige and his power on the line?

Freyberg ordered the Indian Division to attack Monastery Hill without further delay. The division's planners decided to attack both 593 and the monastery on the night of February 17 to 18. Now they were supposed to take two objectives where before they had failed to take one, but none of the handicaps under which the troops up there labored had changed. Getting supplies up to the ridge was still incredibly difficult—on one night only 20 of 200 mules got through —and the soldiers were still short of everything, including the grenades crucial to the attack. The attackers still knew far too little about the treacherous, complicated terrain across which they would have to advance in the dark. This time, however, they would attack in much larger numbers—five battalions compared to the single company of the first attack—although the senior officers had previously decided that many men could not be effectively gathered and sent forward under the circumstances prevailing up there. In the understated words of the division's War Diary: "The difficulties of assembling and deploying a force of nearly two brigades and keeping it supplied in so restricted a space, well ranged by enemy weapons, were serious but had to be accepted."

At midnight the Royal Sussex—the 60 percent that had survived its two previous defeats—and a battalion of Indian troops attacked 593 for the third time. At 2:15 in the morning two battalions of Gurkhas, men from the mountains of Nepal, started off along a route that led to the left of 593 directly to Monastery Hill. The night was clear, and the moon in its fourth quarter shed its light on Gurkhas and Germans alike. The Gurkhas crept and crawled up to Point 445, where Harold Bond a week earlier had watched his mortar hit the abbey. By the weak light of the moon the Gurkhas could see the great ruined building 400 yards away. The Gurkhas were on the edge of the deep ravine through which the American patrol had passed to capture the Germans in the cave under the walls of Monte Cassino. The leading troops of the Gurkhas now dashed toward a line of brush that seemed as if it would provide some shelter. They ran into a deathtrap. The brush was a thicket of throat-high thorn which the Germans had sewn with mines set off by wires. Dead Gurkhas were found later with as many as four trip wires around their legs. Two-thirds of the soldiers in the two leading companies of Gurkhas were cut down within fifteen minutes.

By dawn it was clear that both attacks had failed. The generals had more than doubled the stakes this time, and the price their men had paid was more than twice as high. The Indian Division lost 530 men that night, compared to 64 and 130 in the two previous nights. Freyberg wanted to continue the attack, but on the morning of February 18, Dimoline, the Indian commander, persuaded him to call off the attack on Monastery Hill indefinitely.

That same day, in the valley below Monte Cassino, the New Zealanders' attack on the Cassino railroad station was defeated. Of the 200 men who went forward, 70 returned.

So ended the ground battles for which Generals Tuker and Freyberg had insisted on the bombing of Monte Cassino. The Allies had gained no ground up there. At very high cost, the elite troops of the Indian Division had proved that the theorists of the Italian war college were right: Monte Cassino could not be taken by direct assault.

Two days later German paratroopers occupied the ruins of Monte Cassino. The cellars and vaults of the monastery had not been destroyed by the bombing, and covered with rubble they made ideal defensive positions. The Germans turned the ruins into a fortress from which they withstood successive attacks for the next three months. In March the Indians were replaced on the bloody ridge by Polish soldiers led by General Anders. The Poles in their turn attacked along the ridge and were defeated with great loss of life, just like the Americans and the Indians and the British who had died there before them.

The Germans held the ruins of Monte Cassino until May 18, and when they left they did so voluntarily. The Poles who assaulted Monastery Hill that morning advanced across a landscape strewn with decaying bodies. It was spring: red poppies blew between the corpses. The Poles found the ruins empty, except for a handful of badly wounded men. The Germans had slipped out during the night.

The Germans had left because during May the Allies had at last done what Tuker of the Indian Division had wanted to do in February, what the French general Juin had wanted to do in January, and what the American general Keyes had advocated still earlier under the name "Big Cassino." They went around the German strongpoints instead of assaulting them head on. The North African troops of the French Corps had cut through the Aurunci mountains on the far side of the Liri Valley, over a route so difficult that the Americans, the British, and the Germans thought it was impossible. With the French on the high ground, the German positions of the Gustav Line in the valley became untenable. The Germans retreated up the valley. Monte Cassino fell without a fight.

EPILOGUE

Abbot Gregorio Diamare returned to the ruins of Monte Cassino and died there, of malaria, in 1945. He is buried in the wall by the gate through which he led those who left the ruins two days after the bombing. Tommaso Leccisotti died in 1982. Of the monks who were in the monastery on February 15, 1944, at this writing four are living in the abbey. Martino Matronola, secretary to Diamare, became abbot in his turn and retired in 1982 at the age of 80. The others are Dom Agostino Saccomanno and two lay brothers, Fra Giacomo Ciaraldi and Fra Pietro Nardone.

Among the Allied generals who took part in the decision to bomb Monte Cassino only Mark Clark is alive. He is 87 and lives at the Citadel, the military college of which he became head after his retirement from the army. Gruenther died in 1983 and Keyes in 1967.

General Freyberg became governor-general of New Zealand and died in 1963. General Alexander became governor-general of Canada and died in 1969. Tuker died in 1967, Wilson in 1964. Juin died in 1967.

General von Senger surrendered to Mark Clark in 1945. After two years as a prisoner in Wales, where he worked as a gardener's assistant, Senger became headmaster of Spetsgart School, near Uberlingen on the Bodensee. He died in 1963. Kesselring died in 1960. Baade shot and killed an SS officer who tried to give him an order, went into hiding, was wounded by a British fighter plane, and died of gangrene on the last day of the war.

The memory of war is fresh in Cassino. When the traveler emerges from the railroad station into the town—it has been completely rebuilt—he is greeted by the sight of a rusting tank facing him from the center of a small square. If he is old enough, the traveler is asked, "Were you here during the war?" or, "Do you have relatives here?" That means *buried* here, for the war dead number at least as many as the living people of Cassino. The taxi driver's first offer is a tour of the cemeteries for a fixed price. He enumerates the five military cemeteries in or near Cassino. For an extra fee, he says, he will also take you to the Americans over at Anzio.

Up on the hill the traveler sees the rebuilt monastery. Once again it dominates the landscape, just as it did when Allied soldiers gazed up at it in bitterness from the valley 40 years ago. The road winds like its predecessor in hairpin turns up the abrupt side of the mountain. The massive building that fills your vision at the top of the hill looks like its prewar photographs: it was rebuilt exactly as it had been. The Vatican has long since returned the treasures taken there by the Hermann Goering Division. Everything, it seems, is as it was before they had the war.

Yet today the Abbey of Monte Cassino makes a jarring impression. It is too new. The limestone of the rebuilt monastery is white and raw. Time has not weathered it yellow and gray like the few surviving parts of the old Monte Cassino. Any building must be new once, one tells oneself, but still a medieval building should not look new in the late twentieth century. The new basilica is ornately decorated, and in 1983 the Italian artist Pietro Annigoni was completing a gigantic fresco of *The glory of Saint Benedict* over the entrance. This princely display is from an era long gone: it speaks of the temporal splendor of Monte Cassino in the Middle Ages. And now there is piped music.

Some Benedictines in other monastic communities say that Monte Cassino today does not embody the spirit of their order. "Go to Subiaco," they advise, and they are right. Subiaco, which lies about thirty miles east of Rome, is where Benedict led his first community of monks. Two small monasteries nestle there up in the hills. In the peace and simplicity of the monasteries of Subiaco the visitor can perhaps glimpse, as he cannot at Monte Cassino, the kind of life Benedict was trying to create.

The new Monte Cassino is a strange and melancholy combination of traffic jam and ghost town. The parts of the building that are open to the public—the cloisters and the basilica—swarm with tourists. Even on a midweek morning in late April, far from the height of the season, seventeen tourist buses disgorged their contents all at the same time into the interior of the monastery. This part of Monte Cassino belongs not to the monks but to the tourists just as—it may suddenly occur to the visitor—much the same area belonged to the refugees in the last days before the bombing. A handful of monks are serving the tourists in the abbey's two shops. (Since Monte Cassino is the property of the state, the presence of the tourists is not by decision of the monks.)

One visits the rest of the abbey, the floors above and below ground level, with Dom Agostino Saccomanno. Dom Agostino, a survivor of the bombing, is hospitable and lively at 73. As he leads you down the long, high-ceilinged residence hall he says it has cells for 80 monks. The *foresteria,* the guest quarters, has that many more cells, and the whole complex could easily house hundreds. There are 25 monks here now, and of these only half a dozen are under 60. The building is new, but the community is dying.

Here too the memory of the war, and especially the bombing, is kept fresh. On the right as one enters through the great gate is a shop selling the inevitable postcards. Some of the cards show the ruins after the bombing. On the wall are more photographs of the ruins.

The great bronze doors of the basilica, first cast in the eleventh century, have been remade for the second time. The old doors had panels on which were depicted in relief the three destructions of Monte Cassino. Now a fourth panel has been added. It is dated MCMXLIV and displays a British helmet and the propellor of a B-17 bomber. In the small museum next to the basilica is a display of wartime artifacts that includes a rusting machine gun and an obese unexploded bomb.

A traveler may notice a linguistic oddity about the signs that direct him around the area open to tourists. In present-day Italy, English has become the second language of signs addressed to tourists; French and German lag behind in both frequency and position. But in postwar Monte Cassino none of the signs is reproduced in English.

The monks are quick to tell you that the American government that destroyed Monte Cassino did not contribute a single lira to its reconstruction, despite promises purportedly made by Harold Tittmann and President Roosevelt. What they say is accurate but a bit invidious. Accurate because the government of Italy did in fact pay the whole cost of rebuilding Monte Cassino. Invidious because Italy was heavily dependent on American money at the time, so its government could pay for Monte Cassino only if the Americans financed other more urgent kinds of reconstruction. But somehow the point does not seem worth debating.

About two hundred yards down the hill in front of the monastery, where the slope turns from gentle to steep, a small lookout marks the beginning of the mule path down which Abbot Diamare, bearing the large crucifix, led his little band away from the ruins. The view from here is spectacular. Before the visitor lies the long sweep of the Liri Valley. Immediately below is the new town of Cassino; not one building there dates from before the war. The Rapido River, tiny at this distance, flows across the valley toward the sea 15 miles away. Up the valley, to the right, is the road to Rome for which the long battle was fought. Across from the observer is Monte Trocchio, the hill from which the Allies watched the bombs fall, and to its left are the mountains through which the Fifth Army fought to get here. Somewhere over there are the places from which Dr. Becker and Mark Clark first saw the abbey.

The lookout is a good place to ponder the long dispute over what happened here on February 15, 1944. The controversy about the bombing of Monte Cassino—military necessity, crime, blunder?—began two days after the event, with the first Foreign Office inquiry, and has continued over forty years to the present day. That the bombing had produced nothing of military value was made evident within the first days by the failure of the attacks by the Indian Division. But if the Germans were using the abbey, its bombing could still be justified on military grounds, and the failure to capitalize on it would be no more than a tactical error like many others.

In answer to the Foreign Office request, General Wilson, the Mediterranean commander, sent a cable on March 9 listing twelve pieces of evidence of German use of the abbey or its immediate surroundings.* But Wilson advised that this information "not be given to the Vatican since the Germans might well try to produce faked evidence controverting it." Wilson suggested that "we should confine our statement to the fact that the military authorities on the spot have irrefutable evidence that the Cassino Abbey was part of the main German defensive line."

For the next few years "irrefutable evidence" or some similar phrase was the position of both the American and British governments in response to questions about the bombing. In the fall of 1945, Harold Tittmann was protesting to the Vatican about a booklet which he said was being "distributed to visitors to the abbey,"

---

*This is the evidence described on pages 166–167.

though at the time only a few monks were camped out in the ruins. The booklet stated that "the monastery was made part of the German defense system only after it had been bombed," Tittmann complained, even though he had twice informed the Vatican that his government had "unquestionable evidence" of German use before the bombing.

In 1949, the British government instructed Major F. Jones to conduct an investigation of the circumstances that led to the bombing. After three months of studying the available documents Jones reported: "It is clear that General Wilson was not in possession of conclusive evidence [of German use] prior to the bombing, and it is equally clear that he was not in a position to produce it subsequent to the bombing when asked to do so from London." But the Jones report and its embarrassing conclusion were kept secret by the British for 30 years.

The United States government began to move in small steps away from the certainty of "irrefutable evidence" until, in 1961, the Office of the Chief of Military History said, in reply to a query from the publishers of the *World Book Encyclopedia,* that "there are eyewitness accounts, oral testimony, and documentary evidence from Allied and German sources which support both points of view. At this late date the Department of the Army has no means to check or verify the validity of all the available evidence and cannot, therefore, resolve this controversy." Three years later, this time in response to a congressional inquiry, the same office had retreated still further: "It appears that no German troops, except a small military police detachment, were actually inside the abbey" before the bombing. Also in 1969, the army's official history concluded that "the abbey was actually unoccupied by German troops."

New Zealand remains unyielding in defense of General Freyberg, a national hero, and therefore in defense of the decision to bomb the abbey. This is evident in the affair of the Bloch pamphlet. In 1976 the abbey put on sale a 46-page pamphlet by Herbert Bloch, a classicist at Harvard University who has written extensively on the early history of Monte Cassino. In the pamphlet, originally intended as the preface to a larger work, Bloch describes the bombing as an error and assigns much of the responsibility to Freyberg. The pamphlet has been repeatedly denounced in Britain and especially in New Zealand. As late as October 1982, the prime minister of New

Zealand, R. D. Muldoon, said in Parliament: "Bloch's book . . . is a nasty little piece of work . . . an affront to every New Zealander who served at Monte Cassino, and to the reputation and professional judgement of General Freyberg." Some of the attacks on Bloch have taken a nasty personal turn. Critics have made a point of referring to him as "German-born" to underscore what they see as the pro-German bias of his account. It is true that Herbert Bloch was born in Germany. It is also true that he left when Hitler came to power and that his brother was, in Bloch's words, "murdered at an unknown date in Auschwitz"—credentials that might well give pause to those who cannot match them.

Only the publication of the monks' diary now makes it possible to say with certainty what the Germans did and did not do at Monte Cassino in the months before February 15.

The Germans made no military use of the monastery itself. That is the testimony of the monks and of the civilians who were there before and during the bombing. There is also negative evidence for the same conclusion. Had the Germans been in there, some number of Germans and monks and civilians would have known about it. If the chances that a secret will get out can be calculated by the number of people who know it multiplied by elapsed time, the probability that someone would have talked in 40 years becomes overwhelming. No one has.

But the Germans claimed much more than that. They repeatedly said that they were not using the "immediate vicinity" or "neighborhood" of the abbey. This had usually been interpreted by German writers to refer to the 300-meter neutral zone. German postwar accounts, and Kesselring's statement at the time, would have us believe that the 300-meter zone was still in effect at the time of the bombing. We now know from the monks' diary that this is not true. The 300-meter zone existed for only three weeks: it was announced to the monks on December 12 and abolished on January 5. Even during its brief existence, Abbot Diamare had frequent cause to complain that the Germans were violating the limits they had set.

There is no mystery about the ending of the neutral zone. On December 11, a day *before* the monks were told of the zone, Kesselring ordered that "the building alone is to be spared." And it was General von Senger himself who gave the order to "make defenses right up to the Abbey wall if necessary." That order was dated

December 26, the day after Senger attended Christmas Day mass at Monte Cassino.

In his several postwar accounts of the destruction of Monte Cassino, Senger made much of his desire to save the monastery but said nothing at all about the 300-meter zone or his role in ending it. Senger did not visit the abbey again during the eight weeks between Christmas and the bombing, though he was up on the ridge nearby more than once and though he found time to visit the Benedictine nuns in the valley. If he did not know his artillery was hitting the abbey repeatedly in the last two weeks—there is no evidence as to whether he did know—it is because he never sent anyone to find out what was happening inside the monastery. Yet Senger more than anyone else must have understood what the ending of the 300-meter zone was likely to mean for the monastery and its inhabitants.

Thus the first of several ironies: the main author of the German decision that led to the doom of Monte Cassino was the devout Roman Catholic, friend of the Benedictines, General von Senger. This is not to say that Senger's protestations, then as well as after the war, of concern for Monte Cassino were insincere, though surely self-serving. But when the choice had to be made, Senger, the consummate military professional, made the choice dictated by "military necessity"—the same principle invoked by the Allies in the decisions they made.

From the evidence of the monks and civilians and Allied observers and soldiers, we now know that within the 300-meter zone the Germans had one cave in which they stored munitions, another they used as a command post or bunker (the cave where Germans were captured by the American patrol), at least one and probably several machine-gun positions, at times the two tanks or self-propelled guns, and, perhaps, one or more observation posts.

The difference between the monastery itself and the 300-meter zone is one of sheer size. The building alone covers an area of about twenty-eight thousand square meters, just over seven acres. The zone is ten times as large, about eighty acres with the abbey, in a circle about eight hundred yards across. This means that the Allies, had they been certain that the Germans were not anywhere in the zone, could have aimed their artillery fire and even bombs at legitimate military targets without hitting the abbey more than an occasional accidental blow.

But could the Allies ever have been certain that the Germans were not in either the abbey or the zone? The idea of sending a neutral observer to the scene was discussed at the Vatican, but only in the last days, when it was too late. The monk Leccisotti thought he heard such a proposal much earlier, in late December, in the account of what the German ambassador had told the Vatican, but Leccisotti never reported the idea to his abbot, nor did Abbot Diamare ever suggest a neutral observer. Why no one pushed the idea with any vigor remains one of the minor mysteries of Monte Cassino.

But it is unlikely that a neutral observer at Monte Cassino—even supposing the Germans let him go there and the Allies believed what he said—could have saved Monte Cassino once the Germans had occupied the 300-meter zone. The monastery was not destroyed just by the bombing of February 15 and the two succeeding days. As we now know from the monks' diary, it was being hit daily, by German as well as Allied artillery, for the two weeks before the bombing. Considerable damage had been done before the bombers arrived. And the substantial part of the monastery that was still standing after the bombing was destroyed by the artillery fire that battered Monte Cassino for the three months that the battle continued. Much of this damage before and after February 15 would have occurred without the decision to bomb. A strange irony here is that, had the monks and civilians not been driven out by the bombing, more of them no doubt would have died of shellfire and starvation in the next three months than the one or two hundred killed on February 15. And no one would have blamed the Allies.

"As soon as the decision was made to attack the Monte Cassino feature direct," General Tuker, who insisted on the bombing, wrote after the war, "the monastery was doomed to destruction." That is the truth. The Allied decision to attack the Germans head-on in the Liri Valley, instead of going around them, as Keyes and Juin and Tuker himself had all advocated, was another decision, along with the German abolition of the 300-meter zone, that determined the fate of Monte Cassino. And the man most responsible for the head-on strategy was Mark Clark.

Thus another irony: of the three men on the Allied side most responsible for the destruction of Monte Cassino—the third was Freyberg—one, Tuker, did not want to attack that position at all, and another, Clark, was the most outspoken opponent of the bombing.

The record of the debate in the last few days before February 15 over whether to bomb suggests another observation, this one of application far beyond the bounds of the Liri Valley. Those involved in the debate saw what they wanted to see and did not see what they did not want to see. Two American generals flew in small planes over Monte Cassino to see if the Germans were in there. Keyes thought the Germans were not there, Eaker thought they were. Each general came back from his flight to report that what he had seen confirmed what he believed before the plane took off—and there is no reason to suppose there was any difference on the ground between the two occasions. It is not surprising, then, that no one changed his mind in the various discussions that took place before the bombing.

That the bombing of Monte Cassino did not advance the Allied military cause is generally recognized. Indeed, in one sense it may have done harm. Because of the enormous publicity that attended the bombing, it helped commit the Allied commanders to the long, futile battle on the ridge in which so many died to so little purpose. Tuker again: "A direct attack on the Monte Cassino features meant that we were committed to success. That is, we could not stop short and call it a day without acknowledging complete failure."

Did the fate of Monte Cassino in some way help to save Rome? Abbot Diamare thought so, and the belief may have given him some solace. When he said so to Monsignor Lombardi of the Vatican secretary of state's office, after the Allies had taken Rome and the city was safe, Lombardi answered, "It is revealing no secret to say that the Vatican exploited the disaster of Monte Cassino to obtain respect of Rome from the belligerents." It is true that Cardinal Maglione, the Vatican secretary of state, cited the destruction of Monte Cassino—"falsely described as a German fortress"—in a plea to President Roosevelt on behalf of Rome. It is true, also, that the bombing of Monte Cassino caused more people in the United States and Britain to speak up for Rome. There is even an intricate theory that the Vatican failed to do more than it did for Monte Cassino because its leaders saw the abbey as the sacrifice that would save the Pope's city. But Rome was not saved by any decision the Allies made after the bombing. The Joint Chiefs of Staff rejected the Vatican's plea on the grounds that "it would be unsound from the military viewpoint to make a decision at this time to by-pass Rome." The Allies, in any event, had been avoiding any large-scale bombing of

Rome since long before Monte Cassino. In the end, Rome was saved by Marshal Albert Kesselring's decision not to defend the city during the German retreat, and it is hard indeed to see how that decision could have been influenced by what befell Monte Cassino.

For the Allies, Monte Cassino remains a painful and distressing episode, so much so that it is an orphan. After the war there was no rush to claim parenthood of the bombing, and, as we saw earlier, who escalated Freyberg's original modest request is still a mystery. Certainly Monte Cassino was no war crime, as some have said. But, equally certainly, it was a blunder, and though a blunder need not be worse than a crime, it can be more painful to its authors.

Monte Cassino and Cassino have a far different meaning for the Germans. German veterans of the war can take pride in those names. They represent a very rare bright page in the dark and guilt-ridden German history of those years. The Germans fought here with courage and great skill, and they fought with honor. No Nazi crimes stain the German record here, nor were there any self-inflicted horrors like Stalingrad.

That German soldiers saved the treasures of Monte Cassino and the museum and gallery of Naples is a point of particular pride.* For some it may show that, at one time in one place, the Nazi claim that they were the guardians of European culture was not unfounded. So valued is this memory that there is a lively controversy among veterans of the Hermann Goering Division about which of the two men who first visited the abbey that October—Dr. Becker or Lieutenant-Colonel Schlegel—deserves credit for initiating the rescue. After the war Schlegel wrote a series of newspaper articles in which he gave himself exclusive credit for the idea and its execution. On his death a plaque was attached to his home in Vienna reading:

In diesem Hause
lebte und starb
der verdiente Oesterreicher
Oberstleutnant
Julius Schlegel

---

*The fifteen cases of art sent to Hermann Goering were found at the end of the war by the Americans in a salt mine near Alt-Aussee in Austria. They had suffered only minor damage.

Unter persoenlichem Einsatz
retete er im Herbst '43
die Kuenstschaezse
*des Kloesters Monte Cassino**

Dr. Becker, at this writing, is 73 and is living in retirement in Tecklenburg near the Rhine. In recent years Dr. Becker has devoted a lot of his time and energy and even money to collecting an impressive amount of documentary evidence, in the form of affadavits from other participants, to prove that it was he rather than Schlegel who initiated the rescue in which the veterans of the Hermann Goering Division take such pride, and that he knew nothing about his fellow officers' plan to steal some of the art for Goering.

The new Monte Cassino is once more a site of pilgrimage, as it always was. Since the war Cassino town has also become a site to which pilgrims come. The veterans come from all over the world, as they did 40 years ago, to relive the days of their youth when they fought each other here. The relatives come too. They all come, as the taxi drivers know, to visit the cemeteries where comrades and husbands and brothers and fathers lie. The Poles alone are up on the hill, behind the monastery, on the near slope of Hill 593, now once more known as Monte Calvario. Their cemetery is poorly kept, because, it is said—it is still another Polish tragedy—the present government of Poland does not care to be reminded that the Poles who died here wanted to free their homeland from Stalin as well as Hitler. The British cemetery on the outskirts of town is home also to the New Zealanders, the Indians, and the Gurkhas. The Germans are on the other side of Cassino, on the road up the Rapido Valley. The French and the Italians are down Route 6, and the Americans are 70 miles away at Anzio.

All these cemeteries, with a single exception, bear inscriptions in which leaders invoke god or nation or both to justify or even glorify the deaths of the young men who lie there. The exception is the German cemetery, and it is here that a visit to the war in Cassino should end. Because of the horrors their government unleashed on

*"In this house lived and died the prominent Austrian Lieutenant-Colonel Julius Schlegel. During the fall of '43 he, in his own right, saved the art treasures of the Abbey of Monte Cassino."

the world, the Germans are denied the usual patriotic memorials. What the visitor finds instead is not easily forgotten.

To reach the graves of 20,000 Germans the visitor must pass through a sort of loggia, a small square stone building open to the sky. There is no decor or inscription of any kind here. In the building, otherwise bare, you find the seated figures of a man and a woman sculpted in metal. The woman is bent forward, shattered with grief. The man, erect and somber, has put his hand on her shoulder. These are the parents, and their presence here is the one enduring truth that can be told about what happened in this place.

NOTES AND SOURCES

Chapter 1: The most important source for the events that took place at Monte Cassino from October 1943 through February 1944 is *Il Bombardamento di Montecassino (BMC)*, the collection of wartime accounts published by the monastery. It includes the diaries kept at Monte Cassino by Eusebio Grossetti and Martino Matronola and at Rome by Tommaso Leccisotti, and other first-person accounts. *Echi di Montecassino,* published semiannually by the monastery, also contains useful information. Parts of *BMC* and other Italian texts were translated for the authors by Sylvia Gibot-Behrend. The account by the German monk Emmanuel Munding, *Der Untergang von Monte Cassino* (Beuroner Kuntsverlag, 1954), was translated for the authors by Alexander Leutkemeyer, O.S.B., of Conception Abbey, Conception, Missouri. The authors also interviewed several of the monks at Monte Cassino in 1978 and 1983.

Becker wrote his 78-page "Report on the German Evacuation of the Treasures of Monte Cassino" in German in 1964. Becker has supplied more information in correspondence with the authors. Schlegel's account, "Mein Wagnis in Monte Cassino," was first published in 1951 in *Die Oesterreichischer Furche,* nos. 45–49. Both accounts were translated into English for the authors by Susan Fershee. Both accounts appear in Italian translation in *BMC*.

Since the war, Becker has buttressed his case with statements and affadavits from his commanding officer, Major Hans Sandrock; the quartermaster of the Hermann Goering Division, Lieutenant-Colonel Ulrich Bobrowski; and the two monks from the monastery of San Antonio who accompanied Becker on his first trip to Monte Cassino.

16: Leccisotti on two Germans: *BMC,* p. 113.
18: "Here you will be safe": Munding, p. 13.

Chapter 4: There are, of course, many published accounts of the Allied campaign in Italy, including Clark's own *Calculated Risk.* DWR taped an interview with General Clark on December 29, 1976. The military and government documents referred to here, many of them recently declassified, were found, unless otherwise noted, at the National Archives (NA).

19: Youngest Lieutenant-General: *New York Times Magazine,* September 19, 1943.
19: "I just felt lost": *New York Times,* November 14, 1943.
23: "Each hillside": Clark, p. 210.
23: "One strongpoint after another": Ibid., p. 231.
24: "To reach the Liri": Ibid., p. 237.
24: 'Burma-Shave' sign: Pyle, p. 91.

30: Clark photo caption, *New York Times,* November 5, 1943.

30: "From time to time": U.S. Army message 0-1478.

30: Lieutenant Norris and Monte Cassino: Christopher Norris, letter to DWR, dated October 21, 1978.

34: Germans appeared at Monte Cassino: *BMC,* pp. 12, 21.

37: Becker a British citizen: Letter to the authors, March 30, 1983.

Chapter 6: In addition to General von Senger's book, published in English as *Neither Fear nor Hope,* excerpts from his wartime diary were translated for the U.S. Army (MS # C-095b, "War Diary of the Italian Campaign," Historical Division, Headquarters, U.S. Army, Europe, 1953). Senger's other postwar publications include "Reflections on the Cassino Battles" (*An Cosantoir,* vol. IX, no. 2, 1949, pp. 56–71), and "The Bombing of Monte Cassino" (*The Tablet,* February 15, 1958, pp. 150–51).

The last surviving member of Senger's headquarters staff at Castelmassimo, General Burghard von Cramm, was interviewed for the authors by David Irving on July 21, 1983. Senger's daughter, Maria Gani-Senger, has supplied information to the authors in correspondence and an interview.

39: "He was quite different": DWR interview with Maria Gani-Senger on December 14, 1977.

39: "It is narrow-minded": Senger, p. 34.

40: Italian general and Senger: Morison, Samuel E. *Sicily-Salerno-Anzio (History of U.S. Naval Operations in World War II,* vol. IX). Boston: Little, Brown, 1954, p. 52.

41: "I wonder what": Senger Diary, p. 194.

41: "Creed of Thomas Aquinas": Senger Diary, p. 195.

44: Hitler to Mussolini: Kurzman, p. 39.

45: "Some fine old pictures" and "dessicated face": Senger, p. 198.

Chapter 7: Tommaso Leccisotti's diary for his last days at Monte Cassino and his four months in Rome appears in *BMC,* pp. 111–37. DWR taped an interview with Harold Tittmann on April 30, 1977. Giovanetti's *Roma Città Aperta* describes Vatican policy from the point of view of a young priest working in the Vatican Secretariat of State at the time. Texts of Vatican communications appear in *Actes et Documents de la Sainte Siege.*

48: Diamare's letter: *BMC,* p. 118.

48: Black market prices in Rome: Admiral Franco Maugeri, *From the Ashes of Disgrace,* pp. 198–201, quoted in Aldeman & Walton, pp. 103–04.

49: Scene in St. Peter's Square: Scrivener's diary for September 16, 1943, in Scrivener, pp. 19–21.

50: "Pope is nearer to Himmler": SS "Reports on the Fuehrer's Speech and Events in Italy," September 13, 1943, quoted in Piekalkiewitcz, p. 28.

50: "Occupy Vatican City": Kurzman, p. xxxi.

51: "Not sufficient proof": Tittmann tape.

51: "Little Communist bands": Katz, p. 15.

51: "Holy See confirms": "Nazi-Fascist Relations with the Italian Church Since Italy's Surrender," Office of War Information, December 2, 1943.
53: Vatican message to Washington: Tittmann telegram 203, October 28, 1943.
53: Direct copy: Apostolic Delegate to Acting Secretary of State Edward R. Stettinius, Jr., October 28, 1943.
60: Becker recognized Hofer: Becker letter to DH, Sept. 26, 1983.
63: "Disastrous news": *BMC*, p. 127.
63: "Reassuring news": Ibid., p. 128.
63: "Monte Cassino is still intact": Ibid., p. 130, footnote.
63: Leccisotti reported: Ibid., pp. 132–33, 146.
63: Weizsaecker told Vatican: Giovanetti, p. 213.
63: Vatican message: Enclosure 2, Tittmann dispatch 258, December 8, 1943.
63: Cable to Eisenhower: OPD War Department 330.14.
64: "This headquarters became aware": text in Jones, p. 49.

Chapter 13: Baron von Tieschowitz's actions are described by him in an unpublished postwar report, "The Arrangement of German Art Protection in Italy in November 1943," dated May 29, 1947. The German original is at the Zentral Institut fuer Kunstgeschichte in Munich.

66: "No Nazi": Appendix to "German Publicity on Measures for the Protection of Art in Italy," OSS Research and Analysis Branch Report 1708, December 29, 1943.
66: Tieschowitz in France: Letter from I.G.G. Ramsey, Bury St. Edmunds, in *London Sunday Times,* June 16, 1974, p. 15.
67: "Colonel James Morrison": OSS Report 1708 (see note to p. 66), p. 1.
68: Tieschowitz's identification of two officers: Letter from Tieschowitz's assistant, Ingeborg Lechner, to Dr. Becker, February 8, 1966.
70: The German newsreel of this event, *Die Deutsche Wochenschau* for December 8, 1943, is in the National Archives.
70: "A certain solemnity": De Tomasso diary entry for December 6, 1943, quoted in MFAA "Memorandum on German and Italian Activities with Regard to Works of Art in Italy Prior to the Allied Occupation of Rome," AMG-49, p. 10.
71: Thoughts of Emilio Re: "L'Archivio di Monte Cassino a Roma," by Emilio Re, *L'Urbe,* 1953, vol. 16, no. 6, pp. 9–14.
74: Italian War College: Clark, p. 261.
74: German fortifications: Cramm interview and "Field Fortifications in Central Italy" (interviews with German officers). Historical Division, H.Q. U.S. Army, Europe, Foreign Military Studies Branch, n.d.
74: Location of German installations around Monte Cassino: the locations are given in BMC in the monks' diaries for December 6 and 9, and January 10, 12, and 17, and in the diary of Fulvio de Angelis for January 8, 15, 17, and 21.
76: "astounded and dismayed": Senger, p. 186.
76: Germans had to ration: Westphal, p. 164.

76: "Lacking in spirit": Senger, p. 184.

76: Message to Kesselring: Text in "German Use of the Abbey of Monte Cassino prior to Allied Aerial Bombardment of 15 February 1944," undated OCMH memorandum by Howard McGaw Smyth, p. 5.

77: Osborne's messages: Texts in Jones, pp. 42, 44.

77: Kesselring to Senger: Text in Smyth, "German Use" (see note to p. 76), p. 5.

82: "The stagnation": Churchill, vol. V, p. 429.

83: San Pietro: John Huston's film, The Battle of San Pietro, is at the Donnell Branch of the New York Public Library.

83: Pyle quote: Pyle, p. 98.

84: Mule could carry: Molony, p. 706.

84: Shoe nails short: "Condensed History of the 135th Infantry Regiment," Fort Leavenworth, Kansas, U.S. Army Library.

84: British hanging back: Clark, pp. 223, 263, 269.

85: 925 Allied guns: Ibid., p. 240.

85: Germans played cards: Ibid., p. 311.

85: Eisenhower messages: Texts in Jones, pp. 40, 41.

85: Matthews' correspondence with Eisenhower and Bedell Smith: Papers of Paul J. Sachs, NA.

89: Events in 1504: Gerald de Gaury, The Grand Captain, London and New York: Longmans Green, 1955, pp. 94–5.

89: Senger wrote: "Monte Cassino," New English Review, April 1949, pp. 250–52.

90: Senger's order: Quoted in Molony, p. 695.

93: Weizsaecker's statement: BMC, p. 132; Giovanetti, p. 213.

93: What reached Washington: Tittmann no. 9, January 10, 1944.

93: Neutral observer: Giovanetti, p. 213, and Giovanetti interview with DH, April 7, 1983.

95: "Whole picture": New York Times, January 1, 1944.

95: "We will win": Quoted in Time, January 3, 1944.

95: Newsweek, January 3, 1944.

96: "What Price Success?": Time, January 3, 1944.

96: Americans overseas: New York Times, January 2, 1944.

97: Hitler's proclamation: Quoted in New York Times, January 1, 1944.

97: Dulles "Appraisal": OSS official dispatch, February 2, 1944.

103: Goering's collection: "Annals of Crime: the Beautiful Spoils", part II, by Genet (Janet Flanner), in The New Yorker, March 1, 1947, pp. 33–44.

103: "Ghostly celebration": Speer, p. 322.

104: Hofer story: Report of the American Commission for Protection and Salvage of Artistic and Historical Monuments in War Area (Roberts Commission). Washington, 1946, pp. 75–76.

104: Naples treasures in Rome: "Appreciation of Enemy Methods of Looting Works of Art in Occupied Territories", SHAEF/G-5 report, March 20, 1945.

105: Two trucks delayed: "Works of Art Formerly Stored at Monte Cassino and Later Transferred to the Vatican," MFAA report 20909, July 20, 1944.

105: "Begged to be excused": Schlegel letter to London *Times,* January 1, 1952.
105: The picture showing Schlegel appears in the photo section of *BMC,* after p. 160. No photo credit.
107: Leccisotti's letter: Ibid., p. 189.
108: Vatican to Germans: Giovanetti, p. 214.
108: Letter to Leccisotti: *BMC,* p. 132.
108: German statement of January 12: Ibid.
108: Vatican statements to the Allies on behalf of other monasteries: *Actes et Documents,* vol. IX, no. 480, p. 619 (Subiaco), and vol. X, no. 1, p. 65 (Casamari). The Subiaco statement is dated December 22, 1943, Casamari is dated January 3, 1944.
110: Martin Blumenson, the official American historian of the Italian campaign, describes the Rapido battle in his *Bloody River: The Real Tragedy of the Rapido.* For an excellent view of the locale, in photos, maps and text, see "Cassino Battlefield Tour," *After the Battle,* 1976 (no. 13) especially pp. 23–25.
111: "Every hill": Senger, p. 198.
112: Canaris statement: Blumenson, *Bloody River,* p. 74. In his *Inside Hitler's Headquarters* (New York: Praeger, 1962, p. 410) General Walter Warlimont quotes the OKW Intelligence Section for January 20: "There are no indications that any major undertaking in the Mediterranean area is imminent."
114: Walker's diary: Quoted in Blumenson, *Bloody River,* p. 87.
115: Walker's diary: Ibid., pp. 105, 118.
115: American casualties: Ibid., p. 118.
116: Germans sent troups to Anzio: "14th Panzer Korps Defensive Operations Along the Garigliano, Gari and Rapido Rivers," by Ralph S. Mavrogordato, study for Foreign Studies Branch, OCMH, Washington, November 1955.
116: "Herewith a messenger pigeon": Walker, p. 320

Chapter 34: The story of the French Expeditionary Corps in Italy is told by its commander, General (later Marshal) Alphonse Pierre Juin, in his *Memoires* and his article, "Pelerinage au Mont Cassin," *Mercure de France,* vol. III, 1947, pp. 578–86. Other useful accounts from the French point of view are: (General) Marcel Carpentier, *Les Forces Alliées en Italie,* and Jacques Mordal, *Cassino.*

123: "Sunny Italy": Senger diary, pp. 42, 165.
123: Training for mountain warfare: Ibid., pp. 162, 181, 192.
124: "The tragic part": Ibid., p. 170.
124: Importance of Monte Cifalco: Ibid., p. 69.
126: "le ravin Gandouet": Juin '59, p. 272.
127: Juin to Clark: Ibid., p. 576.

Chapter 36: The story of the American patrol is told in "Small Unit Action at Cassino", in *Infantry Combat,* part II, section V.

136: "Threatened to set fire": Leccisotti's *Montecassino,* pp. 129–30, and Munding (see note to chap. 1), p. 21.
137: Account of four women from Cassino: "Memorandum for Colonel Howard," February 28, 1944. Headquarters, Fifth Army. Office of A C of S, G-2. Text in Jones, p. 69.
137: Fulvio de Angelis diary: *BMC,* p. 156.

Chapter 39: Bond's story appears in Harold L. Bond, *Return to Cassino,* supplemented by an interview with DH on May 28, 1983. Page references are to the Pocket Book edition.

141: Stuart to Bond: Bond, p. 93.
143: "mysterious and beautiful". Ibid., p. 72.
143: Stuart to Bond: Ibid., p. 107.
143: "I replied": Bond interview.

Chapter 40: N.C. Phillips's *Italy,* vol. I: *The Sangro to Cassino* is the official New Zealand history of the Italian campaign. C. J. C. Molony's *Mediterranean and Middle East* also covers this period in great detail. General Kippenberger tells his story in *Infantry Brigadier.* Freyberg is the subject of biographies by W. G. Stevens and Singleton-Gates. Dharm Pal's *The Campaign in Italy, 1943–45* is the official history of the 4th Indian Division in Italy. Fred Majdalany's *The Monastery* is the first-person narrative of a British officer. Other accounts from the Indian Division are George R. Stevens's *Fourth Indian Division* and his *History of Second King Edward VII's Own Goorkha Rifles,* Martineau's *A History of the Royal Sussex Regiment,* and Smith's *The Battles for Cassino.*

146: "Million-Dollar Hill": Pyle, p. 78.
146: "Running Up Highway Six": Kippenberger, p. 351.
147: Evidence of combat: Majdalany, p. 4.
147: "Like Passchendaele": Stevens, *Freyberg,* p. 72.
147: "in spite of considerable weakening": Quoted in Molony, p. 705.
147: Wilson answered: MEDCOS 30.
148: "We have a great need": Churchill, vol. V, p. 487.
149: "Don't your fellows salute?": Singleton-Gates, p. 238.
149: "Boyish fantasy": See, for example, Stevens, *Freyberg,* pp. 15–16, and "Lieutenant-General Lord Freyberg," by Daniel M. Davin, in Carver, p. 591.
150: New Zealand statistics and decisions: Phillips, pp. 25–30.
150: Gurkhas from Nepal: Smith, p. 71.
151: Tuker quotes are from his letter to Donald Bateman, February 20, 1959. Private papers of Major-General Donald R. Bateman, Imperial War Museum, London.
151: "Ever so thankful": Quoted in Graham, p. 68. "I wrote that note": Tuker to Bateman, March 5, 1963. Bateman Papers.
151: Tuker memorandum: In a postwar letter to Dr. Bisheshwar Prasad, general editor of the history of the army of India, dated October 20, 1957, Tuker

provided a copy of the memorandum and said its date was not February 12, as appears on the copy, but "probably February 2." Bateman Papers.

152: "Adopted at Kashmir Gate": quoted in Phillips, p. 205.

153: Situation on the ridge: See, for example, Graham, p. 70.

153: "it was plain": Kippenberger, p. 351.

153: "I always told Freyberg": Tuker letter to Prasad, Bateman Papers.

154: "Requests have been made": Fourth Indian Division Operating Instruction, no. 3, paragraph 11, in War Diary of the New Zealand Corps.

154: Tuker memorandum: H.Q. Indian Division no. 433, February 12, 1944.

155: Gruenther memorandum: U.S. Army Center of Military History, Washington, D.C.

156: "Get back if possible": Clark tape.

156: "Never had more headaches": Ibid.

157: "Only American": Ibid.

157: "Freyberg is a big man": Ibid.

157: Freyberg limit on casualties: Phillips, p. 352.

157: Clark diary: Quoted in Martin Blumenson, *Mark Clark* (New York: Congdon & Weed, forthcoming), msp. 248.

158: Clark to Keyes: Clark, p. 299.

158: "I suggested": Quoted in Jones, p. 178.

158: Eisenhower's order: Text in ibid., p. 48, and other sources.

159: "We cannot agree": Airgram A-107 to Lisbon for Tittmann.

159: Walker's diary: Walker, p. 262.

160: Osborne to Foreign Office: Text in Jones, p. 55.

161: "You don't believe": *BMC*, p. 135.

162: "Steadily creating": Quoted in "Bombing and the American Conscience During World War II," by George E. Hopkins, *The Historian*, May 1966, vol. 28.

163: Heinzerling's dispatch: *Washington Post*, February 12, 1944.

163: Webb: Quoted in a dispatch by George Bernard to the NCWC News Service from London, February 11, 1944.

164: The United Press dispatch was published by the *New York Times* on February 14, 1944.

164: "As the road becomes less crowded": Majdalany, pp. 6–7.

164: Letters to Marshall: Memorandum of the War Department Bureau of Public Relations to the Adjutant-General, February 18, 1944.

166: American Intelligence messages: National Archives records of II Corps and 34th Division; Fifth Army History, part IV, p. 92.

167: Wilson's March 9 messages: MEDCOS 64, text in Jones, pp. 74–75.

167: Original document: Text in Jones, p. 25.

167: German use of Albaneta farmhouse: "90th Armored Infantry Division" in *Mountains, Rivers, Islands,* newsletter of the veterans of the 90th Division: Militargeschichtliches Forschungsamt Bibliothek, Freiburg, p. 18.

168: Colonel Howard: Taped interview with DWR, on November 18, 1978.

168: "Glad to entice": OCMH interview with General Keyes by Howard McGaw Smyth, February 14, 1950.

169: Osborne cable of February 22: Text in Jones, p. 63.

169: General Porter: Taped interview with DWR, on May 8, 1977.

169: "I knew everyone": Clark tape.

171: Alexander to Clark: *The Alexander Memoirs,* p. 126.

172: "I would like you to comply": Clark tape.

173: 300 men a day: Molony, p. 704.

174: Senger calculated: Ibid., p. 709, Phillips, p. 226.

174: Kesselring too naive and "the rotten thing": Cramm interview, July 21, 1983.

174: Campanari house: Anna Campanari letter to DWR, June 15, 1983.

174: "The fight must be hard": H. R. Trevor-Roper, ed., *From Blitzkrieg to Defeat: Hitler's War Directives,* New York: Holt, Rinehart & Winston, 1965, p. 158.

176: On General Baade: See his biography by F. K. von Plehwe, *Reiter, Streiter, und Rebell* (Schauble Verlag, 1976).

176: "I assume": Senger, p. 207.

177: "That's a great favor": Plehwe, p. 234.

177: Baade anecdotes: Senger, p. 207; p. 234.

177: Baade's bunker: Senger, p. 208, pp. 234–35.

177: Senger disapproved: Senger Diary, p. 191.

177: Senger visit to Baade: Cramm interview.

178: Senger did not intervene: Senger Diary, p. 191.

178: Baade immediately saw: Boehmler, p. 154.

179: Heaviest artillery barrage: Ibid., p. 158.

179: American weapons frozen: Wagner, p. 144.

179: Germans hit by own artillery: "The 90th Armored Infantry Division" (see note to p. 167), p. 24.

179: American officer noted: Wagner, p. 145.

179: German dead: "The 90th Armored Infantry Division" (see note to p. 167), p. 24.

179: Truce request: Ibid., p. 25.

180: Walton's account: Adleman & Walton, pp. 180–81.

180: "Mission was scheduled": Staff message 332, dated 1300 hours, February 13, 1944.

180: "Our air officer": 34th Division Journal.

181: Freyberg at Fifth Army: Phillips, p. 209; Graham, p. 73; War Diary, New Zealand Corps, Appendix, p. 6.

181: Allied spokesman: Reported in *New York Times,* February 14, 1944, dispatch from Algiers dated Feb. 13.

181: "Our enemies have unleashed": Reported in "Summary of German Attitude Towards Destruction of Art Treasures as Reported in Enemy-Controlled Broadcasts—January–March 1944." Foreign Broadcast Monitoring Service. (RG-239) NA.

182: General Anders and Polish Corps: Piekalkiewitcz, pp. 101–03.

183: "reinforcements would come": Ibid., p. 103.

183: Glennie's headquarters: Martineau, p. 272.

184: "Barely one blanket": Quoted in Smith, p. 77.

184: "Let's go have a look": Eaker's description of his flight is from an interview with him taped by DWR on May 5, 1977.

184: Slessor to Eaker: JCS 46.

185: Slessor to Eaker: Dated February 8, 1944, no serial.

186: "We clearly identified": Quoted in "The Bombing of Monte Cassino," by Martin Blumenson, *American Heritage,* August 1968, vol. XIX, no. 5.

186: Reese's story: "Intermission at Cassino," by Lieutenant-Colonel Hal Reese, in 36th Division Records, Texas State Archives, Austen. Reese wrote the account in the spring of 1944. He was killed on June 1 near Velletri, Italy.

190: Baade covered up: "90th Armored Infantry Division," p. 25.

190: "It wasn't the Germans": "Press Releases from Reich Propaganda Ministry," February 14–21, 1944, Bundesarchiv, Koblenz, p. 5.

191: "When the shell is observed": Functions of the Fifth Army Combat Propaganda Team," Psychological Warfare Branch, Headquarters Fifth Army, April 5, 1944, p. 34.

191: Leaflet text: Imperial War Museum, London.

193: Commanders on the ridge decided: Stevens, *History of Second King Edward VII's Own Goorkha Rifles,* p. 100

193: Indian Division to Freyberg: War Diary, New Zealand Corps, Appendix, p. 7.

193: Indian Division planning note and pro forma: Texts in Jones, pp. 86–87.

193: Dimoline call to Freyberg: Phillips, p. 209.

194: "He wanted me to know": Ryan letter to DWR, April 4, 1977.

194: Freyberg call to Dimoline: Phillips, p. 209.

195: "Poor Dimoline": Kippenberger, p. 356.

195: Freyberg to Dimoline: Phillips, p. 210; Singleton-Gates, p. 279.

196: Freyberg made no effort: Smith, p. 77.

196: "because it has become": *Actes et Documents,* vol. IX, no. 1709, p. 131.

196: Deiber's command: Boehmler, p. 166.

197: *"Scheiss":* Lieutenant De Grazia report to Psychological Warfare Branch on interviews with refugees, dated March 5, 1944, text in Jones, p. 140.

197: Accounts to Allied reporters: Dispatches by Christopher Buckley, in the *Daily Telegraph,* February 19, 1944, and by Lee McCardell in the *Baltimore Sun,* February 19, 1944.

197: Refugees without food: Jones, p. 140.

198: Evans's flight: The account of the flight is from a letter from Evans to DWR, October 31, 1978, and from Operations Order 341, H.Q. Fifth Wing, 15th U.S. Air Force.

199: "The target is": Intelligence annex to Operations Order 341, signed by Arthur M. Clark, Lieutenant-Colonel, Air Corps.

199: Two of the fliers: Lieutenant-Colonel C. E. Miller, then a bombardier with the 416th Squadron of the 99th Bomb Group, in a letter to DWR, dated August 26, 1976, and Lewis L. Wargo, then co-pilot of plane 465, 419th Squadron, 301st Bomb Group, in a letter to DWR dated March 13, 1978.

200: Eaker said that Wilson: Eaker tape.

200: Wilson "didn't care": John Slessor letter to DWR, dated March 6, 1977.

200: Eaker would have preferred: Eaker tape.

200: "If you say to do it": Clark, p. 318.

202: "Most widely advertised": *Newsweek,* February 28, 1944, p. 27.

202: Group of doctors and nurses: Oyster, Harold and Esther M. (eds.), *The 319th in Action* (Akron, Ohio: 1976).

202: Bond's position: Bond, pp. 120, 134.

202: "They flew in perfect": Buckley, p. 296.

202: View of the bombing: Two films of the bombing are available at the National Archives, one by the U.S. Army (RG 111, ADC 843, NAV 210), and the other by Paramount Newsreel (News Issue no. 54).

203: "Touchdown" and "Boy, oh boy": Quoted in dispatch from Lee McCardell in the *Baltimore Sun,* Feb. 16, 1944.

203: "We acted pretty much": Ray S. Thomson letter to DWR, dated August 11, 1978.

203: "Pennies of American schoolchildren": Bond interview.

203: "Are those bombs going to land": Eaker tape.

203: Bombs near Clark: Clark, p. 319.

203: "What the devil" and "The idiots": Cramm interview.

204: Senger at Baade's bunker: Senger p. 208; Senger Diary, p. 80.

204: "We went to the door" and "At that moment": Quoted in Stevens, *Fourth Indian Division,* p. 285.

204: Dropped twelve bombs: Pal, p. 106.

204: "Indian troops with turbans": Quoted in Stevens, *Fourth Indian Division,* p. 286.

205: Began radioing reports: Texts of the reports are given in "90th Armored Infantry Division" (see note to p. 167), p. 28.

206: "The 90th Panzer Grenadier": Quoted in Smyth, "German Use" (see note to p. 76), p. 6.

206: Westphal to Tenth Army: Quoted in Phillips, p. 213.

206: "At 10:30 I saw": Counterintelligence Corps (CIC), 34th Division, February 20, 1944.

206: "Approximately 200 Germans": telephone message, Journal no. X-15-18.

206: David Hunt story: Hunt, pp. 246–67, and his letter to DWR, dated July 21, 1978.

207: Refugees later said: Quoted in Jones, p. 140.

208: Medium bomber bases: Tannehill, Victor C., *Boomerang! The Story of the 320th Bombardment Group in World War II* (Racine, Wisc.: V. C. Tannehill, 1978).

208: Chappell later recalled: Frank B. Chappell letter to DWR, dated June 15, 1978.

208: Twenty of the 22 planes: Mission Report 172, H.Q. 319th Bombardment Group (M), February 15, 1944.

208: "Target cabbaged": Kenneth E. Chard quoted his diary in a letter to Esther M. Oyster, dated May 27, 1978, sent by Mrs. Oyster to DWR.

208: "Can see white flags" and "II Corps not taking": Telephone message, II Corps to Fifth Army, Journal no. X-15-48.

208: "We laid out": The German account of the interview with Diamare is quoted in Smyth, "German Use" (see note to p. 76).

209: "All went the same way": CIC, 34th Division, February 20, 1944.

211: "Two ounces of whiskey": Miller letter (see note to p. 199).

211: 239 heavy and medium bombers dropped: Wilson report to Combined Chiefs of Staff for January–May 1944.

211: War Diary report: Text in Jones, p. 107.

211: Estimate by local historian: Professor Torquato Vizzaccaro, interview with DWR, on Nov. 28, 1977.

211: 148 skulls: Leccisotti, p. 166.

211: Other estimates: see Phillips, p. 211 footnote.

212: "Had we known": See note to p. 203.

212: "Only rarely": Cox, Geoffrey, *The Road to Trieste* (London: Heinemann, 1947), p. 81.

212: "Sentimentalists in uniform": Waugh's letter is dated March 3, 1944. It and the entries from his diary are reproduced with the permission of the Jones Library, Amherst, Massachusetts.

212: "I remember the actual": Martha Gellhorn letter to DWR, dated July 24, 1979.

214: Four women leave monastery: Jones, p. 136.

214: Osborne to Foreign Office: Text in Jones, p. 57.

214: Similar statement: Tittmann 47, dated February 15, 1944.

214: Roosevelt press conference: Press and radio conference #736, Roosevelt Papers, Hyde Park Library.

215: Commanders of Indian Division had met: Pal, p. 106.

215: Royal Sussex attack: Phillips p. 223; Martineau, p. 273; "Cassino Battlefield Tour" (see note to p. 110), p. 7.

216: 48 fighter-bombers dropped: Air Support Control, H.Q. Fifth Army, report dated April 7, 1944.

217: "We had the superiority complex": Quoted in Smith, p. 83.

219: Italian inscription on a rock: "Una pietra a S. Severo," by Bonifacio Borghini, in *Echi di Montecassino,* January–June 1978 (no. 12), p. 42.

219: Fra Carlo: "Fra Carlomanno," by Bonifacio Borghini, in *Echi di Montecassino,* January–June 1977 (No. 10), pp. 27–29.

220: Kesselring ordered a search: The order was given by Senger's 14th Panzer Korps on February 17. The text, as cited in the Activity Report of the Intelligence Section, 14th P.K., for January–June 1944, p. 66, reads: "1) Troops from the 90th Armored Infantry Division will immediately organize a large search for the abbot and surviving priests, as well as any civilians who were in the monastery at Monte Cassino. 2) [The abbot] is to be brought to Korps command post at Castelmassimo."

220: Silsbee's flight: Silsbee letter to DWR, dated July 27, 1976.

221: Bombing statistics: See note to p. 216.

221: "A sad encounter": *BMC,* p. 106.

222: "In England": Ibid.

222: Senger wrote: Senger Diary, p. 82.

222: Interview in general's living room: A photograph appears in Senger, after p. 160.

222: Accounts of Diamare interview: The German account is quoted in Smyth, "German Use" (see note to p. 76), pp. 6–8. Matronola's account is in *BMC*, pp. 106–108.

223: Car set out for Rome: Senger Diary, p. 82.

223: According to Senger: Ibid., p. 83–84.

224: "Certainly a trump card": Scrivener, p. 115.

224: "The willful destruction" and "again proven their sense": "Press Releases" (see note to p. 190), pp. 2, 6.

224: Kesselring statement: Foreign Office "Outline of News and Enemy Propaganda," dated February 17, 1944, no. 78 in P.I.D. Intelligence Text Series.

224: Message to German diplomats: "U.S. Intelligence Comments." Magic summary no. 700, February 24, 1944, records of National Security Agency.

224: "In this senseless lust": Foreign Office "Outline" (see note to p. 224).

225: Associated Press: *Washington Post*, February 16, 1944.

225: *New York Times:* February 16, 1944.

225: "The Germans evidently": NCWC dispatch from Baltimore, February 16, 1944.

226: Two Benedictine abbots: NCWC dispatch from London by George Barnard, dated February 18, 1944.

226: Dew to Carver: Text in Jones, p. 58.

227: "It is known": Quoted in Tittmann no. 54, dated February 18, 1944.

227: Tittmann notes: Tittmann no. 56, dated February 19.

227: Tittmann denial: Tittmann no. 55, dated February 18, and his letter to secretary of state, dated February 28, 1944.

227: Tardini notes: *Actes et Documents*, pp. 141–42.

228: "The Lord willed it": "Dom Gregorio Diamare," by Giovanni Battista de Felippis, in *Echi di Montecassino*, July–December 1978 (no. 13), p. 54.

228: Indian Division attack: Molony, pp. 714–18; Phillips, pp. 223–29; Stevens, *Fourth Indian Division*, pp. 288–91; "Cassino Battlefield Tour" (see note to p. 110), p. 32.

229: "The difficulties of assembling": War Diary, New Zealand Corps, Appendices, p. 10.

229: Indian Division lost 530 men: Molony, p. 718.

230: New Zealand casualties: Graham, p. 83.

230: Attack called off: Phillips, p. 229.

236: Wilson's cable: MEDCOS 64, text in Jones, p. 74–75.

236: Tittmann protest: Tittmann letter to Tardini, undersecretary of state, dated October 13, 1945.

237: "It is clear that General Wilson" Jones, p. 38.

237: "There are eyewitness accounts": OCMH memo of March 15, 1961, signed by Lieutenant-Colonel Roderick A. Stamey, Jr., acting chief, Historical Services Division.

237: "It appears that no German troops": OCMH memo of November 9, 1964, signed by Colonel R. H. Wiltamuth, deputy chief of military history.

237: "The abbey was actually unoccupied": Blumenson, *Salerno to Cassino,* p. 407.

237: Bloch's pamphlet, "The Bombardment of Monte Cassino," was first published in 1973 in *Benedictina* (Rome). For Muldoon's statement, see *Parliamentary Debates (Hansard),* vol. 447, pp. 3785–86. For the critics of Bloch, see letters in the *Times* of London from John Canning, August 23, 1982, and Raleigh Trevelyan, August 26, 1982.

239: Senger up on ridge: Cramm interview.

240: "as soon as the decision": "Monte Cassino Memories," by F. S. Tuker, undated typescript in Bateman Papers, p. 5.

241: "A direct attack": Ibid., p. 4.

241: "It is revealing no secret": "De Alcune Note de M. Matronola," in *Echi di Montecassino,* January–June 1974 (no. 4), pp. 20–21.

241: Plea to Roosevelt: Letter of Apostolic Delegate, dated March 13, 1944.

241: "it would be unsound": "Proposal for the Military By-pass of Rome," undated JCS memorandum.

242: Schlegel plaque: *Der Soldat,* November 9, 1969.

BIBLIOGRAPHY

Actes et Documents de la Sainte Siege Relative à la Seconde Guerre Mondiale. Vols. IX and X. Lib. Ed. Vaticana, 1980.

Adleman, Robert H., and George Walton. *Rome Fell Today.* Boston: Little Brown, 1968.

Alexander, Harold. *The Alexander Memoirs, 1940–45.* New York: McGraw-Hill, 1962.

Avagliano, Faustino, ed. *Il Bombardamento di Montecassino.* Monte Cassino, 1980.

Blumenson, Martin. *Salerno to Cassino.* (Mediterranean Theatre of Operations. U.S. Army in World War II.) Washington, D.C.: Office of the Chief of Military History (OCMH), 1969.

———. *Bloody River: The Real Tragedy of the Rapido.* Boston: Houghton Mifflin, 1970.

Boehmler, Rudolf. *Monte Cassino.* London: Cassell, 1964. (First published in German: *Monte Cassino,* 1956.)

Bond, Harold L. *Return to Cassino.* New York: Doubleday, 1964, Pocket Books, 1965.

Buckley, Christopher. *The Road to Rome.* London: Hodder & Stoughton, 1945.

Carpentier, Marcel. *Les Forces Alliées en Italie.* Paris: editions Berger-Lerrault, 1949.

Carver, Michael, ed. *The Warlords.* Boston: Little, Brown, 1976.

Churchill, Winston S. *Closing the Ring.* Vol. V of *The Second World War.* Boston: Houghton Mifflin, 1951.

Clark, Mark W. *Calculated Risk.* New York: Harper, 1950.

Giovanetti, Alberto. *Roma Città Aperta.* Milan: Editrice Ancora, 1962.

Graham, Dominick. *Cassino.* (Ballantine's illustrated history of the violent century.) New York: Ballantine, 1970.

Grossi, Tancredo. *Il Calvario di Monte Cassino.* Cassino: Libreria Lamberti, 1977.

Hunt, David. *A Don at War.* London: Kimber, 1966.

Irving, David. *Hitler's War.* New York: Viking, 1977.

Jackson, W. G. F. *The Battle for Italy.* New York: Harper & Row, 1967.

Jones, F. *Report on the Events Leading to the Bombing of the Abbey of Monte Cassino on 15 February 1944.* Unpublished report, written in 1949, available since 1980 at the Public Records Office, London.

Juin, Alphonse Pierre. *Memoires—Alger, Tunis, Rome, vol. I.* Paris: Librairie Artheme-Fayard, 1959).

Katz, Robert. *Death in Rome.* New York: Macmillan, 1967.

Kesselring, Albert. *A Soldier's Record.* New York: Morrow, 1954. (First published in German: *Soldat bis zum letzen Tag,* 1953.)

Kippenberger, Howard. *Infantry Brigadier.* London: Oxford University Press, 1949.

Kurzman, Dan. *The Race for Rome.* New York: Doubleday, 1975.

Leccisotti, Tommaso. *Montecassino.* Monte Cassino, 1967.

Majdalany, Fred. *The Monastery.* Boston: Houghton Mifflin, 1946.

———. *Cassino: Portrait of a Battle.* Boston: Houghton Mifflin, 1957.

Malaparte, Curzio. *The Skin.* Boston: Houghton Mifflin, 1952.

Martineau, G. D. *A History of the Royal Sussex Regiment.* Chichester: Moore & Tillyer, 1955.

Mauldin, Bill. *Up Front.* New York: Holt, 1945.

Molony, C. J. C. *Mediterranean and Middle East.* Vol. V *History of the Second World War.* London: His Majesty's Stationery Office, 1973.

Mordal, Jacques. *Cassino.* Paris: Amiot-Dumont, 1953.

Pal, Dharm. *The Campaign in Italy, 1943–45.* (History of the Indian Armed Forces in the Second World War.) Calcutta: Orient Longmans, 1960.

Phillips, N. C. *The Sangro to Cassino.* Vol. I of *Italy.* (History of New Zealand in the Second World War). Wellington: Department of Internal Affairs, 1957.

Piekalkiewitcz, Janusz. *The Battle for Cassino.* Indianapolis: Bobbs-Merrill, 1980.

Pyle, Ernie. *Brave Men.* New York: Grosset & Dunlop, 1944.

Scrivener, Jane. *Inside Rome with the Germans.* New York: Macmillan, 1945.

von Senger und Etterlin, Frido. *Neither Fear nor Hope.* New York: Dutton, 1964. (First published in German: *Krieg in Europa,* 1960.)

Singleton-Gates, Peter. *General Lord Freyberg VC.* London: Michael Joseph, 1963.

Smith, E. D. *The Battles for Cassino.* New York: Scribners, 1975.

Speer Albert. *Inside the Third Reich.* New York: Macmillan, 1970; Avon, 1971. (First published in German: *Erinnerungen,* 1969.)

Starr, Chester G. *From Salerno to the Alps: A History of the Fifth Army 1943–45.* Washington: Infantry Journal Press, 1948.

Stevens, George R. *Fourth Indian Division.* Toronto: McLaren, 1948.

———. *A History of Second King Edward VII's Own Goorkha Rifles.* Aldershot: Gale & Polden, 1952.

Stevens, W. G. *Freyberg the Man.* Wellington: Reed, 1965.

Trevelyan, Raleigh. *Rome '44.* New York: Viking, 1982.

Wagner, Robert L. *The Texas Army: A History of the 36th Division in the Italian Campaign.* Austin: R. L. Wagner, 1972.

Walker, Fred L. *From Texas to Rome.* Dallas: Taylor, 1969.

Westphal, Siegfried. *The German Army in the West.* London: Cassell, 1951.

ACKNOWLEDGMENTS

Many people have helped one or the other of us in one way or another through the years that led to the publication of this book.

David Richardson owes the most profound thanks to his parents, Mr. and Mrs. F. J. Fitzpatrick, for their indispensable financial support; to his aunt, widow of Major-General Robert Taylor, chief of staff of the 15th Air Force in Italy just after the events described here; and to his wife and children for putting up with some difficult times.

Both of us are grateful to David Irving, who encouraged the idea of the book and later did an interview for us, and to our editor and publisher, Thomas Congdon, who made it a reality.

Father James O'Donnell, O.S.B., was kind enough to read the manuscript in various stages; professors Herbert Bloch, Harold L. Bond, Jeffrey Butler, and Joseph G. LaPalombara offered us valuable information and suggestions; and Professor Henry M. Willard helped us with photographs.

The monks of Monte Cassino, and especially Dom Agostino Saccomanno and Dom Faustino Avagliano, have been hospitable to us and generous with their time on our two visits to their monastery.

Some of those who have helped us are named in the text or in the Notes and Sources. In addition we would particularly like to extend our thanks to: Herbert Agricola, Colonel John R. Angolia, Francis Bartlett, P. Fidelis Beerli, O.S.B.; Baron Heinrich von Behr, John C. Benyo; Betty Bohannon, Walter Brunsmeier, Dottore Vera Signorelli Cacciatore, George C. Chalou, Prof. David G. Chandler, Abbot Primate Victor Dammertz, O.S.B.; Dr. D. C. Derma, Donald S. Detwiler, Douglas C. Earle Lyne, William R. Emerson, Dr. Hans Gerhard Evers, John and Gabriella Felton, Lord Paul Freyberg, Rev. Robert A. Graham, S.J.; Dr. Walter Hagemann, Gerald K. Haines, E. B. Haslam, Dr. Ludwig Heydenreich, Robin Higham, Dr. C. Jaccarini, Rev. Oliver Kapsner, O.S.B.; Deane Keller, Prof. George Kemon, Prof. George O. Kent, Carolyn Lee, Prof. Rensselaer W. Lee, Gen. Lyman L. Lemnitzer, Marianne Loenartz, Col. Dr. Klaus A. Maier, Dr. M. Messerschmidt, Col. C. A. H. M. Noble,

Bro. Columban O'Brien, O.S.B.; Agnes F. Peterson, Prof. N. C. Phillips, Guenther Raebiger, John J. Slonaker, Harold H. Tittmann, Jr.; Lady Cynthia Tuker, Robert van de Velde, J. B. Ward-Perkins, I. McL. Wards, Hon. Justice John White, Group Capt. Fred W. Winterbotham, Abbot James Wiseman, O.S.B.

Our thanks, also, to the members of the 36th "Texas" Division Association, New Zealand Returned Services Association, Bund Deutscher Fallschirmjager e V., and Monte Cassino Veterans Association.

INDEX

266

North Africa, 20, 21, 43, 121, 149, 177
North African troops, French, 122–123, 126–127, 150, 230

Office of the Chief of Military History, U.S., 237
100th Infantry Battalion, U.S., 147
132nd Infantry Regiment, German, 167
133rd Infantry, U.S., 166
135th Infantry, U.S., 166
141st Infantry, U.S., 113–115, 141
143rd Infantry, U.S., 83, 113, 115
168th Infantry, U.S., 166
Operation Michael, 179
Orsogna, 157
Osborne, D'Arcy, 77, 160, 169, 214, 226
OSS (Office of Strategic Services), 66, 97
Osservatore Romano, 226
Oster, Joachim, 174
Overlord invasion, 21–22, 97
Owsnicke, Lieutenant, 222
Oxford University, 39

Pacelli, Eugenio, *see* Pius XII, Pope
Panter-Downes, Mollie, 162
Parable of the Blind (Brueghel), 61
Pastenelle, 106
Paulus, Friedrich von, 41
Pellagalli, Fra Carlomanno, 219, 221
Pétain, Henri Philippe, 121
Pittiglio, Anna, 90
Pius XII, Pope, 26, 49–52, 63, 78, 108, 130, 213, 227
Point 445, 132–135, 142, 229
Point 593, *see* Monte Calvario
Point 862, 127
Polish Corps, 182–183, 230, 243
Pollack, Lieutenant-Colonel, 73
Pompeii, 15, 104, 224
Pontine marshes, 23
Porter, Robert, 169
Portugal, 22
Po Valley, 43
Presenzano, 155, 181, 203
Propaganda Office, German, 81
Pyle, Ernie, 83, 146

Qurinale Palace (Rome), 66–67

Radio Belgrade, 96
Raphael, 104

Rapido, battle of, 110–117, 125, 130, 156
Rapido River, 24, 38, 75, 110, 113, 121, 236
Rapido Valley, 3, 121, 122, 124, 126, 132, 186, 215, 243
Re, Emilio, 71
Red Cross, American, 187
Red Cross, Bavarian, 39
Red Cross, International, 188
Reese, Hal, 186–189
Reinickendorf, 104
Ribbentrop, Joachim von, 223
Roberts, Owen J., 29
Roberts Commission (American Commission for the Protection and Salvage of Artistic and Historic Monuments), 29
Rocca Janula, 63, 147
Roccasecca, 38, 41, 44, 45, 116, 118
Rome, 3, 5, 17, 23, 29, 35–38, 43–53, 56, 62–72, 92–93, 101, 107–110, 131, 161–163, 183, 199, 207, 223–228, 241–242
Rommel, Erwin, 21, 40, 43–44
Roosevelt, Franklin D., 22, 26, 67, 159, 164, 168, 183, 214, 235, 241
Roscher, Alexander, 86–87
Rotterdam, 28
Route 6 (Via Casilina), 3, 4, 5, 18, 21, 24, 31, 36, 44, 72, 82, 110, 146, 153, 173, 200, 236, 243
Route 7 (Via Appia), 23
Royal Air Force, 28, 84, 97
Royal Sussex Regiment, 183, 215, 217, 229
Rule of Benedict, 7, 8, 32, 33, 140, 216
Ryan, Patrick J., 194
Ryder, Charles, 159, 166, 180–181

Saccomanno, Agostino, 208, 209, 233, 235
St. John's College, Oxford University, 39
St. Paul's Outside the Walls, Benedictine monastery at, 17–18, 48, 49, 93
St. Peter's Square (Rome), 49, 50
Saint Scholastica (church), 220
Salerno, 5, 15, 22, 44, 45
San Ambrogio, 112
San Anselmo, Benedictine monastery of, 18, 47–48, 223–224, 228